VENEZUELA. SOME CURRENT LEGA

VENEZUELA.
SOME CURRENT LEGAL ISSUES
2014

Venezuelan National Reports to the *19th*
International Congress of Comparative Law,
International Academy of Comparative Law,
Vienna, 20-26 July 2014

(In memory and in homage of Irene de Valera)

ALLAN R. BREWER-CARÍAS
HILDEGARD RONDÓN DE SANSÓ
EUGENIO HERNÁNDEZ-BRETÓN
CLAUDIA MADRID MARTÍNEZ
ANDREA I. RONDÓN GARCÍA
CLAUDIA NIKKEN
SERVILIANO ABACHE CARVAJAL

Serie Eventos
N° 31

ACADEMIA DE CIENCIAS POLÍTICAS Y SOCIALES

EDITORIAL JURÍDICA VENEZOLANA

Caracas, 2014

© Academia de Ciencias Políticas y Sociales

Depósito Legal: lf54020143401751
ISBN: 978-980-365-257-9

Academia de Ciencias Políticas y Sociales
Avenida Universidad, Bolsa a San Francisco
Palacio de las Academias
Caracas 1010-Venezuela
Teléfonos (058) (02) 483-2674/482-8634
Fax (058) (02) 482-8845, 481-6035
www.acienpoli@cantv.net
academiadecienciaspoliticas@gmail.com

Para la Academia de Ciencias Políticas y Sociales.
Impreso por Ligthning Source, an Ingram Content company
Distribuido por: Editorial Jurídica Venezolana International Inc.
Panamá, República de Panamá.
Email: editorialjuridicainternational@gmail.com

Editado por: Editorial Jurídica Venezolana
Avda. Francisco Solano López, Torre Oasis, P.B., Local 4, Sabana Grande,
Apartado 17.598 - Caracas, 1015, Venezuela
Teléfono (058) (02) 762-25-53 / 762-38-42/ Fax. (058) (02) 763-52-39
Email: fejv@cantv.net
http://www.editorialjuridicavenezolana.com.ve

Diagramación, composición y montaje
por: Mirna Pinto de Naranjo, en letra Times New Roman, 11
Interlineado exacto 11 Mancha 18 x 11,5

FOREWORD

Venezuelan law professors have participated in the works of the International Academy of Comparative Law, mainly through the submission of National Reports on the different topics of the International Congresses of Comparative Law, beginning with the VII International Congress of Comparative Law held in Uppsala, Sweden, in 1966.

The relations with the International Academy were initially established by professors of the Central University of Venezuela, under the guidance of Professor Roberto Goldschmidt, who since his arrival in Venezuela in the fifties, assumed the task of developing the studies of comparative law in the country, first from the Comparative Law Institute of the Ministry of Justice, and later from the Private Law Institute at the Central University of Venezuela.

The National Reports submitted to the Uppsala Congress, compiled under the coordination of Professor Golsdchmidt, were published in the book: *Ponencias Venezolanas al VII Congreso Internacional de Derecho Comparado (Uppsala, agosto 1966), Instituto de Derecho Privado, Facultad de Derecho, Universidad Central de Venezuela, Caracas 1966.*

With the support of Professor Tatiana Maekelt, I succeeded Professor Goldschmidt in the coordination of Venezuela's participation in the International Congresses, and ten years later, the National Reports submitted to the X International Congress of Comparative Law were published in the book: *Ponencias Venezolanas al X Congreso Internacional de Derecho Comparado (Budapest, Hungría, 23/28 agosto de 1978), Facultad de Ciencias Jurídicas y Políticas, Universidad Central de Venezuela, Caracas 1978.* Subsequently, the National Reports submitted to the XI International Congress of Comparative Law held in Caracas were published in the book: *El Derecho Venezolano en 1982, Ponencias al XI Congreso Internacional de Derecho Comparado, Facultad de Ciencias Jurídicas y Políticas, Universidad Central de Venezuela, Caracas 1982*; and the Nacional Reports submitted to the XII International Congress of Comparative Law of 1987 were published in the *Revista de la Facultad de Ciencias Jurídicas y Políticas, Nº 66 (Ponencias Venezolanas al XII Congreso Internacional de Derecho Comparado), Universidad Central de Venezuela, Caracas 1987.*

In my capacity as President of the National Academy of Political and Social Sciences, with the agreement of Professor Maekelt, we decided to establish in the Academy the coordination of Venezuela's participation in the International Congresses. We did so for the Venezuelan National Reports for the XV International Congress of Comparative Law held in Bristol in 1998, which were published in the book: *El Derecho Venezolano a finales del Siglo XX, Ponencias Venezolanas XV Congreso Internacional de Derecho Comparado, Bristol, julio-agosto 1998, Biblioteca de la Academia de Ciencias Políticas y Sociales, Caracas 1998.* Four years later, the National Reports for the XV International Congress of Comparative Law, held in Brisbane in 2002, were published in the *Boletín de la Academia de Ciencias Políticas y Sociales, Ponencias venezolanas para el XVI Congreso Internacional de Derecho Comparado, (Brisbane-Australia), Nº 139, Año LXVIV, Enero-Junio 2002, Caracas 2002.*

All those books contain the Spanish version of the Venezuelan National Reports for the International Congresses of the International Academy. On this occasion, for the Venezuelan participation in the XIX International Congress of Comparative Law to be held in Vienna in July 2014, which I have coordinated with the help of Professor Eugenio Hernández Bretón, we have decided to publish the Venezuelan Reports in their English and French versions, as they were sent to the general reporters; these are the reports included in this book.

When I assumed the task of organizing the XI International Congress of Comparative Law held in Caracas in 1982, I asked Ms. Irene de Valera, a very bright young lawyer, invaluable friend and excellent manager, to help me with this task. She did her job so well, helping in the organization of a Congress attended by more than a thousand participants, that I asked her to continue assisting me in many other academic activities, which she did in the following years. Later, when I assumed the Presidency of the National Academy of Political and Social Sciences in 1997, I proposed her appointment as its Executive Director, a position that she occupied with great efficiency until her death. In that condition, her last contribution in the coordination for Venezuela's participation in the works of the International Congress of the International Academy was for the Congress held in Washington in 2010.

With her departure last year, not only have we lost a very dear personal friend, but also an invaluable human being characterized by her efficiency, dedication, skills, kindness, competence and loyalty, with a passionate devotion to life.

That is why this book is in memory and in homage of Irene de Valera.

Allan R. Brewer-Carías

New York, May 2014

I.B. THEORIE GENERALE DU DROIT/ GENERAL LEGAL THEORY

- ## L'INDEPENDENCE D'UNE ÉLITE MÉRITOIRE: LE GOUVERNEMENTS DES JUGES ET LA DÉMOCRATIE / THE INDEPENDENCE OF A MERITORIOUS ELITE: THE GOVERNMENT OF JUDGE AND DEMOCRACY

THE GOVERNMENT OF JUDGES AND DEMOCRACY. THE TRAGIC SITUATION OF THE VENEZUELAN JUDICIARY

Allan R. Brewer-Carías
PROFESSOR, CENTRAL UNIVERSITY OF VENEZUELA

I. DEMOCRACY AND SEPARATION OF POWERS

The essential components of democracy are much more than the sole popular or circumstantial election of government officials, as it has been formally declared in the Inter American Democratic Charter *(Carta Democrática Interamericana)* adopted by the Organization of American States in 2001,[1] after so many antidemocratic, militarist and authoritarian regimes disguised as democratic because of their electoral origin that Latin American countries have suffered.

---

[1]   See on the Inter-American Democratic Charter, in Brewer-Carías, Allan R. *La crisis de la democracia venezolana. La Carta Democrática Interamericana y los sucesos de abril de 2002*, Ediciones El Nacional, Caracas 2002, pp. 137 ff.; Aguiar, Asdrúbal *El Derecho a la Democracia*, Editorial Jurídica Venezolana, Caracas 2008.

The Charter, in effect, enumerates among the *essential elements of the representative democracy,* in addition to having periodical, fair and free elections based on the universal and secret vote as expression of the will of the people; the following: respect for human rights and fundamental liberties; access to power and its exercise with subjection to the Rule of law; plural regime of the political parties and organizations; and what is the most important of all, *"separation and independence of public powers"* (Article 3), that is, the possibility to control the different branches of government. The *Inter-American Charter* in addition, also defined the following *fundamental components of the democracy*: transparency of governmental activities; integrity, responsibility of governments in the public management; respect of social rights and freedom of speech and press; constitutional subordination of all institutions of the State to the legally constituted civil authority, and respect to the Rule of law of all the entities and sectors of society.

The principle of separation and independence of powers is so important, as one of the "essential elements of democracy", that it is the one that can allow all the other "fundamental components of democracy" to be politically possible. To be precise, democracy, as a political regime, can only function in a constitutional Rule of law system where the control of power exists; that is, check and balance based on the separation of powers with their independence and autonomy guaranteed, so that power can be stopped by power itself. Consequently, without separation of powers and the possibility of control of power, any of the other essential factors of democracy cannot be guaranteed, because only by controlling Power, can free and fair elections and political pluralism exist; only by controlling Power, can effective democratic participation be possible, and effective transparency in the exercise of government be assured; only by controlling Power can there be a government submitted to the Constitution and the laws, that is, the Rule of law; only by controlling Power can there be an effective access to justice functioning with autonomy and independence; and only by controlling Power can there be a true and effective guaranty for the respect of human rights.[2]

The consequence of the aforementioned, is that democratic regimes cannot exist without separation of powers, and in particular, without the possibility of an independent and autonomous Judicial Power with the

---

[2]   See Brewer-Carías, Allan R. "Democracia: sus elementos y componentes esenciales y el control del poder", in González Martín, Nuria (Compiladora), *Grandes temas para un observatorio electoral ciudadano, V. I, Democracia: retos y fundamentos,* Instituto Electoral del Distrito Federal, México 2007, pp. 171-220.

capacity of controlling all the other powers of the State. That is why the most important principle governing the functioning of the Judiciary in democratic regimes, is the independence and autonomy of judges, so they can apply the rule of law without interference from other State's Powers, from institutions, corporation or even from citizens; and only subjected to the rule of the Constitution and of law.

II. THE PROVISIONS OF THE VENEZUELAN CONSTITUTION REGARDING THE JUDICIAL SYSTEM AND ITS GOVERNANCE

For such purpose, in contemporary world, Constitutions have included express provisions in such respect, being no exception the Venezuelan Constitution of 1999.[3] In effect, according to article 253 of the Constitution, the power to render or administer justice emanates from the citizenry and is imparted "in the name of the Republic and by the authority of the law." For such purposes, Article 26 of the Constitution provides that the State must guaranty a "cost-free, accessible, impartial, adequate, transparent, autonomous, independent, accountable, equitable, and expeditious justice, without undue or dilatory delay, formalism, or unnecessary replication of procedures."[4] Consequently, the Constitution denies the Judiciary the power to establish court costs or fees, or to require payment for services (Article 254).

The system of justice, according to the same Article 253 of the Constitution, is composed not only by the organs of the Judicial Branch (Supreme Tribunal of Justice and all the other courts established by law), but by the offices of the Prosecutor General, the Peoples' Defender, the criminal investigatory organs, the penitentiary system, the alternative means of justice, the citizens who participate in the administration of justice as provided in the law, and the attorneys authorized to practice law.[5]

---

[3]   See on the Venezuelan 1999 Constitucion, Brewer-Carías, Allan R. *La Constitución de 1999. Derecho Constitucional Venezulano*, Editorial Jurídica Venezolana, Caracas 2004, 2 vols.

[4]   See Urdaneta Troconis, Gustavo. "El Poder Judicial en la Constitución de 1999", in *Estudios de Derecho Administrativo: Libro Homenaje a la Universidad Central de Venezuela, V.* I. Imprenta Nacional, Caracas, 2001, pp. 521-564.

[5]   See the Law on the Judicial System, *Gaceta Oficial* N° 39.276 of October 1, 2009. See in general Urdaneta Troconis, Gustavo. "El Poder Judicial en la Constitución de 1999," en *Estudios de Derecho Administrativo: Libro Homenaje a la Universidad Central de Venezuela, V.* I, Imprenta Nacional, Caracas, 2001, pp. 521-564; Duque Corredor, Román J. "El sistema de Justicia," en Casal, Jesús María. Arismendi, Alfredo y Carrillo

The principle of the independence of the Judicial Power is set forth expressly in Article 254 of the Constitution, which, in addition, establishes its financial autonomy,[6] and assigns "functional, financial, and administrative autonomy" to the Supreme Tribunal. Fos such purpose the Constitution provides that within the National general annual budget, an appropriation of at least two percent (2%) of the ordinary national budget is established for the judiciary, a percentage amount that cannot be changed without prior approval by the National Assembly.

With the purpose of guaranteeing the impartiality and independence of judges in the exercise of their duties, Article 256 of the Constitution requires that magistrates, judges and prosecutors of the Public Prosecutor and the Public Defenders' offices may not, from the time of entering their respective jobs until they step down, engage in partisan political activity other than voting. This includes political party activism, union, guild and similar activities. Magistrates, judges and prosecutors are also prohibited from engaging in private or business activities that are incompatible with their judicial functions, on their own behalf or on the behalf of others, and they may not undertake any other public functions other than educational activities. In addition, Judges are prohibited from associating with one another (Article 256), which is a limit regarding the constitutional right of association set forth in Article 52 of the Constitution.

According to Article 257 of the Constitution, the fundamental instrument for the realization of justice is the judicial process; regarding which the procedural laws must establish simplified, uniform and effective procedures, and adopt brief, public, and oral proceedings, through which in no case justice should be sacrificed based on the omission of non-essential formalities. These provisions are complemented by Article 26 of the Constitution that set forth that the State must guarantee expeditious justice without undue delay, formalisms, or useless procedural repositions. In addition, being the alternative means of justice part of the judicial system (Article 253), Article 258 of the Constitution imposes on the Legislator the duty to promote arbitration, conciliation, mediation, and other alternative means for conflicts resolution.

Artiles, Carlos Luis (Coord.), *Tendencias Actuales del Derecho Constitucional. Homenaje a Jesús María Casal Montbrun, V.* II, Universidad Central de Venezuela/Universidad Católica Andrés Bello, Caracas 2008, pp. 87-112.

6 See Perdomo, Juan Rafael. "Independencia y competencia del Poder Judicial," in *Revista de Derecho del Tribunal Supremo de Justicia,* Nº 8, Caracas, 2003, pp. 483 a 518.

Finally Article 255 of the Constitution, judges are personally responsible for unjustified errors, delays, or omissions, for substantial failures to observe procedural requirements, for abuse of or refusal to apply the law (*denegación*), for bias, for the crime of graft (*cohecho*) and for criminally negligent or intentional injustice (*prevaricación*) effectuated in the course of performing their judicial functions.

One of the innovations of the 1999 Constitution was to confer to the Supreme Tribunal of Justice "the Governance and Administration of the Judicial Branch," while eliminating the former Council of the Judiciary (*Consejo de la Judicatura*) which exercised these functions under Article 217 of the Constitution of 1961, as one of the organ with functional autonomy separate and independent from all the branches of government, including the former Supreme Court of Justice.

Consequently, since 2000, as provided in Article 267 of the Constitution, the Supreme Tribunal of Justice is charged with the direction, governance and administration of the Judicial Branch, including inspection and oversight of the other courts of the Republic as well as the offices of the Public Defenders.[7] For such purposes the Supreme Tribunal is in charge of drafting and putting into effect its own budget and the budget of the Judicial Branch in general, according to principles set out in Article 254.

In order to perform these functions, the plenary Supreme Tribunal of Justice has created an Executive Directorate of the Judiciary (*Dirección Ejecutiva de la Magistratura*) with regional offices. Judicial Circuits are to be established and organized by statute, as are the creation of jurisdictions of tribunals and regional courts in order to promote administrative and jurisdictional decentralization of the Judicial Power (Article 269).

As mentioned, jurisdiction for judicial discipline is to be carried out by disciplinary tribunals as determined by law (Article 267), which nonethe-

---

[7]   See the Organic Law of the Supreme Tribunal of Justice *Gaceta Oficial* N° 39.522 of October 1, 2010, See Brewer-Carías, Allan R. and Hernández Mendible, Víctor. *Ley Orgánica del Tribunal Supremo de Justicia 2010,* Editorial Jurídica Venezolana, Caracas 2010; Louza, Laura. "El Tribunal Supremo de Justicia en la Constitución de la República Bolivariana de Venezuela," en *Revista del Tribunal Supremo de Justicia,* N° 4. Caracas, 2002, pp. 379-437; Peña Colmenares, Nélida. "El Tribunal Supremo de Justicia como órgano de dirección, gobierno, administración, inspección y vigilancia del Poder Judicial venezolano", in *Revista de Derecho del Tribunal Supremo de Justicia,* N° 8, Caracas, 2003, pp. 391 a 434; and Dos Santos, Olga. "Comisión Judicial del Tribunal Supremo de Justicia", in *Revista de Derecho del Tribunal Supremo de Justicia,* N° 6, Caracas, 2002, pp. 373 a 378.

less was only formally established in 2010-2011 after the sanctioning of the Code of Ethics of the Venezuelan Judge, providing that disciplinary proceedings must be public, oral, and brief, in conformity with due process of law.

III. THE CONSTITUTIONAL REGULATIONS REGARDING THE STABILITY AND INDEPENDENCE OF JUDGES

The basic constitutional provision in order to guaranty the independence and autonomy of courts and judges is established in Article 255, which provides for a specific mechanism to assure the independent appointment of judges, and to guaranty their stability.

In this regard, the judicial tenure is considered as a judicial career, in which the admission as well as the promotion of judges within it must be the result of a public competition or examinations to assure the excellence and adequacy of qualifications of the participants, who are to be chosen by panels from the judicial circuits (Article 255). The naming and swearing-in of judges is to be done by the Supreme Tribunal of Justice, and the citizens' participation in the selection procedure and designation of judges are to be guaranteed by law. Unfortunately, up to 2011, all these provisions have not been applicable because of a lack of legislation implementing them.

The Constitution also creates a Judicial Nominations Committee (Article 270) as an organ for the assistance of the Judicial Branch in selecting not only the Magistrates for the Supreme Tribunal of Justice (Article 264), but also to assist judicial colleges in selecting judges for the courts including those of the jurisdiction in Judicial Discipline. This Judicial Nominations Committee is to be composed of representatives from different sectors of society, as determined by law. The law is required to promote the professional development of judges, to which end universities are to collaborate with the judiciary by developing training in judicial specialization in law school curricula. Nonetheless, none of these provisions have been implemented, and on the contrary, since 1999, the Venezuelan Judiciary has been almost completely composed by temporal and provisional judges,[8] lacking stability and being subjected to political manipulation, altering the people's right to an adequate administration of justice.

---

[8] The Inter-American Commission on Human Rights said: "The Commission has been informed that only 250 judges have been appointed by opposition concurrence according to the constitutional text. From a total of 1772 positions of judges

On the other hand, in order to guaranty the stability of judges according to the express provision of the Constitution, they can only be removed or suspended from office through judicial procedures or trails expressly established by statutes, led by Judicial Disciplinary Judges (Article 255). Nonetheless, up to 2011, because of the lack of implementing the Disciplinary Jurisdiction, judges were removed without due process guaranties by a "transitory" Reorganization Commission of the Judicial Power in charge of the disciplinary procedures, only eliminated in June 2011, which has been substituted by courts but whose judges are appointed by the political organ of the State, the National Assembly, instead of by the Supreme Tribunal of Justice.

IV. THE CATASTROPHIC DEPENDENCE OF THE JUDICIARY IN THE VENEZUELAN AUTHORITARIAN GOVERNMENT

Now, despite all the provisions included in the text of the 1999 Constitution, since 1999, Venezuela has experienced a process of progressive concentration of powers, implemented by controlling the nomination of the head of the State's organs. In effect, on of the mechanism established in the 1999 Constitution in order to assure their independence of powers was the provision of a system to assure that their appointment by the National Assembly was to be limited by the necessary participation of special collective bodies called Nominating Committees that must be integrated with representatives of the different sectors of society (arts. 264, 279, 295). Those Nominating Committees were to be in charge of selecting and nominating the candidates, guaranteeing the political participation of the Citizens in the process.

Consequently, the appointment of the Justices of the Supreme Tribunal, and of all other head of the other State's powers can only be made among the candidates proposed by the corresponding "Nominating Committees," which are the ones in charge of selecting and nominating the candidates before the Assembly. These constitutional previsions, were designed in order to limit the discretional power the political legislative organ tradi-

---

in Venezuela, the Supreme Court of Justice reports that only 183 are holders, 1331 are provisional and 258 are temporary", *Informe sobre la Situación de los Derechos Humanos en Venezuela*; OAS/Ser.L/V/II.118. d.C. 4rev. 2; December 29, 2003; paragraph 11. The same Commission also said that "an aspect linked to the autonomy and independence of the Judicial Power is that of the provisional character of the judges in the judicial system of Venezuela. Today, the information provided by the different sources indicates that more than 80% of Venezuelan judges are "provisional". *Idem*, Paragraph 161.

tionally had to appoint those high officials through political party agreements, by assuring political Citizenship participation.[9] Unfortunately, these exceptional constitutional provisions have not been applied, due to the fact that the National Assembly during the past years, defrauding the Constitution, has deliberately "transformed" the said Committees into simple "parliamentary Commissions" reducing the civil society's right to political participation. The Assembly in all the statutes sanctioned regarding such Committees and the appointment process, has established the composition of all the Nominating Committees with a majority of parliamentary representatives (whom by definition cannot be representatives of the "civil society"), although providing, in addition, for the incorporation of some other members chosen by the National Assembly itself from strategically selected "non-governmental Organizations."[10] The result has been the complete political control of the Nominating Committees, and the persistence of the discretional political and partisan way of appointing the official heads of the non elected branches of government, which the provisions of the 1999 Constitution intended to limit, by a National Assembly that since 2000 has been completely controlled by the Executive.

That is why, that in this context, it was hardly surprising to hear former President Chávez, when referring to the delegate legislation enacted by him, to say in August 2008, simply: *"I am the Law.... I am the State* !!;[11] repeating the same phrases he used in 2001, also referring to other series

---

[9] See Brewer-Carías, Allan R. "La participación ciudadana en la designación de los titulares de los órganos no electos de los Poderes Públicos en Venezuela y sus vicisitudes políticas," in *Revista Iberoamericana de Derecho Publico y Administrativo,* Año 5, N° 5-2005, San José, Costa Rica 2005. pp. 76-95.

[10] See regarding the distortion of the "Judicial Nominating Committee" in Brewer-Carías, Allan R. *Ley Orgánica del Tribunal Supremo de Justicia,* Editorial Jurídica Venezolana, Caracas 2004; the distortion on the "Citizen Power Nominating Committee" in Brewer-Caríasm Allan R. *et al,* Ley Orgánica del Poder Ciudadano, Editorial Jurídica Venezolana, Caracas 2005; and in "Sobre el nombramiento irregular por la Asamblea Nacional de los titulares de los órganos del poder ciudadano en 2007, in Revista *de Derecho Público,* N° 113, Editorial Jurídica Venezolana, Caracas 2008, pp. 85-88; and the distortion on the Electoral Nominating Committee in Brewer-Carías, Allan R. *Crónica sobre la "in" justicia constitucional. La Sala Constitucional y el autoritarismo en Venezuela,* Colección Instituto de Derecho Público, Universidad Central de Venezuela, N° 2, Caracas 2007, pp 197-230.

[11] Chávez Frías, Hugo. August 28, 2008. See in Gustavo Coronel, *Las Armas de Coronel,* October 15, 2008, available at http://lasarmasdecoronel.blogspot.com/2008/10/yo-soy-la-leyyo-soy-el-estado.html

of decree-laws he enacted at that time as delegate legislation.[12] Such phrases, as we all know, were attributed in the seventeen century to Louis XIV, in France, as a sign of the meaning of an Absolute Monarchy – although in fact he never expressed them–;[13] but to hear in our times a Head of State saying them, is enough to understand the tragic institutional situation that Venezuela is currently facing, characterized by a complete absence of separation of powers and, consequently, of a democratic and rule of law government.[14] Consequently, since 1999, a tragic setback has occurred in Venezuela regarding democratic standards, by means of a continuous, persistent, and deliberate process of demolishing the rule of law institutions[15] and of destroying democracy in a way never before experienced in all the constitutional history of the country.[16]

---

[12]   See in *El Universal,* Caracas, December 4, 2001, pp. 1,1 and 2,1. This is the only thing that can explain that a Head of State in 2009 could qualify "representative democracy, separation of Powers and alternate government" as doctrines that "poisons the masses mind." See "Chávez, Hugo seeks to catch them young," in *The Economist,* August 22-28, 2009, p. 33.

[13]   See Guchet, Yves. *Histoire Constitutionnelle Française (1789–1958),* Ed. Erasme, Paris 1990, p.8.

[14]   See the summary of this situation in Petkoff, Teodoro."Election and Political Power. Challenges for the Opposition", en *Revista Harvard Review of Latin America,* David Rockefeller Center for Latin American Studies, Harvard University, Fall 2008, pp. 12. See also Brewer-Carías, Allan R. "Los problemas de la gobernabilidad democrática en Venezuela: el autoritarismo constitucional y la concentración y centralización del poder," in Valadés, Diego (Coord.), *Gobernabilidad y constitucionalismo en América Latina,* Universidad Nacional Autónoma de México, México 2005, pp. 73-96.

[15]   See in *general*, Brewer-Carías, Allan R., "La progresiva y sistemática demolición de la autonomía e independencia del Poder Judicial en Venezuela (1999-2004)," in *XXX Jornadas J.M Dominguez Escovar, Estado de Derecho, Administración de Justicia y Derechos Humanos,* Instituto de Estudios Jurídicos del Estado Lara, Barquisimeto 2005, pp. 33-174; Brewer-Carías, Allan R. , "El constitucionalismo y la emergencia en Venezuela: entre la emergencia formal y la emergencia anormal del Poder Judicial," in Brewer-Carías, Allan R. , *Estudios Sobre el Estado Constitucional (2005-2006),* Editorial Jurídica Venezolana, Caracas 2007, pp. 245-269; and Brewer-Carías, Allan R. "La justicia sometida al poder. La ausencia de independencia y autonomía de los jueces en Venezuela por la interminable emergencia del Poder Judicial (1999-2006)," in *Cuestiones Internacionales. Anuario Jurídico Villanueva 2007,* Centro Universitario Villanueva, Marcial Pons, Madrid 2007, pp. 25-57, available at www.allanbrewercarias.com, (Biblioteca Virtual, II.4. Artículos y Estudios N° 550, 2007) pp. 1-37. See also Brewer-Carías, Allan R., *Historia Constitucional de Venezuela,* Editorial Alfa, T. II, Caracas 2008, pp. 402-454.

[16]   See, in general, Brewer-Carías, Allan R. , "El autoritarismo establecido en fraude a la Constitución y a la democracia y su formalización en "Venezuela mediante la reforma constitucional. (De cómo en un país democrático se ha utilizado el sistema eleccionario para minar la democracia y establecer un régimen autoritario de supuesta "dicta-

This has lead to the complete control of the Judiciary, which after being initially intervened by the Constituent National Assembly in 1999, [17] with the consent and complicity of the former Supreme Court of Justice, which endorsed the creation of a Commission of Judicial Emergency[18] that continued to function, although with another name, in violation of the new Constitution, until 2011.[19] In this matter, in the past fifteen years the country has witnessed a permanent and systematic demolition process of the autonomy and independence of the judicial power, aggravated by the fact that according to the 1999 Constitution, as aforementioned, the Supreme Tribunal that is completely controlled by the Executive is in charge of administering all the Venezuelan judicial system, particularly, by appointing and dismissing judges.[20]

---

dura de la democracia" que se pretende regularizar mediante la reforma constitucional)" in the book *Temas constitucionales. Planteamientos ante una Reforma,* Fundación de Estudios de Derecho Administrativo, FUNEDA, Caracas 2007, pp. 13-74; and "La demolición del Estado de Derecho en Venezuela Reforma Constitucional y fraude a la Constitución (1999-2009)," in *El Cronista del Estado Social y Democrático de Derecho*, N° 6, Editorial Iustel, Madrid 2009, pp. 52-61.

[17] See on the national Constituent Assembly of 1999: Brewer-Carías, Allan R. , "Constitution Making in Defraudation of the Constitution and Authoritarian Government in Defraudation of Democracy. The Recent Venezuelan Experience", en *Lateinamerika Analysen*, 19, 1/2008, GIGA, German Institute of Global and Area Studies, Institute of Latin American Studies, Hamburg 2008, pp. 119-142. On Auguts 19, 1999, the National Constituent Assembly decided to declare "the Judicial Power in emergency." *Gaceta Oficial* N° 36.772 of August 25, 1999 reprinted in *Gaceta Oficial* N° 36.782 of September 8, 1999. See in Brewer-Carías, Allan R. *Debate Constituyente,* tomo I, Fundación de Derecho Público, Editorial Jurídica Venezolana, Caracas 1999, p. 57-73; and in *Gaceta Constituyente (Diario de Debates), Agosto–Septiembre de 1999*, Session of August 18, 1999, N° 10, pp. 17-22. See the text of the decree in *Gaceta Oficial* N° 36.782 of September 08, 1999

[18] "Resolution" of the Supreme Court of Justice of August 23, 1999. See the comments regarding this Resolution in Brewer-Carías, Allan R. *Debate Constituyente,* T. I, Fundación de Derecho Público, Editorial Jurídica Venezolana, Caracas 1999, pp. 141 ff. See also the comments of Hernández Camargo, Lolymar. *La Teoría del Poder Constituyente,* UCAT, San Cristóbal 2000, pp. 75 ff.

[19] See Brewer-Carías, Allan R., *Golpe de Estado y proceso constituyente en Venezuela*, Universidad Nacional Autónoma de México, México 2002, p. 160.

[20] See Chavero Gazdik, Rafael J. *La Justicia Revolucionaria. Una década de reestructuración (o involución) Judicial en Venezuela*, Editorial Aequitas, Caracas 2011; Louza Scognamiglio, Laura. *La revolución judicial en Venezuela*, FUNEDA, Caracas 2011; Brewer-Carías, Allan R. "La progresiva y sistemática demolición de la autonomía e independencia del Poder Judicial en Venezuela (1999-2004)", in XXX Jornadas J.M. Dominguez Escovar, *Estado de derecho, Administración de justicia y derechos humanos*, Instituto de Estudios Jurídicos del Estado Lara, Barquisimeto, 2005, pp. 33-174; and "La

The process began by the National Constituent Assembly, after eliminating the Supreme Court itself, and dismissing its Magistrates, with the appointment, in 1999, of new Magistrates of the new Supreme Tribunal of Justice, without complying with the constitutional conditions, by means of a Constitutional Transitory regime sanctioned after the Constitution was approved by referendum.[21] That Supreme Tribunal, completely packed with the government supporters, has been precisely the one that during the past fifteen years has been the most ominous instrument for consolidating authoritarianism in the country. From there on, the intervention process of the Judiciary continued up to the point that the President of the Republic has politically controlled the Supreme Tribunal of Justice and, through it, the complete Venezuelan judicial system.

For that purpose, the constitutional conditions needed to be elected Magistrate of the Supreme Tribunal and the procedures for their nomination with the participation of representatives of the different sectors of civil society, were violated since the beginning. First, as aforementioned, in 1999 by the National Constituent Assembly itself once it dismissed the previous Justices, appointing new ones without receiving any nominations from any Nominating Committee, and many of them without compliance with the conditions set forth in the Constitution to be Magistrate. Second, in 2000, by the newly elected National Assembly, by sanctioning a Special Law in order to appoint the Magistrates in a transitory way without complying with the Constitution.[22] This reform, as the Inter-American Commission on Human Rights emphasized in its *2004 Annual Report*, "lack the safeguards necessary to prevent other branches of government from undermining the Supreme Tribunal's independence and to keep nar-

---

justicia sometida al poder (La ausencia de independencia y autonomía de los jueces en Venezuela por la interminable emergencia del Poder Judicial (1999-2006)" in *Cuestiones Internacionales. Anuario Jurídico Villanueva 2007*, Centro Universitario Villanueva, Marcial Pons, Madrid 2007, pp. 25-57.

[21]   See in *Gaceta Constituyente (Diario de Debates), Noviembre 1999-Enero 2000*, Session of December 22, 1999, N° 51, pp. 2 ff. See *Gaceta Oficial* N° 36.859 of December 29, 1999; and *Gaceta Oficial* N° 36.860 of December 30, 1999.

[22]   For this reason, in its 2003 *Report on Venezuela*, the Inter-American Commission on Human Rights, observed that the appointment of Judges of the Supreme Court of Justice did not apply to the Constitution, so that "the constitutional reforms introduced in the form of the election of these authorities established as guarantees of independence and impartiality were not used in this case. See Inter-American Commission of Human Rights, 2003 *Report on Venezuela*; paragraph 186.

row or temporary majorities from determining its composition." [23] Third, in 2004, again by the National Assembly by sanctioning the Organic Law of the Supreme Tribunal of Justice, increasing the number of Justices from 20 to 32, and distorting the constitutional conditions for their appointment and dismissal, allowing the government to assume an absolute control of the Supreme Tribunal, and in particular, of its Constitutional Chamber.[24] And fourth, in 2010, once more, the National Assembly reformed the Organic Law of the Supreme Tribunal of Justice, firs in a regular way,[25] and subsequently in an irregular manner,[26] in order to pack the Tribunal with new government controlled members.

After this 2004 reform, the process of selection of new Justices has been subjected to the President of the Republic will, as was publicly admitted by the President of the parliamentary Commission in charge of selecting the candidates for Magistrates of the Supreme Tribunal Court of Justice, who later was appointed Minister of the Interior and Justice. On December 2004, he said the following:

"Although we, the representatives, have the authority for this selection, the President of the Republic was consulted and his opinion was very much taken into consideration." He added: "Let's be clear, we are not going to score auto-goals. In the list, there were people from the opposition who comply with all the requirements. The opposition could have used them in order to reach an agreement during the last sessions, but they did not want to. We are not going to do it for them. There is no one in the group of postulates that could act against us…"[27]

---

[23]   See IACHR, *2004 Annual Report* (Follow-Up Report on Compliance by the State of Venezuela with the Recommendations made by the IACHR in its Report on the Situation of Human Rights in Venezuela [2003]), para.174. Available at: http://www.cidh.oas.org/annualrep/2004eng/cha p.5b.htm

[24]   *Gaceta Oficial* N° 37.942 of May 20, 2004. See the comments in Brewer-Carías, Allan R. *Ley Orgánica del Tribunal Supremo de Justicia*, Editorial Jurídica Venezolana, Caracas 2004.

[25]   *Gaceta Oficial* N° 39.483 of August 9, 2010 and N° 39.522 of October 1, 2010 . See the comments in Brewer-Carías, Allan R. and Hernández Mendible, Víctor. *Ley Orgánica del Tribunal Supremo de Justicia*, Editorial Jurídica Venezolana, Caracas 2010

[26]   See the comments Hernández Mendible, Víctor, "Sobre la nueva reimpresión por 'supuestos errores' materiales de la Ley Orgánica del Tribunal Supremo, octubre 2010," and Silva Aranguren, Antonio, "Tras el rastro del engaño, en la web de la Asamblea Nacional", in *Revista de Derecho Público*, N° 124, Editorial Jurídica Venezolana, Caracas 2010, pp-110-113.

[27]   See in *El Nacional*, Caracas 12-13-2004. That is why the Inter-American Commission on Human Rights suggested in its Report to the General Assembly of the OAS corresponding to 2004 that "these regulations of the Organic Law of the Supreme

This configuration of the Supreme Tribunal, as highly politicized and subjected to the will of the President of the Republic has been reinforced in 2010,[28] eliminating all autonomy of the Judicial Power and even the basic principle of the separation of power, as the corner stone of the Rule of Law and the base of all democratic institutions.

On the other hand, as aforementioned, according to Article 265 of the 1999 Constitution, the Magistrates can be dismissed by the vote of a qualified majority of the National Assembly, when grave faults are committed, following a prior qualification by the Citizen Power. This qualified two-thirds majority was established to avoid leaving the existence of the heads of the judiciary in the hands of a simple majority of legislators. Unfortunately, this provision was also distorted by the 2004 Organic Law of the Supreme Tribunal of Justice, in which it was established in an unconstitutional way that the Magistrates could be dismissed by simple majority when the "administrative act of their appointment" is revoked (Article 23,4). This distortion, contrary to the independence of the Judiciary, although eliminated in the reform of the Law in 2010, also pretended to be constitutionalized with the rejected 2007 Constitutional reform, which proposed to establish that the Magistrates of the Supreme Tribunal could be dismissed in case of grave faults, but just by the vote of the majority of the members of the National Assembly.

The consequence of this political subjection is that all the principles tending to assure the independence of judges at any level of the Judiciary have been postponed. In particular, the Constitution establishes that all judges must be selected by public competition for the tenure; and that the dismissal of judges can only be made through disciplinary trials carried out by disciplinary judges (Articles 254 and 267). Unfortunately, none of these provisions have been implemented, and on the contrary, since 1999, the Venezuelan Judiciary has been composed by temporal and provisional judges,[29] lacking stability and being subjected to the political manipula-

---

Court of Justice would have made possible the manipulation, by the Executive Power, of the election process of judges that took place during 2004". See Inter-American Commission on Human Rights, 2004 *Report on Venezuela*; paragraph 180.

[28]   See Rondón de Sansó, Hildegard , *"Obiter Dicta. En torno a una elección,"* in *La Voce d'Italia*, Caracas December 14, 2010.

[29]   The Inter-American Commission on Human Rights said: "The Commission has been informed that only 250 judges have been appointed by opposition concurrence according to the constitutional text. From a total of 1772 positions of judges in Venezuela, the Supreme Court of Justice reports that only 183 are holders, 1331 are provisional and 258 are temporary", *Informe sobre la Situación de los Derechos Humanos*

tion, altering the people's right to an adequate administration of justice. And regarding the disciplinary jurisdiction of the judges, it was only in 2010[30] when it was established. Until then, with the authorization of the Supreme Tribunal, a "transitory" Reorganization Commission of the Judicial Power created since 1999, continued to function, removing judges without due process.[31]

The worst of this irregular situation is that since 2006 the problem of the provisional status of judges has been "regularized" through a "Special Program for the Regularization of Tenures", addressed to accidental, temporary or provisional judges, bypassing the entrance system constitutionally established by means of public competitive exams (Article 255), by consolidating the effects of the provisional appointments and their consequent power dependency.

V. THE JUDICIARY PACKED BY TEMPORAL AND PROVISIONAL JUDGES AND THE USE OF THE JUDICIARY FOR POLITICAL PERSECUTION

Through the Supreme Tribunal, which is in charge of governing and administering the Judiciary, the political control over all judges has been also assured, reinforced by means of the survival until 2011, of the 1999 "provisional" Commission on the Functioning and Restructuring of the Judicial System, which was legitimized by the same Tribunal, making completely inapplicable the 1999 constitutional provisions seeking to guarantee the independence and autonomy of judges.[32]

---

en Venezuela; OAS/Ser.L/V/II.118. d.C. 4rev. 2; December 29, 2003; paragraph 11. The same Commission also said that "an aspect linked to the autonomy and independence of the Judicial Power is that of the provisional character of the judges in the judicial system of Venezuela. Today, the information provided by the different sources indicates that more than 80% of Venezuelan judges are "provisional". *Idem*, Paragraph 161.

[30] The Law on the Etics Code of the venezuelan Judges *Gaceta Oficial* N° 39.494 of August, 24, 2010, created the expected Disciplinary Judicial Jurisdiction. In 2011 the corresponding tribunal was appointed.

[31] See Brewer-Carías, Allan R. "La justicia sometida al poder y la interminable emer-gencia del poder judicial (1999-2006)", *in Derecho y democracia. Cuadernos Universitarios*, Órgano de Divulgación Académica, Vicerrectorado Académico, Universidad Metropolitana, Año II, N° 11, Caracas, septiembre 2007, pp. 122-138.

[32] See in general, Brewer-Carías, Allan R. "La progresiva y sistemática demolición de la autonomía e independencia del Poder Judicial en Venezuela (1999-2004),"

In effect, as aforementioned, according to the text of the 1999 Constitution, judges can only enter the judicial career by means of public competition that must be organized with citizens' participation. Nonetheless, this provision has not yet been implemented, being the judiciary almost exclusively made up of temporary and provisional judges, without any stability. Regarding this situation, for instance, since 2003 the Inter-American Commission on Human Rights has repeatedly express concern about the fact that provisional judges are susceptible to political manipulation, which alters the people's right to access to justice, reporting cases of dismissals and substitutions of judges in retaliation for decisions contrary to the government's position.[33] In its *2008 Annual Report*, the Commission again verified the provisional character of the judiciary as an "endemic problem" because the appointment of judges was made without applying constitutional provisions on the matter –thus exposing judges to discretionary dismissal– which highlights the "permanent state of urgency" in which those appointments have been made. [34]

Contrary to these facts, according to the words of the Constitution in order to guarantee the independence of the Judiciary, judges can be dismissed from their tenure only through disciplinary processes, conducted by disciplinary courts and judges of a Disciplinary Judicial Jurisdiction. Nonetheless, as aforementioned, that jurisdiction was only created in 2011, corresponding to that year the disciplinary judicial functions to the already mentioned transitory Commission, [35] which, as reported by the

---

in *XXX Jornadas J.M Dominguez Escovar, Estado de Derecho, Administración de Justicia y Derechos Humanos*, Instituto de Estudios Jurídicos del Estado Lara, Barquisimeto 2005, pp. 33-174; Brewer-Carías, Allan R. "El constitucionalismo y la emergencia en Venezuela: entre la emergencia formal y la emergencia anormal del Poder Judicial," in Brewer-Carías, Allan R. *Estudios Sobre el Estado Constitucional (2005-2006)*, Editorial Jurídica Venezolana, Caracas 2007, pp. 245-269; and Brewer-Carías, Allan R. "La justicia sometida al poder. La ausencia de independencia y autonomía de los jueces en Venezuela por la interminable emergencia del Poder Judicial (1999-2006)," in *Cuestiones Internacionales. Anuario Jurídico Villanueva 2007*, Centro Universitario Villanueva, Marcial Pons, Madrid 2007, pp. 25-57, available at www.allanbrewercarias.com, (Biblioteca Virtual, II.4. Artículos y Estudios N° 550, 2007) pp. 1-37. See also Brewer-Carías, Allan R. *Historia Constitucional de Venezuela*, Editorial Alfa, T. II, Caracas 2008, pp. 402-454.

[33]   See *Reporte sobre la* Situación *de Derechos Humanos en Venezuela*; OAS/Ser. L/V/ II.118. doc.4rev.2; December 29, 2003, Paragraphs 161, 174, available at: http://www.cidhoas.org/coun tryrep/Venezuela2003eng/toc.htm.

[34]   See *Annual Report 2008* (OEA/Ser.L/V/II.134. Doc. 5 rev. 1. 25 febrero 2009), paragraph 39.

[35]   The Politico Administrative Chamber of the Supreme Tribunal has decided that the dismiss of temporal judges is a discretionary power of the Commission on the

same Inter-American Commission in its *2009 Annual Report*, "in addition to being a special, temporary entity, does not afford due guarantees for ensuring the independence of its decisions,[36] since its members may also be appointed or removed at the sole discretion of the Constitutional Chamber of the Supreme Tribunal of Justice, without previously establishing either the grounds or the procedure for such formalities."[37]

The Commission had then "cleansed" the Judiciary of judges not in line with the authoritarian regime, removing judges in a discretionary way when they have issued decisions not within the complacency of the government.[38] This lead the Inter-American Commission on Human Rights, to observe in its *2009 Annual Report*, that "in Venezuela, judges and prosecutors do not enjoy the guaranteed tenure necessary to ensure their independence." [39]

One of the leading cases showing this situation took place in 2003, when a High Contentious Administrative Court ruled against the government in a politically charged case regarding the hiring of Cuban physicians for medical social programs. In response to a provisional judicial measure suspending the hiring procedures, due to discrimination allegations made by the Council of Physicians of Caracas, [40] the government

---

Functioning and Reorganization of the Judiciary, which adopts its decision without following any administrative procedure rules or due process rules. See Decision N° 00463-2007 of March 20, 2007; Decision N° 00673-2008 of April 24, 2008 (cited in Decision N° 1.939 of December 18, 2008, p. 42). The Chamber has adopted the same position in Decision N° 2414 of December 20, 2007 and Decision N° 280 of February 23, 2007.

[36] See Decisión N° 1.939 of December 18, 2008 (Case: *Gustavo Álvarez Arias et al.*)

[37] Véase *Annual Report 2009*, Par.481, en: http://www.cidh.org/annualrep/2009eng/Cha p.IV.f.eng.htm.

[38] Decision N° 1.939 (Dec. 18, 2008) (Case: *Abogados Gustavo Álvarez Arias y otros*), in which the Constitutional Chamber declared the non-enforceability of the decision of the Inter American Court of Human Rights of August 5, 2008, Case: *Apitz Barbera y otros ("Corte Primera de lo Contencioso Administrativo") vs. Venezuela* Serie C, N° 182.

[39] See *Informe Anual de 2009*, paragraph 480, available at: http://www.cidh.oas.org/an nual-rep/2009eng/Chap.IV.f.eng.htm

[40] See Decision of August, 21 2003, in *Revista de Derecho Público*, N° 93-96, Editorial Jurídica Venezolana, Caracas, 2003, pp. 445 ff. See the comments in Nikken, Claudia, "El caso *"Barrio Adentro"*: La Corte Primera de lo Contencioso Administrativo ante la Sala Constitucional del Tribunal Supremo de Justicia o el avocamiento como medio de amparo de derechos e intereses colectivos y difusos," in *Idem*, pp. 5 ff.

after declaring that the decision was not going to be accepted [41] seized the Court using secret police officers, and dismissed its judges after being offended by the President of the Republic.[42] The case was brought before the Inter-American Court of Human Rights and after it ruled in 2008 that the dismissal effectively violated the American Convention on Human Rights,[43] the Constitutional Chamber of the Supreme Tribunal response to the Inter-American Court ruling, at the request of the government, was that the decision of the Inter-American Court could not be enforced in Venezuela.[44] As simple as that, showing the subordination of the Venezuelan judiciary to the policies, wishes, and dictates of the President.

In December 2009, another astonishing case was the detention of a criminal judge (María Lourdes Afiuni Mora) for having ordered, based on a previous recommendation of the UN Working Group on Arbitrary Detention, the release of an individual in order for him to face criminal trial while in freedom, as guaranteed in the Constitution. The same day of the decision, the president publicly asked for the judge to be incarcerated asking to apply her a 30–year prison term, which is the maximum punishment in Venezuelan law for horrendous or grave crimes. The fact is that judge has remained to this day in detention without trial. The UN Working Group described these facts as "a blow by President Hugo Chávez to the independence of judges and lawyers in the country," demanding "the immediate release of the judge," concluding that "reprisals for exercising their constitutionally guaranteed functions and creating a climate of fear among the judiciary and lawyers' profession, serve no purpose except to undermine the rule of law and obstruct justice."[45]

---

[41]   The President of the Republic said: "*Váyanse con su decisión no sé para donde, la cumplirán ustedes en su casa si quieren ...*" (You can go with your decision, I don't know where; you will enforce it in your house if you want ..."). See *El Universal, Caracas*, August 25, 2003 and *El Universal*, Caracas, August 28, 2003.

[42]   See in *El Nacional*, Caracas November 5, 2004, p. A2.

[43]   See Inter-American Court of Human Rights, case: *Apitz Barbera et al. (Corte Primera de lo Contencioso Administrativo) v. Venezuela*, Decision of August 5, 2008, available at www.corteidh.or.cr. *See also, El Universal*, Caracas, October 16, 2003; and *El Universal*, Caracas, September 22, 2003.

[44]   Supreme Tribunal of Justice, Constitutional Chamber, Decision N° 1.939 of December 18, 2008 (Case: *Abogados Gustavo Álvarez Arias et al.*) (Exp. N° 08-1572), available at: http://www.tsj.gov.ve/decisiones/scon/Diciembre/1939-181208-2008-08-1572.html

[45]   See the text of the UN Working Group in http://www.unog.ch/unog/website/news_media.nsf/%28httpNewsByYear_en %29/93687E8429BD53A1C125768E 00529DB6?OpenDocument &cntxt=B35C3&cookielang=fr. In October 14, 2010, the

The fact is that in Venezuela, no judge can adopt any decision that could affect the government policies, or the President's wishes, the state's interest, or public servants' will, without previous authorization from the same government. [46] That is why the Inter-American Commission on Human Rights, after describing in its *2009 Annual Report* "how large numbers of judges have been removed, or their appointments voided, without the applicable administrative proceedings", noted "with concern that in some cases, judges were removed almost immediately after adopting judicial decisions in cases with a major political impact", concluding that "The lack of judicial independence and autonomy vis-à-vis political power is, in the Commission's opinion, one of the weakest points in Venezuelan democracy".[47]

In this context of political subjection, the Constitutional Chamber, since 2000, far from acting as the guardian of the Constitution, has been the main tool of the authoritarian government for the illegitimate mutation of the Constitution, by means of unconstitutional constitutional interpretations, [48] not only regarding its own powers of judicial review, which have been enlarged, but also regarding substantive matters. The Supreme Tribunal has distorted the Constitution through illegitimate and fraudulent "constitutional mutations" in the sense of changing the meaning of its provisions without changing its wording. And all this, of course, without any possibility of being controlled, [49] so the eternal question arising from the uncontrolled power, –*Quis custodiet ipsos custodes*–, in Venezuela also remains unanswered.

---

same Working Group asked the venezuelan Goberment to subject the Judge to a trail ruled by the due process guaranties and in freedom." See in El Universal, October 14, 2010, available at: http://www.eluniversal.com/2010/10/14/pol_ava_instancia-de-la-onu_14A4608051.shtml

[46] See Canova González, Antonio, *La realidad del contencioso administrativo venezolano (Un llamado de atención frente a las desoladoras estadísticas de la Sala Político Administrativa en 2007 y primer semestre de 2008)*, Funeda, Caracas 2008, p. 14.

[47] See in ICHR, Annual *Report 2009*, paragraph 483, available at: http://www.cidh.oas. org/-annualrep/2009eng/Chap.IV.f.eng.htm

[48] See Brewer-Carías, Allan R. *Crónica sobre la "In" Justicia Constitucional. La Sala Constitucional y el autoritarismo en Venezuela*, Editorial Jurídica Venezolana, Caracas 2007.

[49] See Brewer-Carías, Allan R. *"Quis Custodiet ipsos Custodes*: De la interpretación constitucional a la inconstitucionalidad de la interpretación," in *VIII Congreso Nacional de Derecho Constitucional*, Fondo Editorial and Colegio de Abogados de Arequipa, Arequipa, Perú, 2005, 463-89; and *Crónica de la "In"Justicia constitucional: La Sala constitucional y el autoritarismo en Venezuela*, Editorial Jurídica Venezolana, Caracas 2007, pp. 11-44 and 47-79.

On the other hand, regarding some fundamental rights essentials for a democracy to function, like the freedom of expression, contrary to the principle of progressiveness established in the Constitution, it has been the Supreme Tribunal of Justice the State organ in charge of limiting its scope. First, in 2000, it was the Political-Administrative Chamber of the Supreme Tribunal that ordered the media not to transmit certain information, eventually admitting limits to be imposed to the media, regardless of the general prohibition of censorship established in the Constitution.

The following year, in 2001, it was the Constitutional Chamber of the Supreme Tribunal, the one that distorted the Constitution when dismissing an *amparo* action filed against the President of the Republic by a citizen and a nongovernmental organization asking for the exercise of their right to response against the attacks made by the President in his weekly TV program. The Constitutional Chamber reduced the scope of freedom of information, eliminating the right to response and rectification regarding opinions in the media when they are expressed by the president in a regular televised program. In addition, the tribunal excluded journalists and all those persons that have a regular program in the radio or a newspaper column, from the right to rectification and response.[50]

In addition, in 2003, the Constitutional Chamber dismissed an action of unconstitutionality filed against a few articles of the Criminal Code that limit the right to formulate criticism against public officials, considering that such provisions could not be deemed as limiting the freedom of expression, contradicting a well established doctrine in the contrary ruled by the Inter-American Courts on Human Rights. The Constitutional Chamber also decided in contradiction with the constitutional prohibition of censorship, that through a statute it was possible to prevent the

---

[50]   See Brewer-Carías, Allan R., "La libertad de expresión del pensamiento y el derecho a la información y su violación por la Sala Constitucional del Tribunal Supremo de Justicia", en Brewer-Carías, Allan R. (Coordinador y editor), Faúndez Ledesma, Héctor, Nikken, Pedro, Ayala Corao, Carlos M., Chavero Gazdik, Rafael, Linares Benzo, Gustavo and Olavarría, Jorge, *La libertad de expresión amenazada (Sentencia 1013),* Edición Conjunta Instituto Interamericano de Derechos Humanos y Editorial Jurídica Venezolana, Caracas-San José 2001, pp. 17-57; and Davila Ortega, Jesús A., "El derecho de la información y la libertad de expresión en Venezuela (Un estudio de la sentencia 1.013/2001 de la Sala Constitucional del Tribunal Supremo de Justicia)," *Revista de Derecho Constitucional* 5, Editorial Sherwood, Caracas 2002, 305-25.

diffusion of information when it could be considered contrary to other provisions of the Constitution.[51]

Regarding other cases in which the Judiciary has been used for political persecution, they are referred to the exercise of freedom of expression, concluding in the shutdown of TV stations that had a line of political opposition regarding the government and the persecution of their main shareholders. One leading case was the *Radio Caracas Televisión* case, referred to a TV station that, in 2007, was the most important television station of the country, critical of the administration of President Hugo Chavez. In that case, it was the Supreme Tribunal in 2007, the State organ that materialized the State intervention in order to terminate authorizations and licenses of the TV station, whose assets were confiscated and its equipment assigned to a state-owned enterprise through an illegitimate Supreme Tribunal decision. [52] The case is the most vivid example of the illegitimate collusion or confabulation between a politically controlled Judiciary and an authoritarian government in order to reduce freedom of expression, and to confiscate private property. For such purpose, it was the Constitutional Chamber of the Supreme Tribunal of Justice and the Political Administrative Chamber of the same Tribunal that in May 2007, instead of protecting the citizens' right of freedom of expression, conspired as docile instruments controlled by the Executive, in order to kidnap and violate them. In this case, it was the highest level of the Judiciary that covered the governmental arbitrariness with a judicial veil, executing the shout down of the TV Station, reducing the freedom of expression in the country, and with total impunity, proceeded to confiscate private property in a way that neither the Executive nor the Legislator, could have done, because being forbidden in the Constitution (art. 115). In the case, it was the Supreme Tribunal, which violated the Constitution, with the aggravating circumstance that the conspirators knew that their actions could not be controlled. This case has also been recently submitted before the Inter American Court of Human Rights.

---

[51]   See *Revista de Derecho Público* 93-94, Editorial Jurídica Venezolana, Caracas 2003, 136ff. and 164ff. See comments in Arteaga Sánchez, Alberto, et al., *Sentencia 1942 vs. Libertad de expresión*, Caracas 2004.

[52]   See the Constitutional Chamber Decision N° 957 (May 25, 2007), in *Revista de Derecho Público* 110, Editorial Jurídica Venezolana, Caracas 2007, 117 ff. See the comments in Brewer-Carías, Allan R. "El juez constitucional en Venezuela como instrumento para aniquilar la libertad de expresión plural y para confiscar la propiedad privada: El caso *RCTV*, en *Revista de Derecho Público*", N° 110, (abril-junio 2007), Editorial Jurídica Venezolana, Caracas 2007, pp. 7-32.

Other cases of political persecution, also related to freedom of expression are the cases against Guillermo Zuloaga and Nelson Mezerhane; two very distinguish businessman that were the principal shareholders of Globovisión, the other independent TV station that after the takeover of Radio Caracas Television, remained with a critic line of opinion regarding the government. They both were harassed by the Public Prosecutor Office and by the Judiciary; accused of different common crimes that they did not commit; they were detained without any serious base, their enterprises were occupied and their property confiscated. They both had to leave the country, without any possibility of obtaining Justice. Their cases have also been submitted before the Inter American Commission of Human Rights.

The Judiciary, particularly on criminal matters, has also been used as the government instrument to pervert Justice, distorting the facts in specific cases of political interest, converting innocent people into criminals, and liberating criminals of all suspicion. It was the unfortunate case of the mass killings committed by government agents and supporters as a consequence of the enforcement of the so-called Plan Avila, a military order that encouraged the shooting of peoples participating in the biggest mass demonstration in Venezuelan history which on April 11, 2002, was asking for the resignation of President Chávez. The soothing provoked a general military disobedience by the high commanders, in a way witnessed by all the country in TV, which ended with the military removal of the President, although just for a few hours, until the same military reinstated him in office. Nonetheless, in order to change history, the shooting and mass killing were re-written, and those responsible that everybody saw in live in TV, because being government supporters were gratified as heroes, and the Police Officials trying to assure order in the demonstration, like the Officers Simonovic and Forero, were blamed of crimes that they did not commit, and condemned of murder with the highest term of 30 years of prison. The former Chief Justice of the Criminal Chamber of the Supreme Tribunal of Justice, general Eladio Aponte Aponte, confessed last year 2012 in a TV Program (SolTV) in Miami, when answering about if there were "political persons in prison in Venezuela, saying "Yes, there are people regarding which there is an order not to let them free," referring particularly to "the Police Officers," mentioning Officer Simonovic. The same former Justice, answering a question about *"Who gives the order"*, simply said: "The order comes from the President's Office downwards", adding that "we must have no doubts, in Venezuela there are no sewing point if it is not approved by the President." He finally said, answering a question if he *"received the order not tolet free Simonovis"* he explained that: "the position of the Criminal Chamber" was "To validate all that arrived already done; that is, in a few words, to accept that these gentlemen could not be freed". [53]

To hear this answers given by one who until recently was the highest Justice in the Venezuelan Criminal System, produce no other than indignation, because it was him, as Chief Criminal Justice, the one in charge of manipulating justice, in the way he confessed; condemning the Police Officers to 30 years in prison, just because obeying orders from the Executive.

VI. THE USE OF THE JUDICIARY TO FACILITATE THE CONCENTRATION OF POWER AND THE DISMANTLING OF DEMOCRACY

On different matters, regarding the organization of the State, the same illegitimate constitutional mutation has occurred regarding the federal system of distribution of competencies among territorial entities of the State, which in Venezuela is constitutionally organized as a "decentralized federal State"; a distribution that cannot be changed except by means of a constitutional reform. Specifically, for instance, the Constitution provides that the conservation, administration, and use of roads and national highways, as well as of national ports and airports of commercial use, are of the exclusive powers of the states, which they must exercise in "coordination" with the Federal government.

One of the purposes of the rejected 2007 constitutional reform was precisely to change this competency of the States. But in spite of the popular rejection of the reform, nonetheless, it was the Constitutional Chamber, through a decision adopted four month after the referendum (April 15, 2008), the State organ in charge of implementing the reform. The Chamber, in effect, when deciding an autonomous recourse for the abstract interpretation of the Constitution filed by the Attorney General, modified the content of that constitutional provision, considering that the exclusive attribution it contained, was not "exclusive", but a "concurrent" one, to be exercised together with the federal government, which even could reassume the attribution or decree its intervention. [54]

---

[53]   See the text of the statement on, in *El Universal*, Caracas 18-4-2012, available at: http://www.eluniversal.com/nacional-y-politica/120418/historias-secretas-de-un-juez-en-venezuela.

[54]   See Brewer-Carías, Allan R. "La Sala Constitucional como poder constituyente: la modificación de la forma federal del estado y del sistema constitucional de divi-

With this interpretation, again, the Chamber illegitimately modified the Constitution usurping popular sovereignty, compelling the National Assembly to enact legislation contrary to the Constitution, which it did in March 2009, by reforming of the Organic Law for Decentralization.[55]

In other cases, the Constitutional Chamber has been the instrument of the government in order to assume direct control of other branches of government, as happened in 2002 with the take-over of the Electoral Power, which since then has been completely controlled by the Executive. This began in 2002 after the Organic Law of the Electoral Power[56] was sanctioned and the National Assembly was due to appoint the new members of the National Electoral Council. Because the representatives supporting the government did not have the qualified majority to approve such appointments by themselves, and did not reached agreements on the matter with the opposition, when the National Assembly failed to appoint the members of the National Electoral Council, that task was assumed, without any constitutional power, by the Constitutional Chamber itself. Deciding an action that was filed against the unconstitutional legislative omission, the Chamber instead of urging the Assembly to comply with its constitutional duty, directly appointed the members of the Electoral Council, usurping the Legislator's functions, but without complying with the conditions established in the Constitution for such appointments.[57] With this decision, the Chamber assured the government's complete control of the Council, kidnapping the citizen's rights to political participation, and allowing the official governmental party to manipulate the electoral results.

---

sión territorial del poder público, in *Revista de Derecho Público*, N° 114, (abril-junio 2008), Editorial Jurídica Venezolana, Caracas 2008, pp. 247-262; and "La ilegitima mutación de la Constitución y la legitimidad de la jurisdicción constitucional: la "reforma" de la forma federal del Estado en Venezuela mediante interpretación constitucional", en *Memoria del X Congreso Iberoamericano de Derecho Constitucional,* Instituto Iberoamericano de Derecho Constitucional, Asociación Peruana de Derecho Constitucional, Instituto de Investigaciones Jurídicas-UNAM y Maestría en Derecho Constitucional-PUCP, IDEMSA, Lima 2009, tomo 1, pp. 29-51

[55] See *Gaceta Oficial* N° 39 140 of March 17, 2009

[56] See *Gaceta Oficial* N° 37.573 of November 19, 20022

[57] See Decision N° 2073 of August 4, 2003, Case: *Hermánn Escarrá Malaver y otros*), and Decision N° 2341 of August 25, 2003, Case: *Hermann Escarrá y otros*. See in Brewer-Carías, Allan R. "El secuestro del poder electoral y la conficación del derecho a la participación política mediante el referendo revocatorio presidencial: Venezuela 2000-2004", in *Stvdi Vrbinati, Rivista tgrimestrale di Scienze Giuridiche, Politiche ed Economiche*, Año LXXI –2003/04 Nuova Serie A– N° 55,3, Università degli Studi di Urbino, pp.379-436

Consequently, the elections held in Venezuela during the past decade have been organized by a politically dependent branch of government, without any guarantee of independence or impartiality. This is the only explanation, for instance, of the complete lack of official information on the final voting results of the December 2007 referendum rejecting the constitutional reform drafted and proposed by the President. The country, nowadays, still ignored the majority number of votes that effectively rejected the constitutional reform draft tending to consolidate in the Constitution the basis for a socialist, centralized, militaristic, and police state, as proposed by President Chávez.

The Constitutional Chamber of the Supreme Tribunal has also been the instrument in order to attack the democratic principle, limiting the right to be elected, imposing non elected officials as Head of State, or revoking the popular mandate of elected officials without having competency or jurisdiction.

Between January and March 2013, the Constitutional Chamber of the Supreme Tribunal, openly violated the democratic principle by imposing a non elected official as head of State, during the illness of former President Chávez and after his death, in two decisions adopted, in addition, without proving anything. The decisions were issued after deciding interpretations recourses of the Constitution: The first decision, N° 2 of January 9, 2013, was issued to resolve the legal situation of the non attendance by the President elected to his Inauguration for the presidential term 2013-2019, refusing the Constitutional Chamber to consider that the situation was one of absolute absence of the elected President, and instead constructing, without proving anything on the heath condition of the elected and ill President, a supposed "administrative continuity" of Chávez, affirming that even been absent of the country (he was said to be in an Hospital in La Habana), he was supposedly effectively in charge of the Presidency, so his nonelected Vice President (N. Maduro) was to be in charge of the Presidency.[58] The second decision, N° 141, of March 8, 2013, was issued after the announcement of the death of President Chávez, but without proving such fact or when it did effectively occurred, in order to assure that the Vice President (N. Maduro), already imposed as President in charge by the same Supreme Tribunal, was to continue in charge of the Presidency; and additionally allowing him, contrary to the text of the

---

[58]   See the text of the decision in http://www.tsj.gov.ve/decisiones/scon/Enero/02-9113-2013-12-1358.html

Constitution, to be candidate to the same position in the subsequent election, without leaving the post.[59]

In other decisions, also contrary to the democratic principle, the Constitutional Chamber of the Supreme Tribunal revoked the popular mandate of two mayors, a decision that according to the Constitution only can be adopted by the people that elected the officials by means of a referendum (art. 74). The Supreme Tribunal, ignoring such principle and provision, without having constitutional competency and usurping the jurisdiction of the criminal courts that are the only competent to impose criminal sanctions to officials for not obeying judicial decisions, issued decision N° 138 of March 17, 2014,[60] condemning the Mayors by considering that they had committed a crime (not to obey a preliminary injunction), and imprisoning them, without guarantying a due process of law. The common trend in this case was that both Mayors were from the opposition to the government

In another case, the Constitutional Chamber of the Supreme Tribunal also revoked the popular mandate of a representative to the National Assembly, which also can only be revoked by the people through a referendum, issuing decision N° 207 of March 31, 2014,[61] in a case that the Tribunal had already concluded because the action was declared inadmissible, proceeding the Tribunal to act ex officio, and interpret an article of the Constitution (Article 93), that prevent representatives to accept another public positions without losing their elected one. The initial petition that was declared inadmissible was a requested for the Tribunal to condemn the *the facto* actions of the President of the National Assembly to strip out the elected condition of one representative; being the result of the case, once declared the petition inadmissible, for the Tribunal, to *ex officio* decide to revoke the popular mandate to the representative that was supposed to be protected by the Tribunal. The reason for such decision was that the representative (María Corina Machado), had talked as such representative, before the Permanent Council of the Organization of American States, in a session devoted to analyze the political situation of Venezuela, from the site of the representative of Panama that had invited her to do so.

---

[59] See the text of the decision in http://www.tsj.gov.ve.decisioes/scon/Marzo/141-9313-2013-13-0196.html

[60] See the text of the decision in http://www.tsj.gov.ve/decisiones/scon/marzo/162025-138-17314-2014-14-0205.html

[61] See the text of the decision in http://www.tsj.gov.ve/decisiones/scon/marzo/162546-207-31314-2014-14-0286.html. Also in *Gaceta Oficial* N° 40385 April 2, 2014

Finally, in another decision, the Supreme Tribunal, also in violation of the democratic principle, accepted that the right of a citizen to be elected, which is a constitutional right, could be limited by an administrative body as the General Audit Office, when issuing decisions imposing public officials the sanction of disqualifying them to run for elected positions. In decision N° 1265 of August 5, 2008,[62] the Supreme Tribunal refused to declare that such disqualification for the exercise of a political right was contrary to the American Convention of Human Rights, that in Venezuela had constitutional hierarchy (Article 23). The lack of justice in Venezuela, lead the interested person, a former Mayor, to filed a petition before the Inter American Court of Human Right, seeking the protection of his political right, the result being a decision of such Court pf September 1st, 2011 (case *López Mendoza vs. Venezuela*), condemning the Venezuelan State for the violation of the Convention. Nonetheless, the response of the State was to file before the Supreme Tribunal of Justice, at the initiative of the Attorney General, an action for "judicial review" of the Inter American Court decision, which was astonishingly admitted by the Constitutional Chamber, which through decision N° 1547 of October 17, 2011,[63] declared the Inter American Court of Human Rights as "non enforceable" in Venezuela, recommending the Government to denounce the Convention. This eventually happened in 2012.

SOME CONCLUSIONS

The result of all these facts is that at the beginning of the twenty-first century, Latin America has witnessed in Venezuela the birth of a new model of authoritarian government that did not immediately originate itself in a military coup, as had happened in many other occasions during the long decades of last century, but in a constituent coup d'état and as result of popular elections, which despite its final goal of destroying the rule of law and democracy, have provided it the convenient camouflage of "constitutional" and "elective" marks, although of course, lacking the essential components of democracy, which are much more than the sole popular or circumstantial election of governments.

---

[62] See the text of the decision in http://www.tsj.gov.ve:80/decisiones/scon/Agosto/1265-050808-05-1853.html

[63] See the text of the decision in en http://www.tsj.gov.ve/decisiones/scon/Octubre/1547-171011-2011-11-1130.html

In particular, among all the essential elements and components of democracy, the one regarding the separation and independence of public powers is maybe the most fundamental pillar of the rule of law, because it is the only one that can allow the other factors of democracy to become political reality. To be precise, democracy, as a rule of law political regime, can function only in a constitutional system where control of power exists, so without effective check and balance, no free and fair elections can take place; no plural political system can be developed; no effective democratic participation can be ensured; no effective transparency in the exercise of government can be assured; no real government accountability can be secure; and no effective access to justice can be guaranteed in order to protect human rights.

All these factors are lacking at the present time in Venezuela, where a new form of constitutional authoritarianism has been developed, based on the concentration and centralization of state powers, which prevent any possibility of effective democratic participation, and any possible check and balance between the branches of government. Today, all the State organs are subjected to the National Assembly, and through it, to the President. That is why the legislative elections are so important, particularly bearing in mind that according to the Constitution, the presidential system of government was conceived to function only if the government has complete control over the Assembly. A government that does not have such control will find difficult to govern, being that the reason, for example, for the then President of the Republic, to declare just before the 2010 parliamentary election, that if the opposition was to win the control of the Assembly, "that would signify war."

The fact is that after a fifteen years of demolishing the rule of law and the democratic institutions, by controlling, at the government will, all the branches of government, it will be very difficult for the government and its official party to admit the democratic need they have to share power in the Assembly.[64] They are not used to democracy, that is to say, they are not used to any sort of compromise and consensus, but only to impose their decisions; and that is why they, when in 2010 they lost the 2/3 majority they used to have in the Assembly, they announced that they were not going to participate in any sort of dialogue.

---

[64]   See Brewer-Carías, Allan R. *Dismantling Democracy. The Chávez's Authoritarian Experiment*, Cambridge University Press, New York, 2009; Brewer-Carías, Allan R. *Authoritarian Government v. The Rule of Law*, Editorial Jurídica Venezolana, Caracas 2014.

That is why, even before the new elected representative took their sits in the Assembly in January 2011, the old Assembly approved an unconstitutional legislation in order to enforce what the people had rejected in a referendum of December 2007, the so called "Communal State" which is based on the centralized framework of the so-called "Popular Power" to be exercised by "Communes" and by the government controlled "Communal Councils".[65]

One further example of the perversion of the Constitution and of the will of the people expressed in the September 2010 Legislative election, was the move made regarding the appointment of the new Magistrates of the Supreme Tribunal. What just a weeks before was only a treat of the government, once it lost the 2/3 control of the National Assembly which prevented the government representatives to appoint by themselves in 2011, such magistrates; they immediately proceed to appoint the new magistrates of the Supreme before the inauguration of the new elected members of the National Assembly in January 2011, avoiding the participation in the nominating process of the opposition members of the Assembly. Nonetheless, in order to make such appointments, which required a previous reform the Organic Law of the Supreme Tribunal, for which they had no time to approve it; they proceed to make such "reform," not through the ordinary procedure, but through a completely irregular mechanism of "reprinting" the text of the statute in the *Official Gazette* based in a supposed "material error" in the copying of the text of the statute.[66]

Article 70 of the Organic Law of the Supreme Tribunal, in effect, established that the term in order to propose candidates to be nominated Magistrate of the Supreme Tribunal before the Nominating Judicial Committee "must not be *less* that thirty continuous days;" wording that has been change through a "notice" published by the Secretary of the Assembly in the Official Gazette stating that establishing that instead of the word "*less*" the correct word to be used in the antonym word "*more*" in the sense of the term "must not be more that thirty continuous days". That means that the "reform" of the statute by changing a word (less to more), transformed a minimum term was transformed into a maximum term in order to reduce the term to nominate candidates and allow the current na-

---

[65] See the Organic Laws on the Popular Power, in *Gaceta Oficial* N° 6.011 Extra. de 21-12-2010. See on these Laws, Brewer-Carías, Allan R. *et al.*, *Leyes Orgánicas del Poder Popular*, Editorial Jurídica Venezolana, Caracas 2011.

[66] See *Gaceta Oficial* N° 39.522 of October 1, 2010

tional Assembly to proceed to make the election before the new National Assembly initiates its activities in January 2010.[67] This is the "procedure" currently used in order to reform statutes, by means of the reprinting of the text in the *Official Gazette*, without any possible judicial review.

With this legal "reform," the National Assembly, composed by representatives that by December 2010, after the Legislative elections, can be said that they did not represented the majority of the people, proceeded to fill the Supreme Tribunal of Magistrates members of the Official political party, and even with members of the same Assembly that were finishing their tenure and that did not comply with the constitutional conditions to be Magistrate. As the former magistrate of the Supreme Court of Justice, Hildegard Rondón de Sansó, wrote:

> "The biggest risk for the State of the improper actions of the Nation al Assembly in the recent nomination of the magistrates of the Supreme Tribunal of Justice, lies not only in the lacking, in the majority of the appointed of the constitutional conditions, but having taken into the apex of the Judicial Power the decisive influence of one sector of the legislative Power, due to the fact that for different Chambers, five legislators were elected."[68]

The same former Magistrate Sansó affirmed that "a whole fundamental sector of the power of the State is going to be in the hands of a small group of persons that are not jurist, but politician by profession, to whom will correspond, among other functions, the control of normative acts," adding that "the most grave I that those appointing, even for a single moment realized that they were designating the highest judges of the Venezuelan legal system that, as such, had to be the most competent, and of recognized prestige as the Constitution imposes."[69] She concluded, as aforementioned, recognizing within the "grave errors" accompanying the nomination, the fact of:

---

[67]   See the comments in Hernández Mendible, Víctor, "Sobre la nueva reimpresión por "supuestos errores" materiales de la LOTSJ en la *Gaceta Oficial* N° 39.522, de 1 de octubre de 2010," and Silva Aranguren, Antonio, "Tras el rastro del engaño, en la web de la Asamblea Nacional," published as an *Addendum* to the book of Brewer-Carías, Allan R. and Hernández Mendible, Víctor, *Ley Orgánica del Tribunal Supremo de Justicia de 2010,* Editorial Jurídica Venezolana, Caracas 2010.

[68]   See Rondón de Sansó, Hildegard. "*Obiter Dicta*. En torno a una elección," in *La Voce d'Italia*, 14-12-2010.

[69]   *Id.*

"The configuration of the Nominating Judicial Committee, that the Constitution created as a neutral organ, representing the 'different sectors of society' (Article 271), but the Organic Law of the Supreme Tribunal converted it in an unconstitutional way, into an appendix of the Legislative Power.

The consequence of this grave error was unavoidable: those electing elected their own colleagues, considering that acting in such a way was the most natural thing in this world, and, as example of that, were the shameful applauses with which each appointment was greeted".[70]

Unfortunately, the political control over the Supreme Tribunal of Justice has permeated to all the judiciary, due mainly to the already mentioned fact that in Venezuela, it is the Supreme Tribunal the one in charge of the government and administration of the Judiciary. This has affected gravely the autonomy and independence of judges at all levels of the Judiciary, which has been aggravated by the fact that during the past fifteen years the Venezuelan Judiciary has been composed primarily of temporary and provisional judges, without career or stability, appointed without the public competition process of selection established in the Constitution, and dismissed without due process of law, for political reasons.[71] This reality amounts to political control of the Judiciary, as demonstrated by the dismissal of judges who have adopted decisions contrary to the policies of the governing political authorities.

New York, April 2014

---

[70]   *Id.*

[71]   See Inter-American Commission on Human Rights, *Report on the Situation of Human Rights in Venezuela*, OEA/Ser.L/V/II.118, doc. 4 rev. 2, December 29, 2003, par. 174, *available at* http://www.cidh.oas.org/countryrep/Venezuela2003eng/toc.htm.

- *L'EFFET PROSPECTIF DES DÉCISIONS DE JUSTICE/JUDICIAL RULINGS WITH PROSPECTIVE EFFECTS*

JUDICIAL RULING WITH PROSPECTIVE EFFECT

Hildegard Rondón de Sansó
PROFESSOR, CENTRAL UNIVERSITY VENEZUELA

Abstract. *This study analyzes and presents the situation of Venezuelan jurisprudence or case law with regard to the acceptance of **rulings with prospective effect**, understood as those rulings, the effect of which is intended to control future situations that are fully comparable to the situation currently being dealt with. The analysis of prospective ruling determines the value of **precedent** in the Venezuelan system and, specifically, that with a **binding nature**, like in the case of the provision of Article 335 of the Constitution of the Bolivarian Republic of Venezuela.*

Key Words. *Prospective Effect; Retroactive Effect; "Stare Decisis"; Legal Precedent; "Prospective Overruling"; Temporary or Interim Constitutionality; "Modulation of Sentences: Interpretative or Conditional Rulings; Substitutive Rulings; Rulings with temporary Effects.*

SUBJECT OF THE PAPER

The paper refers to point I.b of the questionnaire prepared for the XIXth Congress on Comparative Law, to be held in Vienna in 2014. This point deals with the "*General Theory of Law,*" and this paper delves into the subject of *Judicial Rulings with prospective Effect*". The subject in French is found under the title: "*L'effet prospectif des décisions de justice.*"

In Venezuelan law, the use of the term *"prospective"* as an adjective is uncommon, even though it is understood as referring to a future effect. It is possible that in other Latin American countries, which have been more intensely influenced by the Anglo-Saxon Law, the use of this term to refer to the effectiveness of rulings or actions in general is widespread. If one thing is true is that in our system, the term *"retroactive"* to refer to past effects is very usual even in regulatory texts, unlike the *"prospective"* effect, which is seldom mentioned.

We now proceed to answer the questions made by the General Rapporteur, following the same order in which they were posed.

I. COULD YOU BRIEFLY DESCRIBE HOW DOES THE CONCEPT OF PRECEDENT OPERATE IN YOUR LEGAL SYSTEM? IS THERE ANY PARTICULAR PROVISION ESTABLISHING PRECEDENT? ARE THERE PRACTICAL, LEGAL OR CONSTITUTIONAL RULES ON THIS MATTER?

Even though the question refers to *"your legal system,"* we can infer from its context that the aim of the question is to address the **judicial** application of precedent.

We will deal with judicial precedent in a brief manner, before delving into it in more detail throughout this paper, by noting that it is a decision made ahead of the cases that are being heard by a judge, which refers to identical or similar circumstances to those submitted to the said decision. Therefore, a precedent could guide the judge in the issuance of the corresponding ruling. If a precedent has been classified as *"binding"*, it will be mandatory for the judge and becomes a true legal rule in itself with full force and effect of a repealing law of any source deciding in a different sense. Therefore, it could repeal laws with different contents.

It should be borne in mind that Western legal systems are divided into those that address precedent as a fundamental source, like the Common Law or the Anglo-Saxon system, and the German-French or legalist system the essential source of which is the written law.

The principle of *"stare decisis"*, a Latin phrase that is interpretatively translated as *"to stand by decisions and not disturb the undisturbed,"* is applied in the legal system based on Common Law. This phrase is used in Law to refer to a doctrine according to which rulings handed down by a court give rise to a **judicial precedent** and are binding, as jurisprudence or case law, on those that may be issued in the future on similar matters.

This shortened phrase comes from a longer one: "**Stare decisis et non quieta movere**," which refers to the condition of an individual who has to quietly wait, without any disturbance, for the decision to be made.

According to the principle of *stare decisis* quoted above, previous rulings on identical matters should be assumed by courts, which, therefore, are obliged to abide by or comply with already resolved matters. This is a general maxim that expresses that when a matter has been resolved by means of a ruling that sets a precedent, said precedent shall be applied, unless other circumstances modify the *status quo*. Standing by the ruling issued before makes it necessary to back up the change adopted in a robust manner; therefore the *stare decisis* doctrine does not prevent previous decisions from being revised and, if necessary, annulled, with the added difficulty of considering a number of factors, including: the age of the preceding decision that is to be followed; the nature and degree of public and private confidence on which variation is supported and its compatibility or incompatibility with other legislative rules.

However, judges in the Common Law system, above all the American, are relatively free to dissent from the doctrine set by the precedent and have the power to create their own rule, thus emerging a **new precedent**, which allows Common Law to maintain a continuous dynamics of change.

The Royal Courts of Justice of Westminster developed the *stare decisis* system referred to above, according to which once a judge had decided on a cause, the other judges were obliged to follow suit.

The second branch of English law is "equity" which was a way to overcome the main flaw of Common Law, i.e. the fact that the precedent stopped Law from evolving. The Court of Chancery handed down its rulings based on equity.

Concerning countries of Roman-German tradition, they receive Roman rules directly, because in almost all peoples dominated by the Roman Empire, general law rules were applied. This circumstance led to a limited adoption of the custom system which, if existed, only constituted a subsidiary source. This means that due to the existence for historical reasons of general legal rules imposed by public power, those countries did not have to provide judicial rulings with an imperative and mandatory character for their judges; even rulings issued by the Constitutional Courts or the Courts of Cassation had a merely informative characters and could be an interpretation reference for lower court judges, without them having to restrict their possibility of dissenting and separating from jurisprudence decisions of higher courts.

Most systems, however, recognize that reiterated jurisprudence should somehow bind judges, because, while they are independent, it is necessary to prevent their rulings from being fully unforeseeable or that contradictory rulings are handed down.

The current Constitution of the Bolivarian Republic of Venezuela, dated December 30 1999,[1] announces that a severe legalism is imposed in its Article 137 when it reads that the Constitution and the Law shall define powers of entities exercising the Public Power, which they shall abide by during the development of their activities.

In principle, articles of the Constitution do nothing but praise the **supremacy of law**, noting, in this regard, in its Preamble, as purposes of the Constitution *"the rule of law for this and future generations."* In defining sovereignty, Article 5 *ejusdem* reads that sovereignty resides in a non transferable way in the people, who exercise it directly in the manner provided for in this Constitution and in the law.

Article 7, in turn, provides for the **principle of constitutional supremacy**, pointing out that the Constitution is the supreme law and foundation of the legal order and individuals and bodies exercising Public Power are subject to it. At all time, throughout the Constitution, but especially in the enunciation of duties, rights and guarantees, the law is described as the supreme source of Law and power regulation.

The Civil Procedure Code contains the sources governing civil proceedings. For instance, Article 9 of the Code stipulates that procedural law has been applied since the Code's entering into force, regardless whether proceedings were still ongoing. Article 12 of the same Code, in turn, requires judges to adjust their rulings to *"legal rules,"* unless the law empowers them to decide based on equity.

According to the Civil Procedure Code, the law only ceases to govern when it collides with any constitutional provision. In this regard, Article 20 of the aforementioned Code points out that *"in the event that the current law which application is requested collides with any constitutional provision, judges shall preferably apply the latter"*. This rule allows the so-called *"diffuse control of the Constitution,"* because any judge may *"disregard"* the law that is breaching the Constitutional provision.

---

[1]   *Official Gazette* N° 36.860, same date; however, it was published again in the *Official Gazette* Extraordinary N° 5.453 dated March 24, 2000 and was amended on February 15, 2009 and published in the *Official Gazette*, Extraordinary Issue, N° 5.908 dated February 19, 2009

Up to this point, the system appears to be properly legalist; however, a number of elements have made us abruptly go from said system to the theory of precedent as the **main** source of law. In this sense, 1999 Constitution, in its Article 335, surprisingly, provides for that interpretations by the Constitutional Chamber with regard to the content, scope and principles of the Constitution shall be considered **binding** on the other Chambers of the Supreme Tribunal and the other courts of the Republic.

The Organic Law of the Supreme Tribunal of Justice, dated October 1, 2010[2], underscores this trend by remembering that the Constitution foresaw the **binding interpretations of the Constitutional Chamber** when the said Law speaks about the *"content or scope of Constitutional provisions and principles,"* which operates on the other Chambers of the Supreme Tribunal of Justice and the other courts of the Republic, as already seen.

To strengthen this principle, the Organic Law of the Supreme Tribunal of Justice stipulates as a competence of the Constitutional Chamber that of *"reviewing final rulings handed down by courts of the Republic, **in the event that they have ignored any precedent set by the Constitutional Chamber"***. Numbers 11 and 12 *ejusdem* also empower the Chamber to *"review rulings issued by the other Chambers,"* provided they have **ignored a precedent** set by the Constitutional Chamber and also when **diffuse control of constitutionality of the laws** or other rules has been exercised by the remaining Chambers of the Supreme Tribunal of Justice and the other courts of the Republic.

A judge's disregarding a **precedent** set by the Constitutional Chamber constitutes grounds for **nullification of the ruling** and penalization of the judge.

In this regard, the Constitutional Chamber, in its ruling of June 18, 2013, concerning an extraordinary appeal against a decision issued by the Superior Court on Civil, Mercantile, Transit, Labor, Minor and Labor Stability-related Matters of the Judicial District of the State of Aragua, stated that judges that, at the time of deciding on a similar case, refuse to accept the precedent set by the aforementioned Chamber will be held responsible for misconduct in the exercise of their function. In this case, the Chamber found that the judge issuing the ruling pointed out in the same that the Constitutional Chamber had regarded as binding a ruling and that this faced him with the following conflict of consciousness: *"applying the doctrine set in the referred ruling or disregarding in favor of justice, for*

---

[2]   *Official Gazette* N° 39.522

the upholding of which the law is conceived as an instrument". The judge opted for disregarding the precedent, due to which he was fined with fifteen days of salary, following a warning that *"henceforth, you shall abstain from disregarding precedents established as binding by the Constitutional Chamber"*.

The Organic Law of the Supreme Tribunal of Justice insists in the supreme hierarchy of the Constitutional Chamber concerning the interpretation of constitutional rules, empowering it to declare total or partial nullity of national laws and further acts with full force and effect of law passed by the National Assembly, provided they may collide with the Constitution[3]; as well as constitutions and laws of the different states of the country, municipal ordinances and other acts by deliberating bodies of states and municipalities, which are issued in direct and immediate enforcement of the Constitution of the Republic but may collide with it, and also acts by the National Executive, which may collide with the Constitution of the Republic and with those of the different state bodies exercising Public Power.

The aforementioned Law also empowers the Constitutional Chamber – and it is at this point where the figure of **precedent** appears– to *"review final rulings handed down by the courts of the Republic, when the said rulings have disregarded a **precedent** set by the Constitutional Chamber..."* (Art. 25, number 10); this rule is also applied to rulings by other courts that fulfill the aforementioned assumption (Art. 25, number 11). The Chamber has also powers to review final rulings through which diffuse control of the constitutional character of laws has been exercised (Art. 25, number 12).

It is in these rules relative to powers of the Constitutional Chamber of the Supreme Tribunal of Justice where jurisdictional precedent is expressly mentioned.

Outside the judicial sphere, precedent is also mentioned in the Organic Law of Administrative Procedures, published in the *Official Gazette*, Extraordinary Issue, N° 2.818 of July 1, 1981, but only in relation to an *administrative res judicata* (a matter already judged). In this regard, number 2, Article 19 of the aforementioned Law provides for that administrative acts will be absolutely void *"when they resolve a case that has previously awarded a final ruling and that has created particular rights, unless expressly authorized by law."*

---

[3]   Organic Law of the Supreme Tribunal of Justice, Art. 25, number 1°.

A further rule linked to **precedent** is contained in Article 13 of the same Law referred to above: "*under no circumstances whatsoever an administrative act may violate a decision made in another act of higher hierarchy; or those of particular nature may violate an administrative provision of general character, even though they were issued by an authority equal to or higher than the one that issued said general provision*".

Non-retroactivity of the **previous criteria** is established by a rule of the Organic Law of Administrative Procedures as follows: "Article 11. *Criteria set by the different entities of the public administration may be modified, but the new interpretation may not be applied to previous situations, unless said interpretation is more favorable than the previous one. In any case, changing the said criteria shall not give rise to a right to review final acts*".

II. WHAT IS THE STATUS OF THE JUDGE-MADE LAW IN YOUR LEGAL SYSTEM? IS THERE ANY THEORY THAT DESCRIBES JUDICIAL II. RULINGS IN AN ANALOGOUS MANNER AS DECLARATORY THEORIES? WHAT IS THE NATURE OF THE JOINT EFFECT OF LAW AND PRECEDENT AS SOURCES OF LAW?

Before answering these questions, it should be pointed out that the concept of Declaratory Theory is presented in the literature as the thesis by virtue of which judges' rulings **do not create rights, but are intended to grant evidence of what Law is**; this is, to effect a judicial declaration.

The Declaratory Theory establishes that the judge does not create or change Law, but states, utters what Law has always been. Moreover, the judge may review past cases without changing the characterization of Law.

In the XXth century, the Declaratory Theory of State recognition, applicable to International Law, and according to which for a State to exist, other States have to recognize it, prevailed, vis-à-vis the Constitutive Theory of State (XIXth century). We have referred to these latter concepts because they can help to determine the scope of the Declaratory Theory in the judicial sphere.

However, in the specific case of the constitutional judge, whose decisions may be binding, said decisions do not necessarily consist of mere declarations. While original theses concerning constitutional jurisdiction only recognized the *negative judge*, this is, judges with nullifying powers, in the evolution of the system, these judges have been granted greater decision powers, because they are increasingly seen as the owners of the situations submitted to them, i.e. the most suitable individuals to solve them upon interpretation of the Constitution.

Meanwhile, in relation to the formulation of the second question, we observe that it is, in fact, composed of three different questions:

a. The judge has the power to create, modify or extinguish the legal rule, since, as previously stated, originally, judges had been only granted the function of "*negative lawmaker*", in the sense that the judge has powers to extinguish the legal rules. However, with the recent development of constitutional jurisdiction, the constitutional judge has been granted the possibility to bridge the gap of a rule that has to be eliminated, thus finding a situation consistent with the principles the judge has to safeguard.

b. Is the thesis of the merely declarative character of the ruling also employed in constitutional jurisdiction?

The answer derives from the question itself, because if judges may modify legal situations, condition their decisions and carry out the so-called **modulations**, which are accepted in almost all systems having constitutional justice and consist of providing judges' decisions with different contents and, at the same time, changing their effectiveness by modifying or broadening them, it is evident that their function is not limited to confirming a situation, but they are able to create, transform or extinguish legal situations.

Last of all, in constitutional jurisdiction, it is not possible to talk about a merely declarative effect of the sentence.

c. The third question is that of determining how law and precedents coexist in a juridical system.

We have said that our system is legalist in the sense that the highest source of law resides in the formal law, obviously after the Constitution. This principle permanently appears in the constitutional text, in such a way that it would appear to be an inarguable axiom. When Article 335 of the Constitution refers to its defense, it considers that the main guardian of sovereignty is the Constitutional Chamber, which, as an instrument to perform its task, is granted the power to hand down rulings on the interpretation of the Constitution, which are binding, that is, they are mandatory for all other courts of the Republic, including the other Chambers of the Supreme Tribunal of Justice.

If rulings of the Constitutional Chamber are binding for the judge, what happens if the judge finds a rule that contradicts the interpretation given by the Chamber? Which one should the judge follow? The ruling or the pure and simple rule? Several answers are possible to elucidate the preeminence of the binding ruling of the Constitutional Chamber over the rule contradicting it, because, above all, you have to precisely determine what the rule is. If it is a legal rule, it would appear that the ruling will prevail, since in this situation, it represents the constitutional text, as interpreted by the body with competence to do it. However, the situation is other if the conflict exists between said interpretation and the text of the Constitution, which has been drafted unambiguously and in a clear and accurate manner. In this case, the ruling misinterpreting this text should be disregarded with the justification of the corresponding judge, because applying it would constitute a violation of the Constitution. That is, if the rule is constitutional and it clearly expressed an opinion that was distorted or disregarded by the ruling, the judge has the power to disregard the ruling and apply the constitutional rule.

In fact, when the judge decides a case by means of an interpretation of a constitutional rule, the binding element in this case is the meaning given to the constitutional rule, which should be applied as a precedent for the case on which the judge must rule.

The judge's interpretation can never prevail over the specific rule contained in the text of the Constitution, because interpretation is nothing but a jurisdictional act that, because it is interpreting the sense of the Constitution, and it is going to have a high hierarchy among ancillary sources; however, the plain text of the constitutional rule cannot cease to be applied as a result of said interpretation if the same is openly contrary to its meaning.

Therefore, we believe that a legalist system, like ours, where the Constitution is at the top of the legal hierarchy, cannot be ignored by a jurisdictional act, even though the same is trying to be the one determining the meaning of the constitutional rule, because jurisprudence on hierarchy of sources is logically found at a lower level than the express text of the constitutional rule, even though it deals with its interpretation.

Therefore, we believe that in the debate on the validity of the meaning and the scope of the constitutional rule, between the solution given by the Constitutional Chamber to the case and what can be inferred from the plain meaning of the words contained in the text of the article, this latter should prevail.

III. IN YOUR LEGAL SYSTEM, WHAT ARE THE PROBLEMS RELATED TO JURISPRUDENCE THAT DERIVE FROM THE CASE LAW AND THE RULES OF PRECEDENT, IN PARTICULAR THOSE EMERGING FROM COURTS ACTING AS LAWMAKERS, IN WHICH BOTH CATEGORIES (CASE LAW AND PRECEDENTS) HAVE NOT BEEN CONFRONTED?

Let us remember that the concept of **case law** is understood as the rules that have been created based on the interpretation by courts regarding specific cases. Accordingly, case law is not created by the lawmaker, but by the court based on a concrete case or the interpretation of the laws that the court has applied.

The question has been made in relation to the eventual conflict between case laws and the rules of precedent and, in this last instance, in those cases in which courts have assumed the role of lawmakers. In this regard, we have to insist in an idea that is repeatedly referred to in this paper, i.e. that Venezuela is not a system embracing the case law, but, on the contrary, Venezuela's is, in principle, a legalist system in which judges are obliged to apply the written law, naturally subjecting themselves to the hierarchical order of sources.

According to this hierarchical order, the Constitution is the supreme rule, which illustrates the entire system and has an essentially regulatory content. The other rules appear by means of *"implementing acts"* that are understood as the process by virtue of which a general rule is particularized and an abstract rule becomes *concrete*, i.e., it comes to life through a specific assumption.

The immediate subsequent step in the order of sources after the Constitution is the rule with force and effect of a law; that is, it is immediately enforceable after the constitutional text which, in turn, may be object of implementing acts. In fact, the result of the implementing act that gives rise to the legal rule, when it is implemented, results in sub-legal acts that will also acquire their own hierarchy.

Specifically in relation to the question made, the case law doctrine is not applicable in the Venezuelan legal system, because judges should consider **the law** they are supposed to enforce; only if there is a precedent, i.e. a ruling on a case that is identical because it deals with similar assumptions as those pondered in the case object of the decision, the judge **may** apply it to settle the specific lawsuit.

To this effect, a distinction has to be made between non-binding and binding precedent. In this regard, applying a non-binding precedent is optional for the judge, whereas in the case of a binding precedent, like the one that **contains the interpretation of a constitutional rule by the Constitutional Chamber, its application is mandatory**, to such an extent that failing to apply a binding precedent may constitute grounds for the removal of the judge. However, as stated in relation to the previous question, the judge may consider that the constitutional interpretation by the Chamber departs from the true meaning of the rule when the said rule is simple and easily understandable.

For instance, the constitutional rule says that a certain action cannot be undertaken without any exception whatsoever if the ruling enunciates determined exceptional assumptions as existent. The judge should abide by the provisions of the constitutional rule and disregard the interpretation of said rule as it departs from the constitutional terms and norms.

In consequence, there is not any conflict between case law and precedent in Venezuelan law, but it does exist between precedent and implementation of the express rule. With regard to precedent, the same, according to Article 335 of the Constitution, shall be preferably and exclusively applied if it is originated by the Constitutional Chamber and deals with the interpretation of a constitutional rule, in which case, it will prevail over any other source, provided it respects the assumptions of the said rule, as we will explain in the subsequent answers.

IV. HAVE JUDICIAL RULINGS WITH RETROACTIVE EFFECT BEEN CRITICIZED IN YOUR JURISDICTION? SINCE WHEN? BY WHOM? LIKE IN FRANCE, HAS THIS SITUATION LED TO THE CREATION OF WORKING GROUPS INTENDED TO DISCUSS THE SETTING OF LIMITS TO THE RETROACTIVE EFFECT OF JUDICIAL RULINGS?

In this regard, we should point out that in the Venezuelan system the principles of the General Theory of Law are applied. According to these principles, the ruling declaring some acts void, alleging that they are vitiated by absolute nullity, has retroactive effect, because it declares that the act was vitiated from its origin and that, accordingly, it cannot be effective altogether; in this case, it is referred to as *ex tunc* effectiveness, which, as such, has a retroactive effect.

Among us, the distinction between the forms of termination of acts is clear. These differences are based on the effect that said acts of termination produce. The most important **modalities of termination** of legal acts include **nullity, repeal, derogation** (when it is general), **abatement of the act, exhaustion of the act** and **abatement** and **modification of its**

content or of any of its characteristic elements. We are going to briefly refer to the effectiveness of each one of these figures, once their existence has been declared.

Nullity of an act occurs because said act is so severely vitiated that it can result in absolute nullity or voidability. The main difference between absolute nullity and voidability is that the first cannot be validated, is not susceptible to be corrected; that is, the individual controlling the act (judge or general official empowered to do this) cannot modify the act to correct the defects affecting it, because absolute nullity is an irregularity with such a nature that the act extinguishes by itself and there is not any means to provide it with new life. Meanwhile, relative nullity or voidability is characterized because both the author of the act or any individual empowered by law to do it can modify it to add or remove some elements. Therefore, if a non-essential stage of the proceedings is missing, it can be exhausted; or if essential documents have to be added to demonstrate the facts, this situation does not appear in the file. Likewise, any missing requirement, the existence of which has been evidenced in the file, is a true judgment element. All acts mentioned above constitute validation or correction acts and, of course, the corrected act has normal effects. Unlike, the act vitiated of absolute nullity, which is declared as such, totally extinguishes. In this case, the Latin aphorism "what is void cannot produce any effect" is applied.

It is therefore unquestionable that the declaration of absolute nullity of an act has a retroactive effect; and it could not be otherwise, because what is stated is that if the act is considered irremediably vitiated, nothing can correct it and it is as if it would have never existed. In consequence, the declaration is retroactive because it confirms that the act was irregular in the past and declares its ineffectiveness from the time when it appears in the judicial world.

The second termination figure is *"repeal"*. This term has many meanings and some of them point out that it is determined based on whether the termination of the act is produced by the same entity dictating it. Another thesis states that repeal is a termination through the administrative way, unlike nullity that essentially takes place by the judicial way. This thesis is not correct, since the Organic Law of Administrative Procedures provides for the figure of nullification which the Administration may declare of its own vitiated acts. That is, that it is not necessary that an entity alien to the administrative sphere, like a judge, operates for the act to be terminated by means of nullity. Therefore, how is it terminated? Repeal does not refer to nullity or formal defects of acts, but to inconvenience or inopportuneness of the act in terms of the law. The act does not satisfy the interests of the administration or does not satisfy them fully, even though it is a perfectly valid act, constituted in accordance with the more demanding standards of the administrative procedure.

The problem is other when it is related to the possibility that the judge may repeal the act due to its timing or convenience. We have to be very clear in this regard. Let us remember that the "merit" of the act, that is, deciding if it is useful or effective, corresponds to the Administration, something in which judges cannot interfere, because they do not have the power to decide whether it is convenient or opportune for the Administration to dictate or omit a measure. This can only be qualified by the entity empowered to dictate it. However, what the judge can determine is whether there is motivation for the act and whether it is consistent with the situation presented; that is, the only thing a judge can do is verifying whether there is or not a motive and if said motive, regardless of its decisive content, is clear enough and is not contradictory (that is, formal elements that do not constitute an opinion of law).

The Italian doctrine has imposed the notion of the "*lack of merit*" of the act, that is, the fact that the same does not refer to the purposes and satisfaction of interests for which it has been dictated. The lack of merit occurs as the inopportuneness of the act itself, i.e. the act does not obey to the interests being safeguarded or pursued at that time, or is inconvenient or became inconvenient to satisfy the purposes pursued by the administration. The effects of the inopportune act that is to be repealed i.e. the effects of the repeal are *ex nunc*, that is, operative in the future.

Another form of termination of acts is *abatement*, which is the circumstance under which the act loses one of the elements justifying its existence. This happens, for instance, in the case of an act intended to authorize a patent to deal with a determined illness, and later an experimental and innovative drug which cures said illness is developed. In this case, the effects of the act have been abated, i.e. the act has lost its intended purpose and no longer has to pursue it.

A further form of termination is *caducity*, which consist of termination of the act due to the lack of compliance by the recipient with the burdens the said act imposes. It is known that some administrative acts submit their recipients to the compliance with a series of duties. When these burdens or obligations of the recipient are not complied with and this lack of compliance is verified by the Administration; the act terminates due to caducity. An example of this is the lack of payment of a fee or good, the failure to take a step such as delivering a notice. We just have to point out that in the case of abatement and caducity, the effects always occur upon verification of the fact producing them and toward the future; that is, there are no retroactive effects.

Another form of termination of the administrative act is the one result-ing from the **modification of its contents** or **any of its characteristic elements**. If the author of the act considers that any of the assumptions comprising its typology has to be changed, it is worth asking if in this case, a new act has emerged or it is the same act that has changed in ap-pearance. The doctrine has not unanimously decided what has to be **the answer**, but that the same is **casuistic** depending on the opportunity.

The description of the different modalities of termination of the act leads us to the conclusion that all of them only have effect toward the fu-ture, except for nullity, the effect of which is retroactive.

Furthermore, it is possible that the lawmakers grant a specific type of act an only immediate effectiveness, even though it is nullifying. In this same vein, this power can be granted the ruling judge or the administra-tion, even without an express legal provision existing, but leaving the granting of the power of providing or not the act emerging from a deter-mined proceeding with a retroactive effect, once the consequences derived from the effectiveness, either postponed or not, have been valued, to the opinion of the deciding entity or individual.

However, there is a ruling by the Constitutional Chamber, which sur-prisingly orders to retroactively apply a provision of the Criminal Code in relation to a crime of the disappearance of a person, on the grounds that the crime had a **continuous effect**, and, therefore, even though the crime was committed before the facts had been typified as crimes, said facts will continue to operate under the new law.

1. Analysis of Ruling N° 174706-1656, presented by judge Carmen Zuleta de Merchán

The Constitutional Chamber heard the request to review ruling N° 318 handed down on July 11, 2006 by the Criminal Cassation Court, deciding on the change of venue requested by Casimiro José Yánez in relation to the action against him for the crime of forced disappearance of people in prejudice to Marcos Antonio Monas-terios Pérez.

2. On the Ruling to be reviewed

The ruling to be reviewed was issued by the Criminal Cassation Cham-ber on July 11 2006 by judgment N° 318. which considers that the perpe-tration of the actions on file leads to presume the commission of crimes typified in Articles 177 and 182 of the Criminal Code (individual free-dom), aggravated by the concurrence of the circumstance established in

Article 77, numbers 1, 10 and 11, i.e. that the crime was committed with premeditation, taking advantage of the disaster that had occurred due to the heavy rains in the State of Vargas and in conjunction with other individuals to assure impunity. Therefore, the Chamber annulled the previous *habeas corpus* proceedings and demanded the public prosecutor to continue with the investigation and the Direction of Intelligence and Prevention Services of the Ministry of the Interior and Justice to open a disciplinary investigation against Casimiro José Yánez.

On the date when the crime was allegedly committed, forced disappearance of people was not typified as a crime in the corresponding Criminal Code. However, the Chamber considered that it was a continuous crime, i.e. a crime against freedom, of an instantaneous nature but with a permanent effect. The fact is that with this decision, the constitutional principle of non-retroactivity of sentences and penalties (Art 24) was disregarded.

V. HAS THE TECHNIQUE KNOWN AS PROSPECTIVE OVER-RULING BEEN USED BY COURTS IN YOUR COUNTRY? BY WHAT COURTS? ON WHAT CRITERIA? ON WHAT BASIS? HAS IT BEEN APPLIED IN AN IMPLICIT OR AN EXPLICIT MANNER? COULD YOU DEFINE PROSPECTIVE OVERRULING IN A GENERAL MANNER FROM THE POINT OF VIEW OF YOUR JURISDICTION AND TELL WHAT SITUATIONS ARE DEALT WITH BY THE SAID TECHNIQUE?

We should point out that the expression "prospective overruling" is unknown in the Venezuelan Law, unlike to other Latin American countries, like Peru or Colombia where, as we have seen in the specialized literature, the concept is frequently and broadly used. In Venezuela, this concept has not been upheld in any ruling; we could even say that no even in any commentary.

However, the above does not mean that the very meaning of the prospective overruling has not been applied in our Law.

In its broadest sense, prospective overruling refers to the sentence or judicial act intended to be applied in the future, i.e. it will regulate situations that have occurred subsequently its issuance. In this sense, it should be pointed out that this does not mean applying the classic difference as to the temporary effects of sentences, which distinguishes between retroactive effect (toward the past) and the immediate effect, i.e. upon and subsequently to the ruling. This difference is expressed with the Latin phrases: *ex tunc and ex nunc*, the first of which refers to the effect toward the past and the other to the fact that the act is only applied upon issuance of the ruling and thereafter.

Note that these categories refer to effects that are applied to **situations that exist at the time when the ruling is handed down and the difference** between them lies in the fact that the *ex tunc* **effect operates back in time with respect to the origin of the act or at a later time as stated by the sentencing judge, but always in the past**; whereas the *ex nunc* effect refers to the immediate effect. The condition of prospective effect in the ruling is going to regulate situations that have not been born at the time of its rendering.

The **prospective** effect is something more than the *ex nunc* effect, because it refers to the application of the precept contained in the ruling not only to situations that could be foreseen in the future, but also to others that have a similar assumption as that which was object of the ruling.

The prospective effect is underpinned by the force of the precedent, because it is intended to apply a judicial solution established in the ruling to analogous situations that may arise in the future.

The technique of prospective overruling is essentially intended to follow the **principle of procedural economy**, together with the **necessity of equitable treatment** of identical situations, so that to avoid juridical **discrimination**, which is contrary to the safeguard of human rights. In fact, the prospective overruling is that which has to be applied to one or more future situations; therefore its value is similar to that of the precedent because it is a precedent itself, that is, a decision the content of which is to have an effect on future situations that are equal to those that gave rise to it and have the same content.

To understand prospective overruling, it is necessary to analyze, albeit briefly, the different types of rulings based on their effectiveness, which operate in Procedural Law, more specifically, in Constitutional Procedural Law, which is where this concept has been most applied.

1. *Classical or traditional Modulation*

According to the most widespread and known criterion, constitutional rulings are classified into **affirmative**, which uphold the decision, and **disallowing**, which dismiss the ruling.

Martínez Caballero remembers that, in Colombia, constitutional rulings cannot be challenged or rectified in the internal legal system and the only possibility of over-coming incorrect interpretation is the procedure of nullification of the constitutional ruling which, in spite of being established, has almost never been successfully exercised. It is pointed out that the force of these rulings may lie in the ironical phrase of Judge

Jackson: *"We are not final because we are infallible, but we are infallible only because we are final."*[4]

2. *Modulation impacting the Content*

According to the content, rulings are classified into *"manipulative"* because they derive from the possibility of the constitutional court to *"manipulate the law."* The type of rulings that can result from manipulations or modulations of their contents include:

- Interpretative or conditional
- Additive
- Substitutive,
- Exhortative; and,
- With temporary effects.

An analysis of the types of rulings above follows.

3. *Interpretative or conditional Rulings*

Interpretative rulings are those in which the court restricts the scope of the challenged provision, either by limiting its application or its effects. These rulings are said to be manipulative because the text of the rule survives, but with an interpretation criterion that was not probably the one intended by the lawmaker.

Interpretative rulings may represent a rejection of any of the assumptions of the rule, which have been expelled from the legal framework, even though the regulatory statement from which they emerge remains unaltered. Opposite there are those rulings establishing interpretation according to the constitution of the regulatory statement. It would appear that in the Colombian Constitutional Court the practice of issuing this type of rulings has become rooted; this custom was inherited from the Supreme Court of Justice in those cases in which said Court controlled the constitutional character of laws; that is, before said function was assigned to it. In summary, interpretative or conditional rulings try to preserve the rule, only eliminating interpretations and applications that can be contrary to the legal order.

---

[4]   Judge Jackson of the US Supreme Court.

4. *Additive Rulings*

These rulings declare constitutional illegitimacy of the lawmaker's omission. *In this ruling, the Court does not annul the provision, but adds content to it to render it constitutional.* It adds a new element to the regulatory statement, expanding the rule for it to contain a factual assumption that it did not initially considered. It is unquestionable that in these cases, the constitutional court is stating a legislative omission, because its regulation is insufficient, since it has not provided for determined aspects that were required for the rule to adjust to the Constitution.

In our case, this situation is similar to the decision with respect to the provision in number 7, Article 336 of the Organic Law of the Supreme Tribunal of Justice, which empowers the Constitutional Chamber to hear the *unconstitutionality by omission*, when it states that the aim of the Article is "to dictate **rules or measures**" referred to in enforcement actions. In fact, Article 336, number 7 of the Constitution states as one of the powers of the Constitutional Chamber "*to declare the unconstitutionality of omissions by the municipal, state, national or legislative bodies, in failing to promulgate rules or measures essential to guarantee compliance with the Constitution, or promulgate them in an incomplete manner; and to establish the time limit and, where necessary, guidelines for correcting the deficiencies.*" Meanwhile, Article 24, number 7 of the Organic Law of the Supreme Tribunal of Justice reads as follows: "*To declare the unconstitutionality of omissions by the municipal, state, national or legislative bodies, in failing to promulgate rules or measures   essential to guarantee compliance with the Constitution, or promulgate them in an incomplete manner; and to establish the time limit and, where necessary, guidelines for correcting the deficiencies.*"

This rule has been taken from number 7, Article 336 of the Constitution, but with a significant addition; upon stating the power to establish the time limit for rules to be issued, as well as overall essential guidelines, the following phrase was added: "*Without this implying usurpation of functions of other entities of the Public Power or overstepping attributions of the competent Chambers*". We believe that this addition responds to the experience acquired by the Chamber throughout the long process of controlling the National Assembly's appointment of the members of the National Election Board, which eventually were appointed by the Chamber.

5. *Substitutive Rulings*

These rulings were developed in Italy to refer to those cases in which the Court expels from the legal system a challenged provision and fills the regulatory gap with a specific rule that is rooted in the Constitution. In some sense, said rulings are a combination of unconstitutionality and additive rulings, because through their decision, they annul the challenged provision, thus giving rise to a vacuum that is filled by a new mandate stated by the ruling itself.

Undoubtedly, these rulings, given that they fill regulatory gaps, would appear to be fulfilling a legislative function, since, under the Constitution, they have to correct a failure, because the constitutionality control should always be subject to the supreme values of the Constitution.

6. *Exhortative Rulings*

This type of ruling urges lawmakers to change preexistent situations within a time limit expressly determined by the Court, with the additional consequence that if this does not happen, the court will directly apply the constitutional mandate in the future, thus being able to determine the nullity of the respective legal rule. These rulings include from a mere advice to lawmakers to coactive formulas that urge them to regulate a matter dealt with in the Constitution.

These rulings undoubtedly limit the freedom to shape the legal order developed by the lawmaker, because they warn about situations that should be addressed by the lawmaker to avoid unconstitutional results.

7. *Rulings with temporary Effects*

In accordance with their nature, rulings classified based on their temporary nature may include the following modalities: a) Retroactive or *ex tunc* unconstitutionality ruling; b) *Ex nunc* rulings or rulings with prospective effects; and c) deferred unconstitutionality or temporary constitutionality rulings.

8. *Retroactive unconstitutionality or ex tunc Ruling*

According to this ruling, the Court may modulate temporary effects and in exceptional cases, apply them to situations consolidated while the rule that was declared as unconstitutional remained in effect. It has to be pointed out that in spite of the sensible nature of the criterion on which this assumption was typified, the same is very risky, because these rulings may impair legal security considering that they influence situations and/or rights already acquired and effects already produced.

9. *Rulings with prospective Effects or ex nunc Rulings*

These rulings imply that the challenged provision is removed from the legal apparatus once the ruling has been notified; however, this does not change situations consolidated while the challenged provision was in force. A constitutional court may even go further and determine a transition period to avoid inconveniences for the economic and political stability of societies. It is recommended to set a sensible effectiveness term. This kind of ruling was literally invented by German constitutional jurisprudence for reasons of practical necessity. Opinions regarding the doctrine are divided and it has been criticized alleging whether it is possible from the legal viewpoint to require the citizen affected by an unconstitutional rule to support the effects of said rule, in spite of its irregular condition, which has been already known and declared.

In fact, the previous analysis leads us to the so-called deferred unconstitutionality or temporary constitutionality rulings, which are those that, while declaring unconstitutionality of a challenged legal provision, do not withdraw or annul it immediately, but delay the nullifying effect of the ruling for a determined time period, within which lawmakers may proceed to modify the challenged provision to render it compatible with the text of the Constitution, or replace it with other compatible legal provision. The court may also determine **temporary or interim constitutionality of the rule** until the legislative body modifies or replaces it with another rule that is compatible. This type of ruling is aimed at avoiding the damage that may arise from declaring unconstitutionality and nullity of the law, since this could lead to a regulatory gap and could also impact law expectations that are derived from the enforcement of the challenged provision.

Hans Kelsen[5] stated that the main characteristic of concentrated jurisdictional control is the issuance of general or *erga omnes* rulings with prospective effect. In this regard, Kelsen wrote that "*it would be convenient for the Constitutional Court to be able to rule that the nullification, especially of laws and international treaties, will not have any effect until the expiration of certain periods upon its release, regardless of whether it is*

---

[5] "La garantía jurisdiccional de la Constitución", Editorial Kipus, 2006, p. 69.

to provide the Parliament with the opportunity to replace the unconstitutional law with a law that abides by the Constitution, without the matter governed by the annulled law being out of regulation for a relatively long time."

Two different formulas can be used in deferred rulings: a) certain constitutional courts declare unconstitutionality of the challenged legal provision, but also decide to expressly defer the effect of the ruling for a determined term, at the same time urging the lawmaker to replace the legal provision or to correct the unconstitutionality defects within the said term; b) other constitutional courts declare temporary constitutionality of the challenged legal provision, setting an effectiveness term and urging the lawmaker to replace the provision or correct the defects.

Modulating the effects of rulings has been defended, pointing out that far from being a contrived technique of constitutional courts, or an interference of the constitutional judge in the lawmaker's competences, it has emerged from the very needs of the practice and, as such, it deserves to be applied considering the practical advantages it offers.

VI. BY WHAT COURTS? ON WHAT BASIS? TO WHAT EXTENT? COULD YOU DEFINE THE TERM PROSPECTIVE OVERRULING IN A MORE GENERAL MANNER FROM THE POINT OF VIEW OF YOUR JURISDICTION AND TELL WHAT SITUATIONS ARE DEALT WITH BY SAID TECHNIQUE?

The repealed Organic Law of the Supreme Court of Justice, in its Article 131, granted the judge the power to decide *"the effects of the ruling over time"*. This power was referred both to rulings aimed at overall actions and those intended for particular actions; this implies, for instance, that nullity of an act that creates an individual legal situation may influence from the very moment of its inception, from the moment of its declaration and even at any other time the court may consider convenient.

The possibility of determining the effects of a ruling in time, above all in relation to particular acts, revealed a significant degree of discretion by the administrative litigation judge at the closing of the cognition phase of the crux of the appeal, and the said judge acquired the power of safeguarding the administrative order. It is no longer a matter of a controversy that has been settled, but of the administrator of the solution resulting from the content of the ruling and, therefore, the same will have to determine whether his decision will change or not the sphere of interests within which said decision will operate.

Unlike the case of individual acts, in rulings establishing total or partial nullity of a regulatory act, the necessity for the judge's decision to set the effects over time is evident. The above derives from the fact that the authority deciding on the permanence or termination of a regulatory act is exercising a legislative function, because by means of the ruling, said authority can modify the legal order. In this regard, the question is in which sense the jurisdictional body can perform in the time-related sphere.

To this effect, the ruling can be brought back to the past, to the time when the judge detected the defect giving rise to nullification, because a vitiated rule cannot produce any effect. However, what would happen if we go back a little further, i.e. before the time at which preparatory actions were initiated? The answer could seem to be negative in the sense that the only that would be voided would be the act and its effects, but not the preparatory phase, since its mention in the file plays a mere instrumental role (of the same nature of the existent evidence).

Now, going forward, the solution would not appear simple, but deserving of an in-depth analysis on a case-per-case basis. In fact, a positive answer would allow a vitiated and nullified act to survive for the time that the individual or body with the authority to declare its existence may decide, which would be equivalent to try to keep a dying person on life support. Even though logics inclines to deny the last possibility assumed, the ratio determining the judge's power to change the timing of his ruling tends to give a favorable answer, because the intention of that modifying power is, above all, allowing the judge to chose the timing and convenience of his decision in defense of the interests said judge is to safeguard.

It is worth asking if the above is valid both in the case of absolute or relative nullity. In our opinion, to give an appropriate answer, it has to be remembered that differences between both types of nullity somehow lie in the possibility of the second type to be validated, which is lacking in the first type. A further difference consists of the specific character of grounds for absolute nullity, as established in our system in Article 19 of the Organic Law on Administrative Procedures, which is in contrast with the residual nature that the aforementioned Law attributed to the grounds giving rise to relative nullity. The remaining comparison elements are referred to the powers of the administration in terms of the vitiated act, to such an extent that in the case of absolute nullity, Article 82 *ejusdem* stipulates that the Administration may declare termination of an act at any time. That is, the exercise of the power of termination is not limited by time or by the nature of the legal situation of the administrated ones, because its only obstacle in this regard is the existence of subjective rights that cannot emerge from an act vitiated by irremediable flaws. Last of all, suspension of the effects of an act may be requested through the administrative way and said suspension will be granted if the reason for the challenge is a defect of absolute nullity; a similar provision does not exist regarding relative nullity.

Having stated differences between absolute and relative nullity, it can be inferred that they are not relevant in terms of the timing to lodge the request for nullification by judicial process, because the time limit to exercise it is the same, regardless of the alleged defect. The law does not establish either the differences in relation to legitimacy of the appellant in a case or another; therefore, the main requirements for admissibility (caducity and suitability of the act to be challenged) are unified, regardless of the defect being claimed.

Finally, the law disregards the differences concerning the effectiveness of the declaration depending on whether it has an *ex tunc* or *ex nunc* effect.

This being said, the answer we gave with respect to the effects of the ruling, regardless of the defect of the annulled act, is inferred from the differences between both of them, because if they are not referred to effectiveness, the nullifying power of the judge can hardly be limited to the existence of a special type of defects.

The administration continuously and permanently issues individual acts on matters of its competence. The exercise of the administrative function essentially implies providing the administered party with the essential services the Administration is responsible for. But parallel to this, the Administration's function is also expressed in its power to issue individual acts that, as such, refer to the particular situation of determined individuals or groups or individuals. The individual acts of the Administration are not isolated and exclusive to a unique situation, but they are constantly repeated in an almost analogous sense with regard to different recipients. For instance, permits concerning city planning are not an extraordinary and unique act, but they are everyday procedures related to construction works in general. In the same vein, the different activities concerning citizens' identification (such as issuance for the first time of identity cards, renewal of those already issued; changes in personal data including changes in marital status; correction of birth certificates; issuance of passports, granting of licenses to perform determined controlled activities (sales of alcoholic beverages, for instance) are always routine acts to such as extent that many of them are issued "in series". In contrast with the automation of the procedures mentioned above required by their identical nature, challenges of those acts are personal, barring exceptional circumstances. The necessity to appeal on a case-per-case basis the acts that basically have similar content is a waste of efforts, because the applicant will certainly obtain a response to the particular situation in question identical to those that have been given to many other previous applicants.

From the procedural point of view, where the principle of procedural economy is applied, initiating as many procedures as appealed identical acts exist would appear to be useless when, on the contrary, the effects of an original ruling could be extended to all similar situations, even though parties affected by said situations had belatedly sought the procedural way.

1. *Cases decided in Venezuela having a prospective effect*

A. *Ruling issued by the Political-Administrative Chamber,*
dated July 15, 1999

The first case to be analyzed is that of AIDS patients against the Ministry of Health and Social Assistance of Venezuela. The ruling of the Political-Administrative Chamber of July 15, 1999 decided on a constitutional relief proceeding against said Ministry filed by several individuals, with the applicants being individuals bearers of the human immunodeficiency virus (HIV) of Acquired Immunodeficiency Syndrome (AIDS). The applicants claimed the following:

"1) To order the Ministry of Health and Social Assistance, through their respective agencies, 'to regularly and periodically deliver medical drugs known as Transcriptase Inhibitors and Protease Inhibitors such as AZT or Zidovudine, DDI or Didanosine, DDC or Zalcitabine, D4T or Stavudine, 3TC or Lamivudine, Crixivan or Indinavir, Saquinavir or Invirase, and Norvir or Ritonavir, according to the combined prescriptions of specialist physicians at the Immunology and Infectious Disease Departments of hospitals and health care centers attached to the Ministry...

2) To order the Ministry of Health and Social Assistance to carry out or assume the payment of specialized tests such as "viral load, lymphocyte count, platelet count and all tests to detect opportunistic diseases and those required to have access to combined treatment of Transcriptase and Protease Inhibitors."

3) To order the Ministry of Health and Social Assistance to develop "an information, treatment and comprehensive health care policy in favor of the people we represent, as well as other people living with HIV/AIDS and who are going through a similar situation to that of the people we represent.",

4) To order the Ministry of Health and Social Assistance to supply all medical drugs required for the treatment of opportunistic diseases, including antibiotics, antifungals, antidiarrheal drugs, chemotherapy, cryotherapy and all other drugs required due to their condition as HIV/AIDS patients.

5) Aiming at an equitable treatment and in the pursue of procedural economy and swiftness for a proper functioning of Courts, "to extend the recognized benefits to all citizens living with HIV/AIDS in Venezuela, who require therapy prescribed by specialist physicians, without it being necessary for them to permanently resort to the constitutional relief solution."

The petitioners of the constitutional relief quoted the ruling issued with regard to a similar matter by the same Political-Administrative Chamber on **January 20, 1998**, in the case of a group of troops of the National Armed Forces (FF.AA.), who were protected by the ruling that ordered the Ministry of Defense to deliver the proper antiviral drugs.

Likewise, they referred to the ruling of the Political-Administrative Chamber of **August 14, 1998** in relation to the request by HIV positive patients to obtain antiretroviral therapy and comprehensive health care services; request which was granted.

The Chamber, upon granting the relief, pointed out that the problem of the high cost of treatment for AIDS patients, which was estimated throughout the entire patient's life at about USD 120,000, equivalent at the time of the ruling to about Bs. 72 million, impacted the budget issue. Therefore, to safeguard the right to health on the one part and the effective legal protection, on the other, the Chamber presented two possibilities that would settle the claims of the HIV/AIDS patients: the amending budget procedure provided for in Article 32 of the Organic Law of the Budgetary Regime and the request for supplementary appropriations, depending on approval by the Congress or the Delegate Committee of the Congress. At the same time the Political-Administrative Chamber ratified the criteria it had set in its ruling of August 14, 1998, in the sense that a national prevention program should be established, stating, at the same time, the guidelines for said program.

The significance of the ruling is that its decision is extended to subjects that tare in the same situation as the original actors. To this effect, the ruling established as follows:

"Upon declaring the existence of a violation of the rights to health, this Chamber shall decide on the request of the petitioners, in the sense that aiming at an equitable treatment and in the pursue of the procedural economy and swiftness for a proper functioning of Courts, "the benefits recognized are extended to all citizens living with HIV/AIDS in Venezuela, who require therapy prescribed by specialist physicians, without it being necessary for them to permanently resort to the constitutional relief solution."

B. *Ruling issued by the Supreme Court of Justice in Full Court on July 14, 1999*

Another case in which the subjective effectiveness of the ruling was extended is the petition for unconstitutionality against the Regulations of the Free Port in the State of Nueva Esparta, which were issued through Decree N° 3.144 of December 30, 1998 (published in the *Official Gazette* Extraordinary Issue N° 5.293 of January 26, 1999). To this effect, the Court granted an unnamed precautionary measure which was extended to cover parties adhering to the plea.

Said extension was justified as follows:

"In this regard, it is worth highlighting that the new trends in Comparative Law have recognized the possibility of extending the effects of a final ruling to all those individuals that are in analogous situations to those originally favored.

It has to be pointed out as a basis for the measure in question that the administrative litigation procedure operates on the Administration's functions; it is well known, however, that when said functions are materialized in individual acts, they shall be repeated in time, given their existence in multiple situations, because they almost always operate on current and necessary circumstances. The individual acts of the Administration are not, therefore, isolated acts exclusive to a unique situation, but they will be repeated permanently in analogous cases related to different recipients. For this reason, the Administration must dictate the so-called "serial acts", which, in turn, are subject to isolated challenges, given the individuality distinguishing them. The necessity to challenge on a case-per case basis the acts that have analogous contents substantially hinders the ability to exert actions. At the same time, it requires a necessary identity in rulings dealing with said challenges. As a consequence of this evident fact typical of the administrative dynamics, a rule like the Spanish one emerges.

This Court observes that the telos *of these juridical criteria seen from the procedural point of view is to avoid the inconvenience of forcing an individual to undertake an entire contradictory proceeding that will eventually prove said individual right in the final ruling, basing the decision on the same reasons that have repeatedly underpinned identical or similar cases already decided and declared final. Therefore, the court finds that the request is evidently appropriate. However, regarding precautionary issues, neither Venezuelan law nor comparative law reveal the possibility of extending to those intervening parties that have been admitted as such, the effects of an interlocutory judgment that accords to the original petitioners a preventative measure subsequently to the granting thereof; therefore said intervening parties are in the same condition as the original petitioners and they would be not only damaged in the event that elements contrary to their interest would derive from the file, but that they could also be benefited from acts already performed in the process in which they are intervening. This would be the case of benefits resulting from an incidental judgment that grants a precautionary measure like the one in file, provided they prove that they are in an identical situation as the petitioner who was granted the preventative measure. That is, the intervening party should prove that in this case, the requirements that should inescapably coexist for the precautionary measure to be legitimate have been verified; said requirements include fumus boni juris, periculum in mora, as well as the specific one set forth in paragraph one, Article 588 or the Civil Procedural Code.*

In this regard, this Court considers that the fact that fumus boni juris and the periculum in mora are verified with respect to the intervening party is not enough for the preventative measure to be granted, but that, as in the case in question, who is requesting the extension of the effects of an incidental ruling granting the precautionary measure, has to request it expressly, present elements demonstrating that the current situation is identical to that of the original beneficiary of the precautionary measure and, finally, the extension of the measure should be agreed by means of express ruling by the court hearing the case.

Therefore, if as stated above, the intervening parties have the same interests as those of the original petitioners and considering that precautionary measures find their raison d'être in their own instrumental nature, in the sense that they are issued to prevent the petitioner from suffering damage that the final ruling cannot correct, this Court considers that it is appropriate to extend to the intervening parties the effects of the precautionary measure previously issued, with the proviso that, in the event that a reason may occur that justifies the repeal of the precautionary measure to the prejudice of the original petitioner, the same consequence would operate with respect to them; and it is hereby declared this way."

C. Ruling issued by the Political-Administrative Chamber of the Supreme Court of Justice on July 7, 1999

A further case regarding the extension of the effects of a judgment in the administrative litigation sphere is the ruling issued on October 7, 1999 by the Political-Administrative Chamber in relation to an action for failure to act[6] introduced by two retired teachers of the Ministry of Education, who were asking the Ministry to order the entity for which they worked the

---

[6]   The topic of action for failure to act should be addressed.

regular readjustment of the amount of the pensions they were receiving, in accordance with Articles 199, 105 and 143 of the Organic Law of Education.

Other retired and pensioned teachers, amounting to about three thousand teachers, attached to the same entity, adhered to the action claiming the same as the original petitioners.

A previous item of the ruling by the Political-Administrative Chamber established that issuing a declaration limited to the original petitioners was useless, because the recipients *"of an eventual compliance by the Administration with the decision would be all those individuals described in the rule providing for the requirement in Article 100 of the Organic Law of Education...teachers performing teaching or administrative functions."* In this regard, the Chamber considered that based on the nature of the procedural action exercised, which was intended to obtain from the judicial body an enforcement order under the same terms provided for by the rule establishing the obligation, said order, according to the Chamber's opinion, should comprise all those individuals addressed by the same, because this would guarantee its effects and, consequently, the attainment of the political-social or economic purposes it pursued. Before deciding on the issue, the Chamber expressly pointed out that the ruling to be handed down *"would entail an erga omnes effect, either for the Administration to comply with the legal provision with respect to all teachers pensioned by the Ministry of Education, or for it to refrain from complying, in absolute terms, in the event that the inexistence of that obligation is determined."*

In the operative part of its decision, once the action for failure to act was admitted, the Chamber proceeded to order the Ministry of Education to take the corresponding budgetary measures as from the next fiscal year to increase the remuneration of retired and pensioned teachers by said Ministry, by the amount resulting from applying to the wage percentage allotted to said teachers when they were retired or pensioned, the increases in the base wage of the posts corresponding to teachers that are still active, or their equivalents in the event that their denomination has been changed. In other words, resuming the originally established criterion, the ruling is not exclusively limited to the original petitioners, but extends to all pensioned and retired workers that are in the same condition.

Ruling of July 26, 2000

Case file: 00-0856

Speaker: Héctor Peña Torrelles

Subject: Clarification of the ruling handed down by the former Supreme Court of Justice in Full Court on December 14, 1999, declaring partially founded the request for nullification on the grounds of unconstitutionality filed against the provision contained in Article 59 of the Organic Tax Code, nullifying the sole paragraph of the said Article 59.

To understand the problem, it has to be remembered that the Organic Law of the Supreme Tribunal of Justice, which was in force on the date of the ruling, in its Articles 119 and 131 provided for as follows: Article 119: *"In its final ruling, the Court shall declare whether nullification of the act or of the articles challenged is founded or not, upon examination of the reasons on which the claim is based, and* **shall determine, in its case, the effects of the ruling over time**...*"* Article 131, in turn, has a similar content and points out: *"In its final ruling, the Court shall declare whether nullification of the act challenged is founded or not and* **shall determine the effects of its ruling over time**...*"*

As seen, the lawmaker did not determine the *ex tunc* or *ex nunc* effect of nullification over time, leaving these effects over time of nullifying rulings in the hands of the judge. In the case in question, the ruling did not determine the effects of the nullifying decision, therefore, it should be necessary to abide by the jurisprudence of the former Supreme Court of Justice that stated that it produces *ex tunc* effects, i.e. with effect back in the past.

Furthermore, the Full Court of the Supreme Court stated in the clarification that the ruling provided the nullifying decision with an *ex tunc* effect by setting the terms of the enforcement, that is, the parameters and the time period based on which those affected by the nullified rule could exercise their rights.

At that time, the Political-Administrative Chamber stated that **determining the effects of rulings regarding nullification of general regulatory or other acts** has been related to the preservation of a proper balance between safeguarded rights and the principles of legal security and the preservation of overall interests, taking into account the impact a ruling may have within the structure of the State. To this effect, the Chamber considered that the constitutional interpretation of legal rules should be intended to redirect them to the general principles of Law, upholding essential legal values.

Constitutional values operate this way to provide judges with meaning and orientation and, therefore, judges are able to contribute with a harmonic evolution of State and society.

Every legal operator should inspire the interpretation of the legal framework in the light of constitutional values. Judgments upholding unconstitutionality are presented as the required link between the instrumental function of constitutional values and the political system, the effects of which are crucial to the delicate task of balancing social dynamics and political values declared by the constituent.

Articles 119 and 131 of the Organic Law of the Supreme Court of Justice attributed the power to determine the effects over time of the unconstitutionality declaration of a legal rule, with a view to correcting unfavorable effects and ,thus, providing the ruling, according to the circumstances, with *ex tunc* (starting in the past) or *ex nunc* (starting now) effects.

In the case in question, the Full Court stated that the values of equality and justice that would imply recognizing as valid the claims of tax payers with regard to tax effects of rules that are subsequently declared unconstitutional are in contrast to the principle of social solidarity, when it comes to establishing the future effect of judgments.

Based on this reasoning and the principles of justice, legal security and social accountability inspiring the new Constitution of the Bolivarian Republic of Venezuela, the Chamber decided to grant *ex nunc* effects to the ruling issued by the Full Court of the former Supreme Court of Justice, starting from the publication of the decision. In consequence, the Chamber declared that nullity of the rule does not influence the validity and effectiveness of acts issued based on the said sole paragraph of article 59, which might have been declared final by virtue of an administrative act that has not been contested due to the decision by a court declaring it final. Therefore, the ruling estimated that tax payers' obligation to pay default interest as per article 59, part one, of the Organic Tax Code should be understood as emerging when there exist liquid or due credits; that is, nullity of article 59 of the Organic Tax Code does not impact the validity and effectiveness of acts issued based on the sole paragraph of said article 59, provided they have been declared as final.

Ruling of June 5, 2003

Case file: 03-0124

Speaker: Antonio García García

Subject: Request for constitutional relief, lodged by the President of the Medical Association of the Metropolitan District of Caracas in defense of the party he represents and the diffuse interests of all Venezuelans, against the provision contained in Article 63, number 5, of the Law on Partial Reform of Value Added Tax imposing a Value Added Tax (VAT) corresponding to an 8% aliquot, on all medical, dental, surgical and hospitalization services provided by private entities as from January 1, 2003, alleging that the said provision breaches Articles 83 and 84 of the Constitution of the Bolivarian Republic of Venezuela.

D. *Decision on the request*

The request for constitutional relief filed is based on the grounds that the provision violates Articles 83 and 84 of the Constitution consecrating guarantees and the rights to health, access to health services and to a national health public system. The appellant puts forward the "alleged unfairness of the tax", on the grounds that high costs of general administration services, to which solution the provision is intended to contribute, have been provoked in this case by the State itself, because if a true and efficient health protection and health public system would exist, only a minority of the population would use the services provided by private clinics and hospitals, in which case, the tax would not represent a burden and, as such, it would be legal and fair.

A request was made to disregard the provision contained in Article 63, number 5 of the Law on Partial Reform of Value Added Tax, on the grounds that the said provision violates Articles 83 and 84 of the Constitution, because a higher number of Venezuelans would not be able to afford the high costs of private clinics and hospitals to solve their health problems.

E. *Ruling*

The Constitutional Chamber remembered that the petition for constitutional relief against a rule, like in this case, contests the specific application of the rule to a concrete legal situation; therefore, the target of the constitutional relief action is said concrete legal situation whose violation is alleged, unless this case concerns challenging a self-performing rule, because its mere enactment implies that it is effectively and mandatorily enforceable by people covered by it, i.e. payers of the value added tax; the Chamber alto stated that the ruling to be handed down, if appropriate, will have *erga omnes* effects.

The Chamber proceeded to analyze each one of the rights to health set forth in the Constitution of the Bolivarian Republic of Venezuela and concluded that it is a duty of the State to implement and maintain a universal, comprehensive and efficient social security system, as well as a national public health system which provides free, universal, comprehensive, equitable, continuous, quality and supportive health services.

In this regard, the Chamber considered that since the rule object of the petition for relief taxes private health, dental, surgical and hospitalization services, it affects a substantial part of the population having access to them, because public health services are not efficient. Therefore, the free nature of health services would be undermined in relation to the right to profits that private health care providers derive from this activity, which cannot be demanded to maintain public burdens.

Based on its analysis, the Chamber ordered to disregard the provision of Article 64, number 5 of the law establishing the value added tax. Likewise, the Chamber pointed out that to guarantee an effective tax justice, health care, dental, surgical and hospitalization services rendered by private entities are declared exempted from value added tax, for which purpose, Article 3 of the aforementioned law is also disregarded in relation to these services.

The Chamber finally stated that individuals or legal persons that would have been subject to the tax and had paid the same cannot demand reimbursement from the National Treasury or from the entity that billed the service.

F. *Ruling issued by the Constitutional Chamber on August 10, 2011*

Another ruling granting prospective effect to a decision is the one issued on August 10, 2011 by the Constitutional Chamber (case file 11-0283), regarding a request for change of venue filed by an individual in a trial for moral damages against a mercantile society. In this case, the Chamber held that it had jurisdiction to hear the request, and ordered the court which had the file to forward it to its offices. Once the Chamber analyzed the file, it stated that municipalities have a series of procedural privileges, none of which is extensible to firms owned by them. Furthermore, the Chamber pointed out that the Organic Law of the Attorney General's Office does not provide for extending the privileged condition of public entities to the firms mentioned above. The important element of this ruling is that the Chamber **ordered to extend its effects** *"provided it is verified that the other susceptible cases are in a situation identical to those dealt with in this ruling."* Therefore, the Chamber ordered that such cases had to be decided based on its ruling *"provided the extension of effects is appropriate."*

VI. IN YOUR JURISDICTION, HAVE COURTS EVER REFERRED TO CIRCUMSTANCES (CONTEXT), THE USE OF WHICH WOULD BE APPROPRIATE AS A GUIDE, OR, ON THE CONTRARY, HAVE THEY RECOMMENDED TO REFRAIN FROM USING THIS TECHNIQUE (IN THE LAST CASE, THE EXAMPLE PRESENTED IS PREVENTING AN INDIVIDUAL FROM CLAIMING THE VIOLATION OF HIS HUMAN RIGHTS)? HAS THE TIME AT AND THE TERMS UNDER WHICH THE OVERRULING MAY HAVE EFFECT BEEN ALSO ESTABLISHED?

While, as stated in the answer to the previous question, in Venezuela in some cases a court with constitutional jurisdiction, in fact, the Political-Administrative Chamber of the former Supreme Court of Justice (which according to the 1999 Constitution became the Supreme Tribunal of Justice) as well as the Full Court of the said Court, and presently the Constitutional Chamber of the Supreme Tribunal of Justice, has ruled giving effect to their decisions on future cases that are based on the same situations in such a manner that they impose the obligation to issue an identical ruling in the case in question, the category of ***prospective overruling***, as per the Anglo-Saxon Law terminology, has never existed. The Venezuelan doctrine has never referred to the prospective effect of the ruling but at most it has talked about the "peculiarity" or specific characteristics of some rulings issued by administrative litigation courts[7]. In consequence, since in our system there does not exist a specific category of prospective rulings, the highest jurisdictional bodies could hardly establish rules on how to set out the content, narrative and operative part of these type of rulings.

With regard to the second question contained in question N° 6 above, of whether the time and terms under which an ***overruling*** may have effect have been set, it is evident that since this type of judgment does not constitute a special category and an *ad hoc* rule does not exist, hardly could the term and conditions to apply this ruling have been determined. However, having the rulings mentioned above, which have had a prospective nature, stated how the doctrine set should be applied, they have necessarily established some overall criteria that can be summarized as follows:

1.   To be identified with that of the original ruling, the situation has to be based on an identical factual situation.

---

[7]   Rondón de Sansó, Hildegard, "*Las Peculiaridades del Contencioso Administrativo*". Fundación Estudios de Derecho Administrativo (FUNEDA), Caracas, 2001.

2.   The fact that the situation is identical obliges the judge to automatically apply the solution taken in the original ruling.

3.   The proceeding of the subsequent cases is reduced to verifying the existence of the situation giving rise to the original ruling; therefore, the petitioners of the request in question do not have to bear the burden of proof because it is enough for them to allege the same elements that underpinned the original ruling.

In cases in which the technique of the mandatory effect was applied, the court did not face situations different to those giving rise to the original judgment; therefore, we cannot state if judges in subsequent cases would have the power to, upon application of the original ruling doctrine, hear and decide on the new aspects they are presented with. However, we believe that logic indicates that in relation to matters that do not fit into the mandatory ruling, judges should decide based on their own criteria.

VII. WHAT ARE THE ADVANTAGES AND DISADVANTAGES OF THE PROSPECTIVE OVERRULING, WHICH HAVE BEEN IDENTIFIED IN YOUR JURISDICTION?

Judgments in which the prospective effect was applied set out the main advantage of using this technique, i.e. not having the inconvenience of forcing the plaintiff to go through a contradictory proceeding which, eventually, will prove said plaintiff right in the final ruling, with said ruling being based on the same motives that have repeatedly grounded identical or similar cases previously decided and declared final. Therefore, the court declares that the request is well founded.

It can be seen that this case is about the application of the principle of *procedural economy* that implies that the process has to be swift and courts have to operate in a more appropriate manner. Based on this principle, the unnecessary step should not be required, but it is replaced with proofs and evidence presented in the previous proceeding.

A further advantage that the system expects to protect is receiving an *equitable treatment*, because once the obligation of the State to protect sick citizens with the resources specifically stated has been declared, citizens suffering from the same or similar diseases should be granted the same assistance.

The argument favoring the prospective effect rests on the fact that all individual acts by the administration are not isolated and exclusive to a unique situation, but they will always be repeated in the same manner vis-à-vis different recipients. This is why the Administration dictates the so-called *"acts in series,"* which is a category recognized in the typology of administrative proceedings. The necessity to appeal on a case-per-case basis with respect to situations with a similar content hinders the ability to take actions and, at the same time, entails the risk of making contradictory decisions.

It is worth stating that in those cases in which the decision dealt with precautionary measures, the ruling was provided with the prospective effect, because it was considered that these decisions have their raison d'être in their own instrumental character, in the sense that they are issued to protect the petitioner against damages that the final ruling cannot correct. This reason requires that all situations in which the same risk may exist are identical, but with the warning, as the Court did, that in the event that the precautionary measure is annulled in prejudice to the original petitioner, the same consequence would operate with respect to subsequent petitioners.

This *erga omnes* effect granted by the prospective overruling is the one used to justify other decisions which estimated that all subjects submitted to the same rule, upon strict adherence to the situations, well could be benefited, in the same sense, with the ruling establishing final and unchallengeable effects in any of the situations pondered in an isolated fashion.

A further circumstance that, to some extent, plays in favor of the application of the prospective effect is the identity between situations and the institution of the jurisdictional precedent. The prospective effect is said to strengthen the force of the precedent; therefore everything referred to the precedent both in a positive and a negative sense, is applicable to the prospective effect.

Possible disadvantages are mainly related to the unforeseeable mistakes in qualifying the assumptions of the cases, because the judge could subsume in the case setting a precedent a circumstance with some common elements, but which is not fully identifiable as typical of a situation deserving a prospective effect.

This remark corresponds to all court proceedings in which a mistake can always result from a false assessment of the facts. The problem in these cases lies in the unappealable character of rulings emerging from the constitutional judge who has the power to apply the theses under study. This means that a decision, which under no circumstance is identified with the jurisprudential thesis the effects of which have been intended to be extended into the future, can be rendered permanent.

VIII. HAS THE ARGUMENT THAT PROSPECTIVE OVERRUL-ING SHOULD NOT BE USED WHEN A DECISION IS EXCLU-SIVELY INTENDED TO "ESTABLISH A STATUTE" BEEN ALLEGED IN YOUR COUNTRY?

Undoubtedly, the decision related to a statute refers to duties, rights and overall legal situations, typical of subjects belonging to an organization. Of course, in cases concerning members of the same organization, it is convenient to apply the prospective overruling, because the equality and non-discrimination principle is strengthened, as well as that of procedural economy, given the identity of the regimes. This means that the answer to whether the statutory rule duly construed in a prospective overruling may be applied to other cases of subjects covered by the same statute necessarily has to be affirmative.

The situation is different when it is believed that the ruling could be applied *ipso jure* to individuals and entities subject to other statutes. The possibility of it being applied cannot be denied a priori if the conditions that we have set out as essential for said application to occur are present. On the contrary, the answer should be negative because the mere fact that the situations from which the conflict is derived may emerge from the fact that individuals and entities are subject to a statute is not enough to justify the application of the prospective overruling. Notwithstanding, while many professional statutes have similar rules, it is possible that in the specific case the set of rules governing them is completely different.

IX. HAS IT BEEN SAID IN THE SYSTEM THAT YOU REPRE-SENT THAT PROSPECTIVE OVERRULING TRANSFORMS JUDGES IN "DISGUISED LEGISLATORS"?

The mere fact that the precedent is the rule to be followed by judges in their *"binding"* rulings leads judges to have a power similar to that of legislators. When the precedent becomes the main source, the judge replaces the legislator in the creation of the rule.

1. *Precedent and constitutional res judicata*

The constitutional *res judicata* is the effectiveness of a judicial ruling when no means of appeal allowing said ruling to be modified can be filed against it, because it has the special quality of being immutable and uncontestable. Therefore, the decision issued to safeguard the right to due process cannot be challenged or contradicted in subsequent rulings by judicial entities.

In consequence, *res judicata* implies that **facts that were object of the proceeding in which a ruling was handed down cannot be again the object of controversy**.

The modern German doctrine states that *res judicata* is the declaration of certainty contained in the mandatory and undisputable ruling that excludes a new and different ruling.

According to the Italian doctrine, *res judicata* prevents any new decision on the substance of the same litigation and not only a different one.

Res judicata only operates when the judicial ruling decides on the question put forward in the proceeding, that is, **claims presented by the parties.** Therefore, *res judicata* **does not operate with regard to formal decisions.**

Res judicata is not considered an effect but a quality of the ruling, which is materialized in the application of the ***non bis in idem*** principle, that is, in the banning to try twice the same question or the same facts.

In the constitutional sphere, rulings are issued in the exercise of the regulatory control, i.e. unconstitutionality pleas; therefore it is worth asking what the binding part of the constitutional ruling is?

Two theses have been put forward with regard to the binding nature of the constitutional ruling: the one that sustains that the binding character only lies in the content of the operative part of the ruling; or if the part related to the reasoning elements that underpin the decision or constitute the *ratio decidendi* is also binding. It is worth remembering that the Colombian case is exceptionally quoted, because Article 48 of Statutory Act 270 of the Administration of Justice of 1996 expressly sets forth as follows: "*only the operative part of the ruling shall be mandatorily enforceable and shall have erga omnes effects. The grounds for the decision only constitute an ancillary criterion for the judicial activity and for the application of overall rules of Law.*"

Unlike the Colombian case, legal rules in Bolivia, Chile, Ecuador, Peru and Venezuela governing constitutional courts and their resolutions, are silent on this matter.

Rulings of constitutional courts in both European Comparative Law and South America render *res judicata* when the said ruling determine or disregard unconstitutionality of a legal rule on grounds of substance, because the internal legal order of the State does not provide for any action that allows rulings to be challenged, thus preventing the problem to be put forward on an identical content and with them being mandatory for all State organs.

For the denial of unconstitutionality of a rule to have the effect of *res judicata*, it is necessary for the ruling of the constitutional court to have decided on all aspects that may influence the regulatory statement, eliminating other eventual grounds for unconstitutionality that were not considered in the corresponding ruling. If such overall decision has not been made, the *res judicata is relative*. A relative *res judicata* exists when the constitutional court has not taken into account in its analysis determined feasible hypotheses of unconstitutionality of the normative statement, which can be recognized through two possible ways: a) when the same constitutional court in the ruling states that its decision deals with the elements challenged by the plaintiff, which makes it possible that new requests for unconstitutionality are filed, based on different matters that were not considered in the initial ruling; b) when the constitutional court does not refer in the ruling to having examined the regulatory statement only form determined standpoints, but from the analysis of the basis of the ruling no element is derived that leads to reasonably consider that a new constitutional problem was pondered.

The **apparent *res judicata*** occurs if when a constitutionality or unconstitutionality decision is sustained, **rational and legal grounds of the decision** declaring one among several regulatory instruments as constitutional **have not been established**. In this case, *res judicata* is only apparent, because it has not been effectively examined if the specific normative text is constitutional or unconstitutional vis-à-vis the Constitution. It should be borne in mind that a ruling issued by an entity with jurisdiction has to be motivated, based on current sources of Law, and consistent. No ruling or *res judicata* exist without the proper legal support of the decision.

It is worth noting that a rule in all South American systems is that *res judicata* of the ruling of the constitutional court is binding on all courts and state organs, except the very same constitutional court, which, in a future case, may review its case law or precedent and, on solid grounds (because otherwise, it would be arbitrary and equality before the law would be impaired), change its interpretation thus allowing constitutional case law to evolve and adapt to new contexts and situations. Accordingly, in subsequent litigations, unconstitutionality of a law can be declared, even though it had been previously declared constitutional. This situation also exists in Spain and Italy, among other countries, because it is possible for a law with respect to which an abstract control decision has been made can be questioned again through concrete control by invoking new circumstances or different motives.

2. *Binding character of Rulings of the Supreme Tribunal of Justice*

We have referred before to Article 335 of the current Constitution, which consecrates the guarantee of constitutional supremacy through the Constitutional Chamber, strengthening this role by granting a binding character on all courts of the Republic, including the other Chambers of the Supreme Tribunal of Justice, to *"interpretation established...regarding the content or scope of constitutional rules and principles."* The power of the Constitutional Chamber is further strengthened when it is authorized to **review rulings** handed down by all other courts of the Republic (number 10, Article 336 of the Constitution). This constitutional action, which allows the Constitutional Chamber to review final rulings, both in terms of constitutional relief and control over the constitutionality of laws or legal rules, was broadened in the Organic Law of the Supreme Tribunal of Justice by allowing the Chamber to review final rulings issued by the other Chambers (number 12, Article 24, Organic Law of the Supreme Tribunal of Justice):

> *"to review final rulings, in which diffuse control of constitutionality of laws or other legal rules issued by the other Chambers of the Supreme Tribunal of Justice and other courts of the Republic, has been exercised."*

Furthermore, the legislator was even more generous by granting the power to review *"rulings handed down by the other Chambers, which are subsumed in the cases set out in the previous number (failure to know a precedent set by the Constitutional Chamber; undue application of a constitutional rule or principle; serious interpretation mistake or non-application of a constitutional rule or principle),"* as well as the violation of fundamental legal principles contained in the Constitution of the Republic, international treaties, pacts or agreements signed and validly ratified by the Republic or violations of constitutional rights".

In other words, to guarantee constitutional supremacy, the Constitutional Chamber is granted the ample power to review rulings issued by all other courts of the Republic, including the other Chambers of the Supreme Tribunal of Justice, based on multiple grounds that can be summarized in any violation of the constitutional order contained in internal and external rules applied. The character given to rulings handed down to decide on said actions is binding; therefore, the first question emerging is whether said character is applied to all rulings, that is, those that decide on general and abstract cases, or if their scope only refers to the resolution of concrete cases.

The Constitutional Chamber through ruling of July 19, 2001 established a distinction between *jurisdictio* and *jurisdatio*. *Jurisdictio* would consist of the decision of the Chamber on concrete cases, in which the Chamber states that from these concrete cases, individualized rules emerge, the binding nature of which *"could only be invoked based on the technique of precedent."* Therefore, *jurisdatio* would be the ruling that interprets in a general and abstract manner the Constitution with an *erga omnes* effect, *"with this being an authentic or paraconstituent interpretations,"* expresses the contents constitutionally declared by the Constitution.

Literally, the Constitutional Chamber in ruling issued referring to Articles 334 and 335 of the Constitution states as follows: *"as can be seen, the Constitution of the Bolivarian Republic of Venezuela does not duplicate in these articles the competence to interpret the Constitution, but it rather consecrates two classes of constitutional interpretation, namely: individualized interpretation that is presented in the ruling as individualized rule and general or abstract interpretation provided for by Article 335, which is a true "jurisdatio" because it declares erga omnes and ex nunc, the content and scope of constitutional principles and rules the interpretation of which is requested through the corresponding extraordinary action. This jurisdatio is different to the function which controls constitutionality of laws, since this nomophylactic function, as per Kelsen, is a true negative legislation that decrees nullity of rules colliding with the Constitution; in addition, general or abstract interpretation mentioned above does not address sub-constitutional rules but the very same constitutional system"*.

In the same ruling, the Constitutional Chamber considered that the extraordinary action of constitutional interpretation is founded in Article 335 and has to be admitted, because, otherwise, said article would be redundant in relation to the provision in Article 334 *ejusdem*, which can only give rise to individualized rules, such as rulings handed down by the Constitutional Chamber in relation to constitutional relief matters.

The Chamber estimated that the difference between both types of interpretation is patent and brings about decisive legal consequences in the exercise of constitutional jurisdiction. These consequences are referred to the diverse effect of *jurisdictio* and *jurisdatio*, because the effectiveness of the individualized rule is limited to the resolved case; whereas the general rule derived from the abstract interpretation has *erga omnes* value and constitutes, as a true *jurisdatio*, a "para-constituent" interpretation…"

X. BIBLIOGRAPHY

HERNÁNDEZ, Adrián T.M. *"Aproximación crítica a los sistemas de precedentes judiciales vinculantes"*. Revista de Derecho Constitucional N° 8, julio-diciembre, Caracas, 2003, p. 259.

ALVARADO ESQUIVEL, Miguel de Jesús. *"¿Son retroactivos los nuevos criterios aislados o juriprudenciales?"*. Revista del Instituto de la Judicatura Federal N° 32, México, 2011.

CIENFUEGOS MATEO, Manuel. *"Los efectos jurídicos de las sentencias prejudiciales interpretativas del tribunal de justicia de las comunidades europeas y su aplicación judicial en los estados miembros"*. Universidad Pompeu Fabra, Facultad de Derecho, Barcelona, 1995.

ESKRIDGE, William N. *"Overruling Statutory Precedents"*. Yale Law School, Faculty Scholarship Series, 1988.

ESPINOSA-SALDAÑA BARRERA, Eloy. *"El precedente constitucional: sus alcances y ventajas, y los riesgos de no respetarlo o de usarle en forma inadecuada en la reciente coyuntura peruana"*, Estudios Constitucionales, Año 4 N° 1, Universidad de Talca, 2006.

GOZAÍNI, Osvaldo Alfredo. *"Sobre sentencias constitucionales y la extensión erga omnes"*. Instituto Iberoamericano de Derecho Procesal Constitucional, N° 8, 2008.

MARTÍNEZ CABALLERO, Alejandro. *"Tipos de sentencias en el control constitucional de las leyes: La experiencia colombiana"*. Revista Estudios Socio-Jurídicos, Vol. 2, N° 1, Colombia, 2000.

NOGUEIRA ALCALÁ, Humberto. *"Consideraciones sobre las sentencias de los tribunales constitucionales y sus efectos en América del Sur"*. Fondo Nacional de Desarrollo Científico y Tecnológico (Fondecyt), Chile, 2003.

OLANO GARCÍA Hernán Alejandro *"Tipología de nuestras sentencias constitucionales"*, Universitas, 2004.

RIVERA SANTIVÁÑEZ, José Antonio. *"Los efectos de las sentencias constitucionales en el ordenamiento jurídico interno"*. Estudios Constitucionales, Año 4, N° 2, Universidad de Talca, 2006.

RONDÓN DE SANSÓ, Hildegard. *"Ab imis Fundamentis. Análisis de la Constitución Venezolana de 1999. Parte Orgánica y Sistemas"*, Tercera Edición Revisada, Gráficas Lauki, Caracas, 2013.

——————————— *"Análisis de la Ley Orgánica del Tribunal Supremo de Justicia. Una ley fuera de contexto"*. Printer Colombiana, S.A., Caracas, 2006.

I.C. DROIT COMPARÉ ET UNIFICATION DU DROIT/COMPARATIVE LAW AND UNIFICATION OF LAWS

- LE CONTRÔLE ET LA RECONNAISSANCE DES SENTENCES ARBITRALES ÉTRANGERES – L'APPLICATION DE LA CONVENTION DE NEW YORK PAR LES JURIDICTIONS NATIONALES / RECOGNITION AND ENFORCEMENT OF FOREIGN ARBITRAL AWARDS: THE APPLICATION OF THE NEW YORK CONVENTION BY NATIONAL COURTS

RECOGNITION AND ENFORCEMENT OF FOREIGN ARBITRAL AWARDS: THE APPLICATION OF THE NEW YORK CONVENTION BY NATIONAL COURTS

Eugenio Hernández-Bretón
PROFESSOR, CENTRAL UNIVERSITY OF VENEZUELA

I. IMPLEMENTATION

1. *In what form has the New York Convention been implemented into national law?*

Following constitutional provisions, the New York Convention was approved by a law of congress published in Special *Official Gazette* N° 4.832 of December 29, 1994. The adhesion instrument was deposited on February 8, 1995. From the standpoint of Venezuelan law, international treaties are not transformed into domestic laws, they remain to be treaties, and as such they must be interpreted and applied by national courts. Thus, it is an international treaty binding on Venezuela.

2. What declarations and/or reservations, if any, did your country make?

Pursuant to Article I(3), upon adhesion to the New York Convention Venezuela made two interpretative declarations, namely (i) the application of the Convention is subject to reciprocity, and (ii) the commerciality under domestic law reservation.

3. What is the definition of an "arbitral award"? of a "foreign arbitral award"?

Under Venezuelan law, there is no statutory definition of an "arbitral award". The Commercial Arbitration Law, published in *Official Gazette* N° 36.430 of April 7, 1998, which is applicable to both domestic and international arbitration, deals mostly with awards in the sense of "final awards" as the usual form of decision of the merits of controversies subject to arbitration (ex-Articles 29 et seq.). The Commercial Arbitration Law also contemplates the possibility of rendering other decisions in the course of an arbitration proceeding different from the final award. This is the case of decisions related to the jurisdiction of the arbitration panel (Articles 7 and 25) and to the granting of precautionary measures (Article 26). Some authors appear to limit the notion of awards to final awards (See Luciano Lupini Bianchi, "Naturaleza, efectos, requisitos y modalidades del laudo arbitral", Luis A. Araque Benzo et al. (*coordinadores*), *El arbitraje en Venezuela. Estudios con motivo de los 15 años de la Ley de Arbitraje Comercial*, Caracas, Centro de Arbitraje de la Cámara de Caracas et al., 2013, p. 359 et seq., at p. 363-364 with more citations; see also in the same publication Andrés A. Mezgravis et al., "El recurso de nulidad contra el laudo arbitral", p. 503 et seq., at. p. 530 et seq.).

Similarly, there is no statutory definition of a "foreign award". Commentators are of the view that based on the interpretative declaration made by the Venezuelan government when adhering to the New York Convention, a foreign award would be an award issued in the territory of another State (Eugenio Hernández-Bretón, "International Arbitration and the Venezuelan Law on Commercial Arbitration", Nuray Eksi et al., *International Commercial Arbitration. A Comparative Study*, Istanbul, ICOC Publication N° 2007/45, 2007, p. 127 et seq., esp. p. 144). This is also the approach adopted by the Political Administrative Chamber of the Supreme Court in the *Pepsi Cola* case (October 9, 1997, published in *Revista de la Facultad de Ciencias Jurídicas y Políticas*, N° 109, Caracas, Universidad Central de Venezuela, 1998, p. 150 et seq., at p. 164). Other commentator, however, based on the same *Pepsi Cola* decision, does not share this view and consider that an award with "foreign contacts" may qualify as an award subject to the New York Convention even if rendered in Venezuela (Javier Ochoa, "Reconocimiento de laudo arbitral extranjero", Irene de Valera (*coordinadora*), *Arbitraje comercial interno e interna-cional. Reflexiones teóricas y experiencias prácticas*, Caracas, Academia de Ciencias Políticas y Sociales, p. 239 et seq., at p. 248).

4. When if ever are measures of provisional relief ordered by an arbitral tribunal considered to constitute "awards" within the meaning of the Convention?

As mentioned before, pursuant to the Commercial Arbitration Law, arbitral tribunals may order measures of provisional relief. Such measures are considered to be awards within the meaning of the Convention (Andrés A. Mezgravis, "Las medidas cautelares en el sistema arbitral venezolano", Milagros Betancourt C., *Memoria Arbitral*, Caracas, Centro Empresarial de Conciliación y Arbitraje CEDCA, 2011, p. 277 et seq., at 311-312) or awards for the purposes of their enforcement under the Commercial Arbitration Law (see Claudia C. Madrid M., "Medidas cautelares y arbitraje. Especial referencia a la Ley de Arbitraje Comercial, Fernando Parra Aranguren (*editor*), *Liber Amicorum Homenaje a la obra científica y académica de la profesora Tatiana B. de Maekelt*, Tomo II, Caracas, Universidad Central de Venezuela, 2001, p. 87 et seq., at p. 114-115).

5. May a party seeking recognition or enforcement of a foreign arbitral award, at its option, also rely upon a means other than the New York Convention? If so, which means?

Because Venezuela is also a party to the Panama Convention on International Commercial Arbitration, approbatory law published in *Official Gazette* N° 33.170 of February 22, 1985, deposit of the instrument of ratification on May 16, 1985, it is also possible to rely on its terms in order to obtain recognition or enforcement of a foreign arbitral award. The same applies to the Montevideo Convention on the Extraterritorial Effect of Foreign Court Decisions and Arbitral Awards, approbatory law published in *Official Gazette* N° 33.144 of January 15, 1985, deposit of the instrument of ratification on February 28, 1985. Theoretically, the provisions of the Accord on the Enforcement of Foreign Acts of 1911 (*Acuerdo Boliviano*) are also available. However, because all of the State parties to the *Acuerdo Boliviano* are also parties to the Panama Convention, it should be affirmed that the latter has replaced the former on matters of recognition and enforcement of foreign awards (see for example *M.V. Villavicencio* case, decision of the Political Administrative Chamber of the Supreme Court of Justice, October 21, 1999, *Ramírez & Garay*, Tomo CLVIII, Caracas, 1999, p. 785). If no international treaty is applicable, then the provisions of the Commercial Arbitration Law will apply.

Venezuelan courts have also allowed the successful challenge of foreign arbitral awards by way of a petition for constitutional relief (*acción de amparo constitucional*) in cases where the affected party invokes the violation of his/her constitutional rights and guarantees by the arbitrators, and even if the seat of the arbitral tribunal or the place of hearings are located abroad (see for example *Consorcio Barr v. Four Seasons Hotel* case, decision of the Political Administrative Chamber of the Supreme Court of Justice, November 19, 2004, http://www.tsj.gov.ve/decisiones/scon/noviem bre/2635-191104-04-0163%20.HTM). This continuous to be an available parallel avenue to torpedoed foreign arbitral awards, especially when the defendants named in the petition for constitutional protection are arbitrators of a foreign nationality and not residents of Venezuela (*Gabriel Castillo Bozo v. Adolfo E. Jiménez* et al. case, decision of the First Superior Court on Civil, Commercial, Transit and Banking Affairs of the Judicial Circuit of the Metropolitan Area of Caracas, April 22, 2013, http://cara cas.tsj.gov.ve/DECISIONES/2013/ABRIL/2138-22-AP71-O-2012-00004 2-13.006-DEF(AMP)-CONS.HTML).

II. ENFORCEMENT OF AGREEMENTS TO ARBITRATE (N.Y. CONVENTION, ARTICLE II)

1. *How do the courts interpret the Convention terms*
"null, void, inoperative or incapable of being performed"?
In interpreting them, do they consult any particular choice-of-law rules?

In the aforementioned *Pepsi Cola* decision the Supreme Court did not address the issue of the meaning of the terms "null, void, inoperative or incapable of being performed" nor did it discuss the question of the law applicable to the arbitration clause. The Supreme Court merely restricted itself to the plain meaning of the written arbitration clause, and to verify that the subject matter was arbitrable under Venezuelan substantive law. However, authors suggest that the arbitration clause must be interpreted under the law chosen by the parties or using the choice of law rules of the forum (Eugenio Hernández-Bretón, "International Arbitration and the Venezuelan Law on Commercial Arbitration", *op.cit.*, at p. 132-133).

2. Which kind of objections to arbitration (whether jurisdictional or non-jurisdictional) are the courts willing to entertain prior to the arbitration, if a party resisting arbitration so requests? And which kind of objections will the courts not entertain, but instead allow the arbitral tribunal to decide in the first instance?

Regardless of the express admission of the principle of *Kompetenz-Kompetenz* in Articles 7 and 25 of the Commercial Arbitration Law, by commentators and case law (See Luis Alfredo Araque Benzo et al., "El acuerdo de arbitraje", Luis Araque Benzo et al. (*coordinadores*), *El arbitraje en Venezuela, op.cit.*, p. 155 et seq., at p. 188 et seq.), Venezuelan courts are prone to entertain and decide any type of objections to arbitration, whether jurisdictional or not (See Political Administrative Chamber of the Supreme Court, *Diques y Astilleros Nacionales (DIANCA) v. Raytheon Marine GmbH* case, decision of July 16, 2013, http://www.tsj.gob.ve/sr/Default3.aspx?url=/decisiones/spa/julio/00847-16713-2013-20).

III. GROUNDS FOR REFUSAL OF RECOGNITION AND EN-FORCEMENT OF FOREIGN ARBITRAL AWARDS (N.Y. CONVENTION, ARTICLE V)

1. *General*

A. When, if ever, do courts recognize or enforce a foreign arbitral award, even though a ground has been established that would permit them to deny recognition or enforcement of the award?

We are not aware of a single case where Venezuelan courts have recognized or enforced a foreign arbitral award when a ground has been established that would allow them to deny recognition or enforcement of the award. Similarly, there are no cases dealing with the recognition or enforcement of foreign awards that have been nullified abroad.

B. *Are any of the grounds for denying recognition or enforcement of a foreign arbitral award under the Convention subject to waiver by the parties? If so, which ones, and what constitutes waiver?*

Although there is no case law on this issue, because the causes for refusal of enforcement and recognition established in Article V(1) of the New York Convention must be alleged and evidenced by the party against which the arbitral award is invoked, it is possible to infer that those causes may be waived. Conversely, the causes established in Article V(2) which fall under the control of the judge may not be waived. Failure to timely allege the causes for refusal of enforcement and recognition established in Article V(1) would be considered to be a waiver. It is unclear if an express or tacit waiver in advance of the award would be valid and enforceable (See Andrés A. Mezgravis et al., "El recurso de nulidad contra el laudo arbitral", Luis A. Araque Benzo et al. (*coordinadores*), *El arbitraje en Venezuela, op.cit.*, p. 503 et seq., at p. 514.). When analyzing the possibility of a waiver of the grounds for nullity of domestic awards, Venezuelan authors consider that the grounds equivalent to Article V(2) of the Convention cannot be waived, and that it would be possible in respect of those of V(1) (Andrés A. Mezgravis, "Recursos contra el laudo arbitral comercial", *Seminario sobre la Ley de Arbitraje Comercial*, Caracas, Academia de Ciencias Políticas y Sociales, Serie Eventos N° 13, 1999, p. 205 et seq., at. p. 265 et seq.).

2. *Particular Grounds*

A. *How do courts interpret and apply* Article V(1)(a) *("The parties to the agreement referred to in article II were, under the law applicable to them, under some incapacity, or the said agreement is not valid under the law to which the parties have subjected it or, failing any indication thereon, under the law of the country where the award was made")*

(In particular, do courts follow the sequence of choice of law rules prescribed here for determining whether an agreement to arbitrate is valid – i.e. "the law to which the parties have subjected [the agreement] or, failing any indication thereon, ... the law of the country where the award was made"?)

There is no case law on this issue. Based on Article 1 of the Commercial Arbitration Law and in Article 1 of the Statute on Private International Law, a Venezuelan court should abide by the sequence of choice of choice of law rules prescribed in Article V (1) (a), rather than resorting to other

Venezuelan rules of conflict of laws, such as those established in other international treaties, or in the absence of such treaties, in the Statute on Private International Law. It is likely, however, that when examining the validity of the arbitration clause Venezuelan courts will also look at Venezuelan substantive rules governing the arbitrability of the subject matter as well as other rules of Venezuelan strict public policy.

B. *How do courts interpret and apply Article V(1)(b) ("The party against whom the award is invoked was not given proper notice of the appointment of the arbitrator or of the arbitration proceedings or was otherwise unable to present his case")*

(In particular, do courts apply the same standards of proper notice and fair hearing as required by domestic constitutional law?)

We have not been able to locate Venezuelan court cases discussing the application of this provision or the standards of proper notice and fair hearing for purposes of the New York Convention. It is most likely that when applying those standards Venezuelan courts will look at Venezuelan constitutional standards safeguarding due process and the right of defense, which, in sum, do not differ much from the common notions generally applied in other Latin American countries or in continental Europe.

C. *How do courts interpret and apply Article V(1)(c) ("The award deals with a difference not contemplated by or not falling within the terms of the submission to arbitration, or it contains decisions on matters beyond the scope of the submissionto arbitration ...")*

(In particular, does an award "deal with a difference not contemplated by or not falling within the terms of the submission to arbitration, or it contains decisions on matters beyond the scope of the submission to arbitration" when the award grants a remedy specifically excluded by the main contract?)

There are no court decisions interpreting and applying Article V(1)(c) of the Convention. According to usual practices in Venezuelan arbitration proceedings, the terms of the main contract are incorporated by reference into the submission to arbitration or the arbitration clause.

Also, the last paragraph of Article 8 of the Commercial Arbitration Law orders that in discharging their duties arbitrators shall always take into consideration the main contract terms as well as usages and commercial customs.

The foregoing makes us to believe that the granting in the award of a remedy specifically excluded by the main contract may be understood to constitute an award dealing with issues not falling or beyond the scope of the submission to arbitration.

D. *How do courts interpret and apply Article V(1)(d) ("The composition of the arbitral authority or the arbitral procedure was not in accordance with the agreement of the parties, or, failing such agreement, was not in accordance with the law of the country where the arbitration took place")*

(In particular, what do courts do in the case in which the parties expressly adopted an arbitral procedure that is not in accordance with the mandatory law of the country where the arbitration took place?

There is no case law discussing this issue. A Venezuelan court is likely to deny recognition to a foreign arbitral award if the arbitral procedure did not respect the mandatory law of the country where the arbitration took place. The parties agreement will be understood to be limited by the mandatory rules of the place of arbitration.

(Also, do courts treat an award as not in accordance with the agreement of the parties if the arbitral tribunal applied to the merits of the dispute a body of law other than the body of law that the parties selected in their contract as the governing law?)

See answer III.B.3. However, in our view this situation will not constitute a violation of Article V(1)(d).

E. *How do courts interpret and apply Article V(1)(e) ("The award has not yet become binding on the parties, or has been set aside or suspended by a competent authority of the country in which, or under the law of which, that award was made.")*

(In particular, under what circumstances, if any, will courts recognize or enforce a foreign arbitral award, even though i has been set aside by a competent court of the place of arbitration?)

There are no cases dealing with the recognition or enforcement of foreign awards that have been set aside abroad. Most likely a Venezuelan court would review independently whether the foreign arbitral award meets the standards of the Convention regardless of its being set aside by a competent court of the place of arbitration.

F. *How do courts interpret and apply* Article V(2)(a)
("The subject matter of the difference is not capable of settlement by arbitration under the law of [the] country")

(In particular, what kinds of disputes are considered legally incapable of settlement by arbitration?)

The issue of arbitrability of disputes has been the subject of much controversy in Venezuela. The basic proposition is that matters may be subject to arbitration if capable of being the subject of a settlement agreement (*contrato de transacción*) (Article 3 of the Commercial Arbitration Law, Article 47 of the Statute on Private International Law, and Article 608 of the Code of Civil Procedure). In any event, arbitration is not permitted in matters contrary to public policy, or related to crimes and felonies, except in respect of the determination of damages, issues related to the sovereign powers of State entities, issues related to status or capacity of individuals or related to assets or rights of individuals subject to legal incapacity except with judicial authorization, and any matters decided with res judicata effect, except for the economic consequences arising there from, but only as between the parties and insofar as they have not been decided already (Article 3 of the Commercial Arbitration Law). International arbitration will not be admitted for matters dealing with in rem rights over Venezuelan situs real estate, matters not capable of being the subject of a settlement agreement or affecting public policy issues (Article 47 of the Statute on Private International Law). The Constitutional Chamber of the Supreme Court has pointed out that matters of public policy are not necessarily excluded from arbitration. Thus, all patrimonial matters that can be brought before a court of law are capable of settlement by arbitration (Decision of October 17, 2008, in re interpretation of Article 258 of the Constitution, http://www.tsj.gob.ve/decisiones/scon/Octubre/1541-171008-08-0763.htm). (See also Víctor Hugo Guerra H. and Ramón Escovar Alvarado, "El ámbito de aplicación de la LAC: Las controversias no susceptibles de arbitraje, las controversias susceptibles de arbitraje y las controversias patrimoniales", Luis A. Araque Benzo et al. (*coordinadores*), *El arbitraje en Venezuela, op.cit.,* p. 123 et seq.). Nonetheless, in the *Diques y Astilleros Nacio-nales (DIANCA) v. Raytheon Marine GmbH* case (decision of July 16, 2013 (http: //www. tsj.gob.ve/sr/Default3.aspx?url=/decisiones/spa/julio/00847-16713-2013-20) the Political Administrative Chamber of the Supreme Court disregarded an international arbitration clause because the subject matter of the arbitration dealt with assets of the public domain (i.e., submarines) owned by the Venezuelan State and used in security operations in the Venezuelan maritime space.

7. How do courts interpret and apply Article_V(2)(b)
("The recognition or enforcement of the award would be contrary to the public policy of [the] country")

(In particular, under what circumstances is a foreign award deemed to be contrary to the public policy of the country? In other words, what constitutes a violation of public policy for these purposes?)

(Also, does the law draw a distinction for these purposes between "international public policy" (ordre public international) and "domestic public policy" (ordre public interne)?)

Venezuelan law clearly distinguishes between international public (*orden público internacional*) policy and domestic public policy (*orden público interno*). The former is regulated in Article 8 of the Statute on Private International Law and the latter corresponds to Article 6 of the Civil Code. The distinction is also acknowledged by commentators on arbitration law matters (Andrés A. Mezgravis, "El recurso de nulidad contra el laudo arbitral", *op.cit.*, p. 529). International public policy protects the essential principles of the Venezuelan legal order, while domestic public policy limits party autonomy. However, Venezuelan courts often mix both notions and treat domestic public policy as international public policy and vice versa. In a recent case, a Venezuelan court annulled an award rendered in Miami, Florida which had adjudicated a contractual controversy between a number of Venezuelan citizens in respect of the transfer of shares of certain Venezuelan financial and insurance entities, based on public policy grounds. The agreement was subject to the laws of Florida. Nonetheless, the court considered that because the arbitral tribunal ignored Venezuelan mandatory rules on governmental authorizations for the transfer of shares of that type of entities, which the parties did not obtain, such a breach constituted a violation of domestic public policy rules aimed at the protection of the interests of the Venezuelan State. The court stated that domestic public policy was a limitation imposed on any arbitral tribunal, whether domestic or international. Accordingly, international arbitration under such circumstances would be to act in fraud of the Venezuelan legal system and a violation of a number of constitutional guarantees such as the right to a natural judge. Therefore, the award was notoriously contrary to the Venezuelan constitutional public policy. The court expressly stated that this type of violations were contrary to "public policy" under Article II of the New York Convention. However, the court did not waste much efforts in differentiating domestic from international public policy (*Gabriel Castillo Bozo v. Adolfo E. Jiménez et al.* case, decision of the First Superior Court on Civil, Commercial, Transit and Banking

Affairs of the Judicial Circuit of the Metropolitan Area of Caracas, April 22, 2013, http://caracas.tsj.gov.ve/DECISIONES/2013/AB RIL/2138-22-AP71-O-2012-000042-13.006-DEF(AMP)-CONS.HTML).

IV. PROCEDURAL ISSUES

1. *What is required in order for a court to have personal jurisdiction over the award debtor an action to enforce a foreign arbitral award?*

It is unclear whether in an action to enforce a foreign arbitral award Venezuelan courts must have personal jurisdiction over the award debtor or if the award creditor's interest in enforcing the award in Venezuela would suffice. According to general rules on jurisdiction, personal jurisdiction will lie if the defendant is domiciled in Venezuela, except if the award deals with in rem rights over real estate located in Venezuela. In this case, the award would be unenforceable in Venezuela. There will be Venezuelan jurisdiction even if the defendant is not domiciled in Venezuela if the defendant has assets in Venezuela, is served within Venezuelan territory, or if the defendant voluntarily submits to the jurisdiction of Venezuela courts (Articles 39 et seq. of the Statute on Private International Law, published in *Official Gazette* N° 36.511 of August 6, 1998).

2. *What is the statute of limitations (i.e. prescription period), if any, applicable to actions to enforce a foreign arbitral award?*

There is no clear guidance on this issue. A possible approach would be to subject the enforcement of the award to the corresponding statute of limitations of the law governing the merits of the case (ex-Article 14 (d) of the Inter American Convention on the Law Applicable to International Contracts, CIDIP-V, 1994, approbatory law published in Special *Official Gazette* N° 4.974 of September 22, 1995, deposit of the instrument of ratification on October 26, 1995). Nonetheless, under Venezuelan law, the statute of limitations for an action to enforce a judgment runs for 20 years from the date of its issuance (Article 1977 of the Civil Code).

3. *On what basis, other than absence of personal jurisdiction or prescription, may a court decline even to entertain an action to enforce a foreign arbitral award?*

The procedure for the enforcement or recognition of a foreign arbitral award is subject to Venezuelan procedural laws (Article 56 of the Statute on Private International Law). Generally, any judicial action will be admitted by Venezuelan courts except if it is contrary to public policy, to bones mores or to some express legal provision (Article 341 of the Code of Civil Procedure). It is likely that petitions for the enforcement or recognition of foreign arbitral awards against State entities will face difficulties based on constitutional public policy grounds (see Eugenio Hernández-Bretón, "El arbitraje internacional con entes del Estado venezolano", *Boletín de la Academia de Ciencias Políticas y Sociales*, N° 147, Caracas, 2009, p. 141 et seq.; same author, "El arbitraje y las normas constitucionales de Venezuela: lo malo, lo feo y lo bueno", *Boletín de la Academia de Ciencias Políticas y Sociales*, N° 149, Caracas, 2010, p. 389 y ss.).

4. *To what extent, if any, does a court that is asked to deny recognition or enforcement of a foreign arbitral award on a particular ground show deference to determinations about that ground previously made by (i) a court that compelled arbitration in the first place, (ii) the arbitral tribunal itself, or (iii) a court of the place of arbitration that was asked to set aside the award?*

Although this is an untested issue in Venezuela, it is highly unlikely that Venezuelan courts will feel themselves bound by a determination made by a foreign court or the arbitral tribunal itself. The Venezuelan court most likely will like to establish ex novo whether the arbitral award meets the standards established in the New York Convention, other applicable treaty or in the Commercial Arbitration Law.

V. ASSESSMENT

1. *In what respects, if any, is the New York Convention subject to criticism in your country?*

The New York Convention has been rarely applied by Venezuelan courts, and has not been the subject of much scholarly attention. Thus, it does not surprise that its provisions have not been subject to close scrutiny and criticism in Venezuela.

2. How would you assess the application of the Convention by the courts of your country?

The first decision applying the New York Convention in Venezuela, i.e., in the *Pepsi Cola* case, rendered by the Political Administrative Chamber of the Supreme Court of Justice on October 9, 1997 (published in *Revista de la Facultad de Ciencias Jurídicas y Políticas*, N° 109, Caracas, Universidad Central de Venezuela, 1998, p. 150 et seq.), generated very positive remarks both in Venezuela (Eugenio Hernández-Bretón, "Lo que dijo y no dijo la sentencia Pepsi Cola", *Revista de la Facultad de Ciencias Jurídicas y Políticas*, N° 109, Caracas, Universidad Central de Venezuela, 1998, p. 141 et seq.) and abroad (Oliver Linnenborn, "Die Derogation der venezolanischen Gerichtsbarkeit durch eine Schiedsvereinbarung", zu venezolanischer OGH, 9.10.1997-Az. 13.354, 1999, *IPRax* 1999, p. 137 et seq.). However, since then the practical application of the New York Convention in Venezuela has been scarce, and in one important subsequent case regarding the validity and enforceability of an arbitration clause the very same Political Administrative Chamber absolutely ignored the Convention as it was pointed out in the dissenting opinion (*Hyundai de Venezuela* case, decision of October 21, 1999, *Ramírez & Garay,* Tomo CLVIII, Caracas, 1999, p. 762 et seq.). The same is true of more recent decisions related to foreign arbitral awards.

3. What have been the principal problems, difficulties or controversies surrounding application of the New York Convention in your country? (In answering, you are NOT confined to the issues specified in this questionnaire)

Until now Venezuelan courts have been more involved in discussing the issue of the derogation of Venezuelan jurisdiction by means of an arbitration clause. This has led to the analysis of the validity and enforceability of such arbitration clauses. Among the questions dealt with by the courts a very significant place is given to the arbitrability of the subject matter and the question of public policy as a bar to arbitration. The enforcement of foreign arbitral awards has been blocked by means of constitutional *amparos* (petition for constitutional relief). Very little effort has been devoted to the enforcement of awards under the Convention or any other issues.

4. *Based on your country's experience, what reforms of the New York Convention, if any, would be useful or appropriate?*

Because of the absence of domestic judicial precedents and commentaries on the New York Convention, it is very difficult to assess what type of reforms would be useful or appropriate. The very limited experience when dealing with the Convention and /or foreign awards shows that public policy based on constitutional grounds would be a very high barrier for foreign arbitral awards to overcome, especially if the losing party is a State-owned entity.

II.B. DROIT INTERNATIONAL PRIVE / PRIVATE INTERNATIONAL LAW

- INFORMATION ET PREUVE DU CONTENU DU DROIT ÉTRANGER / PROOF OF AND INFORMATION ABOUT FOREIGN LAW

PROOF OF AND INFORMATION ABOUT FOREIGN LAW

Eugenio Hernández-Bretón and Claudia Madrid Martínez

PROFESSORS, CENTRAL UNIVERSITY OF VENEZUELA

I. CONFLICT OF LAWS RULES

In Venezuela, the application of conflict of laws rules is mandatory. Article 1 of the Statute on Private International Law mandates the determination of the applicable law, *inter alia*, through conflict of laws rules in cases related to foreign legal systems[1]. In Venezuela, all rules of law, including, conflict of laws rules, are applied *ex officio* pursuant to the principle of *iura novit curia*[2]. Their application is thus mandatory for courts and other public officials. The parties are not required to invoke or prove them. This is also the opinion of commentators[3].

Generally, conflict of laws rules, as embodied in the Statute on Private International Law, are of a bilateral nature, and as such could lead to the

---

[1]   Published in *Official Gazette* N° 35.511 of 6 August 1998.

[2]   Articles 12, 19, 243.4 and 274 of the Code of Civil Procedure, Article 2 of the Civil Code.

[3]   Madrid Martínez, Claudia. *La norma de derecho internacional privado*, Universidad Central de Venezuela, Caracas, 2004, at p. 55 et seq.

application of either the *lex fori* or the *lex causae*, indistinctly, and depending on the facts of the case at stake.

Although court decisions on these issues are limited, the majority of cases concern the application of the laws of the states of Florida and New York, United States of America, and of some Latin American states, like Chile and Colombia.

The Venezuelan conflicts of laws rules are basically comprised in the Statute on Private International Law. According to its Article 1, the sources of norms for dealing with cases connected with foreign legal systems are (i) the norms of Public International Law on the matter, especially those contained in international treaties in force in Venezuela; (ii) the domestic norms on Private International Law; (iii) the analogy; and (iv) the generally accepted principles of Private International Law. Additionally, for international contracts the *lex mercatoria* plays a very important role[4]. Among the treaties in force in Venezuela, and in respect of the subject matter of this national report, it is worth mentioning the following: Articles 408 et seq. of the Bustamante Code; Articles 2 and 4 of the Inter American Convention on General Rules of Private International Law ("GRPIL Convention")[5]; Inter American Convention on Proof of and Information on Foreign Law ("Montevideo Convention")[6]. In addition, Articles 2, 60 and 61 of the Statute on Private International Law regulate the proof and application of foreign law. From among the foregoing, we are of the opinion that the Statute on Private International Law is the main and most important source of all.

However, it is worth mentioning that Venezuelan courts are much more prone to the analysis of procedural rather than substantive law issues, which in turn is reflected in the relatively scarce amount of decisions on the merits applying foreign laws.

---

[4]   Article 31 of the Statute on Private International Law.

[5]   Approbatory law published in *Official Gazette* N° 33.252 of 26 June 1985, deposit of the instrument of ratification on 16 May 1985.

[6]   Approbatory law published in *Official Gazette* N° 33.170 of 22 February 1985, deposit of the instrument of ratification on 16 May 1985.

II. FOREIGN LAW BEFORE JUDICIAL AUTHORITIES

1. *Nature of Foreign Law*

As far as the nature of foreign law is concerned, it is considered as law in Venezuela (Article 408 of the Bustamante Code; Article 2 of the GRPIL Convention; Article 1 of the Montevideo Convention; Article 60 of the Statute on Private International Law). This is also the view of commentators and case law[7].

2. *Application of Foreign Law*

Concerning the application of foreign law before judicial authorities, they are bound to apply foreign law *ex officio*[8]. Nonetheless, the parties may provide information as to the applicable foreign law, and the courts and authorities may order steps to be taken in order to acquire greater knowledge of the same (Article 408 of the Bustamante Code; Article 2 of the GRPIL Convention; Article 1 of the Montevideo Convention; Article 60 of the Statute on Private International Law).

As it will be explained more fully below, although in theory the courts and authorities are obliged to ascertain and apply foreign law *ex officio*, in practice "a party wishing to rely on foreign law is well advised to present evidence of it."[9]

---

[7]   See de Maekelt, Tatiana B. "Tratamiento procesal del derecho extranjero", Artículo 60, Maekelt, Tatiana B. et al. (Coordinación), *Ley de Derecho Internacional Privado Comentada*, T. II, Universidad Central de Venezuela, Caracas, 2005, at p. 1225 et seq.; Monleón, Nicole, *Das internationale Privatrecht von Venezuela*, Max-Planck-Institut fuer auslaendisches und internationales Privatrecht, Studien zum auslaendischen und internationalen Privatrecht N° 204, Tuebingen, Mohr Siebeck, 2008, at p. 219 et seq.; Barrios, Haydée and Marín, Zhandra, "Información, aplicación y tratamiento procesal del derecho extranjero", (Maekelt, Tatiana B. et al. (Coordinación), *Derecho Procesal Civil Internacional*, Academia de Ciencias Políticas y Sociales, Serie Estudios N° 88, Caracas, 2010, p. 619 et seq.

[8]   See, among others, File 000871, Foreign Credit Insurance Association v. Naviera Rassi C.A. et al., 20 December 2001, http:// www.tsj.gov.ve/decisiones/scc/Diciembre/RC-0451-201201-00871.html; File 2012-0532, Export-Import Bank of the United States of America v. Supercable Alk Internacional, S.A., 9 May 2012, http://www.tsj.gov.ve/decisiones/spa/mayo/00499-9512-2012-2012-0532.html.

[9]   Lombard, Richard S. *American*-Venezuelan *Private International Law*, Bilateral Studies in Private International Law N° 14, Parker School of Foreign and Compara-

3. *Ascertainment of Foreign Law*

A. *General Remarks*

With regard to the way how judicial authorities ascertain foreign law, they are required to ascertain it *ex officio*. In this sense, the *iura novit curia* principle is equally applicable to domestic and foreign law. In order to fulfill their duty, the courts and other authorities may issue procedural orders requesting more information on foreign laws as they deem it necessary. The parties have the option, but not the burden, to provide information as to the applicable foreign law. This is a consequence of the formal requirement established in Article 340.5 of the Code of Civil Procedure, which mandates the plaintiff to make express reference in the relevant pleadings to the legal basis of his/her complaint. However, the judge is not bound by any such legal characterization.

As far as the means to ascertain foreign law is concerned (cf. *infra* V), still today, there is no statutory rule of Venezuelan law for the method of presentation of evidence of foreign law. The determination of the means used to ascertain foreign law is largely left to the parties and the courts preferences. The Bustamante Code and the Montevideo Convention allow for several options in order to provide information on foreign laws, including, but not limited to, international judicial cooperation. The Statute on Private International Law does not restrict or limit the means for the ascertainment of foreign law.

B. *Methods used in Venezuela*

(a) *Documents*

It is not uncommon for practitioners, courts and authorities to rely on documents and books when researching foreign legal texts, commentaries and case law, and to produce such materials as evidence of the applicable foreign law. However, due to the limited availability of those materials in Venezuelan libraries, either public or private, the interested parties prefer to opt for other alternatives. In the case of materials obtained abroad or locally which are drafted in a foreign language, parties are required to submit those materials translated into Spanish by a public interpreter admitted to act as such in Venezuela.

---

tive Law, Columbia University in the City of New York, Dobbs Ferry, Oceana Publications, New York, 1965, at p. 95.

(b) *Internet Sources*

Currently more and more judicial authorities and practitioners are resorting to Internet sources for researching foreign laws. This practice has been followed even by the Civil Cassation Chamber of the Supreme Court of Justice when faced with the difficulties of obtaining *ex officio* information about Swedish family law[10]. In this case the Venezuelan court acknowledged the scarcity of information available in Spanish in respect of parental guardianship, and thus resorted to the official webpage of the European Commission, European Judicial Network on Civil and Commercial Matters[11], and also to the official webpage of the Swedish government[12], where it found a Spanish translation of the applicable Swedish law on parental guardianship. This is also the approach favored by Venezuelan authors[13].

(c) *Assistance of the Parties*

As commented before, "a party wishing to rely on foreign law is well advised to present evidence of it"[14]. In almost all cases where foreign law was at stake, parties provided information on foreign law in the widest variety of forms. Very rarely parties let judicial authorities alone with the task to research the contents, interpretation and force of applicable foreign law.

In addition, one could even say that the courts expect that the interested parties devote considerable efforts and time in the process of providing the necessary foreign legal information.

---

[10] File AA20-C-2009-000464, María Julia Méndez Casal v. Domingo José Rodríguez Polanco, 18 February 2011, http://www.tsj.gob.ve/decisiones/ scc/febrero/EXE. 000065-18211-2011-09-464.HTML.

[11] http://ec.europa.eu/civiljustice/parental_resp/parental_resp_swe_es.htm.

[12] http://www.sweden.gov.se/sb/d/3288/a/19570, with a link to: http://www. spaininformation.org/sp_Legaliseringar.html.

[13] Torres Yonekura, Kumeyi. La información sobre derecho extranjero obtenida a través de Internet: Su validez ante el juez en el sistema venezolano de Derecho Internacional Privado, Thesis submitted for the Degree of Master on Private International Law and Comparative Law, Universidad Central de Venezuela, Caracas, 2004; see an abridged and updated version of the foregoing research paper in Víctor Hugo Guerra et al. (coordinadores), Estudios de Derecho Internacional Privado. Homenaje a Tatiana Maekelt: Contribución de sus alumnos, Escovarleón, Universidad Católica Andrés Bello, Caracas, 2012, p. 363 et seq.

[14] Lombard, Richard S. *op.cit.*, at p. 95.

(d) *Expert Witnesses*

In Venezuela, the taking of the testimony of an expert witness on foreign law is gaining prominence among the methods for providing information on foreign law. The testimony is often recorded in an affidavit of law, in which the expert witness explains his/her opinions supported by case law, statutes and quotations from treatises, and not very differently from the usual way in which such affidavits are made in international arbitral practice[15]. In most cases the testimony is sworn before a notary public or similar official, and subsequently legalized or apostilled as applicable. A commentator recommends, "it would be advisable for the notary to state that the affiants are known to him to be lawyers admitted to practice and practicing in the state concerned. The affidavit should state that the affiants are familiar with the law of the state and country concerned."[16]. This will follow the provision of Article 409 of the Bustamante Code as explained herein below. It is worth mentioning, however, that contrary to international practice, it is unfamiliar in Venezuela to have the expert witnesses cross-examined by the opposing counsel. It is unclear whether an expert witness written testimony is subject to personal ratification by the witness before Venezuelan courts[17].

(e) *Inquiry to Expert Bodies or Institutions*

Venezuelan judicial practice is not inclined to the use of court appointed experts or expert institutes. It would be unusual if a court asks or appoints an independent expert or an expert institute, such as the very well known Max-Planck-Institute, to request his/her/its views on a given foreign legal issue, no matter how well his/her/its reputation may be.

As far as the inquiry to domestic judicial or non-judicial authorities is concerned, it is an unknown method for the ascertainment of foreign legal information in Venezuelan practice, and in our experience, Venezuelan courts and authorities have never used it. Theoretically, an inquiry to foreign judicial (or non-judicial) authorities would be available via multilateral treaties. However, in practice Venezuelan judicial authorities never use it.

---

[15] Hernández-Bretón, Eugenio "La participación de 'testigos expertos' en el procedimiento arbitral internacional", *Boletín de la Academia de Ciencias Políticas y Sociales*, N° 150, Caracas, 2011, p. 203 et seq.

[16] Lombard, Richard S. *op.cit.*, at p. 95.

[17] File AA60-S-2008-00309, Michael Sterling Little v. Chevrontexaco Global Technology Services Company, 2 June 2009, http://www.tsj.gov.ve/decisiones/scs/Junio/0894-1609-2009-08-309.html.

Although Venezuela is a party to multilateral treaties (i.e., the Bustamante Code and the Montevideo Convention) providing for mechanisms to facilitate access to information on foreign law, including international judicial cooperation, we are not aware of a single reported case where Venezuelan courts have requested such legal information via bilateral or multilateral treaties.

In our experience, Venezuelan judicial authorities are reluctant to enter into direct communications with foreign judges in order to obtain information on foreign law.

(f) *Other methods*

The most usual methods for providing information on foreign laws are expert witnesses and the Internet. The former works fore mostly for the parties and the latter equally for both parties and judicial authorities.

C. *Qualification of Individuals or Institutions*

As far as the qualification of individuals or institutions to provide legal information is concerned, there is no precise statutory requirement. However, in practice judicial authorities and litigators rely on Article 409 of the Bustamante Code as a generally accepted principle of Private International Law, and demand that two lawyers practicing in the jurisdiction concerned certify evidence on foreign laws.

However, as pointed out before, in some instances courts are satisfied even with the sworn declaration of a single lawyer practicing in the relevant jurisdiction. No further qualifications are required although other academic and professional merits are certainly taken into account when examining the evidentiary value of the legal information provided.

D. *Effects of the Provided Legal Information*

The provided legal information clearly does not have binding effects. Judicial authorities are not bound by the information that is provided to them. They are free to evaluate the information received according to their sound judgment and understanding, as it is acknowledged in the last paragraph of Article 6 of the Montevideo Convention.

Furthermore, there is no statutory and precise mechanism to examine the reliability of the provided legal information. Judicial authorities have ample discretionary powers to determine the accuracy of the provided legal information. Once again, courts and judges are left to their sound judgment in order to evaluate information on foreign law.

E. *Costs*

In Venezuela, access to the courts is free of charge (Article 26 of the Constitution[18]), and judicial authorities cannot demand payment whatsoever for their services (Article 254 of the Constitution). Thus if judicial authorities engage in the research of foreign law the Venezuelan State will bear the costs, but if the parties assume the task then each of them will bear the corresponding costs and expenses associated therewith, provided, however, that they may recover such costs and expenses if successful in the litigation (Article 274 of the Code of Civil Procedure).

F. *Other Issues*

As the number of cases with foreign elements grows, Venezuelan courts have become more familiarized with issues of Private International Law. Awareness of the complexities of these type of situations, and of the needs of the parties involved have caused Venezuelan courts to be more willing to meet their duties and thus research and apply foreign laws *ex officio*. However, parties, to the extent possible, in practice assume the task of providing proof on foreign laws as if they were under the burden to do so.

4. *Interpretation and Application of Foreign Law*

Foreign law must be interpreted and applied as it would be applied in the country of origin (Article 2 of the GRPIL Convention). This means, among other things, that it would be applied in accordance with the principles in force in the country of origin. However, the application of foreign law must be made in such a way as to realize the objectives pursued by the Venezuelan rules of private international law (Article 2 of the Statute on Private International Law). This latter provision has been interpreted as establishing a basic rule for the characterization of foreign laws under a functional approach within the framework provided by the Venezuelan conflict of laws rules, and as a basic rule to determine the scope of reference to a foreign law, in order to permit a *renvoi* of first or second degree under Article 4 of the Statute on Private International Law.[19]

---

[18] Published in Special *Official Gazette* N° 5.908 of 19 February 2009.

[19] Hernández-Bretón,Eugenio, "An attempt to regulate the problem of 'characterization' in private international law", *Festschrift für Erik Jayme*, Band I, Heinz-Peter Mansel et al. (Editors), München, Sellier European Law Publishers, 2004, p. 332 et seq.; id., "Los objetivos de la normas venezolanas de conflicto", Jan Kleinheisterkamp/ Lorenzo

According to the foregoing, a gap in foreign law must be filled up using the rules and principles on construction and interpretation of laws as they are applied in the relevant foreign law, and this irrespective of how dissimilar such rules and principles may be from those of Venezuelan law.

5. *Failure to Establish Foreign Law*

If the foreign law cannot be ascertained, the solution must be sought in an appropriate way. This is an unregulated area of law, and it is left to the discretion of the judicial authorities. In this connection, it should be borne in mind that courts have the duty to decide any case that is brought to their knowledge and are under the prohibition of *non-liquet* (Article 19 of the Code of Civil Procedure). Violation of this prohibition can lead to criminal liabilities (Article 206 of the Criminal Code, Article 83 of the Anticorruption Law[20]). We anticipate that the most likely position to be followed by Venezuelan judicial authorities in the case when foreign law cannot be ascertained would be to apply the relevant Venezuelan substantive rules.

It is a pragmatically simple approach. Because Venezuelan law would be applied, Venezuelan judicial authorities would feel more comfortable when deciding the issue at stake. Probably the underlying rationale would be that it is better to decide a case even under the wrong law than to leave it open and undecided. However, as it will be more fully discussed below, a decision rendered following the approach just described, may be subject to judicial review.

III. JUDICIAL REVIEW

1. *Conflict of Laws Rules*

When conflict of laws rules have erroneously been applied (i.e., the law of State A has been applied instead of the designated law of State B), the

---

Idiarte, Gonzalo A. (Coordinadores), *Avances del Derecho Internacional Privado en América Latina. Liber Amicorum Juergen Samtleben*, Fundación de Cultura Universitaria, Montevideo, 2002, p. 169 et seq.; id., "En materia de calificaciones, reenvío y otros asuntos de Derecho Internacional Privado", *Cuadernos Unimetanos* N° 11/Septiembre 2007, Caracas, p. 227 et seq. See also Parra-Aranguren, Gonzalo. *El régimen de los bienes en el matrimonio en el Derecho Internacional Privado venezolano,* Universidad Católica Andrés Bello, Cátedra Fundacional Caracciolo Parra León, Caracas, 2007, p. 192.

[20]   Published in *Official Gazette* N° 5.637 of 7 April 2003.

parties can appeal to higher courts including the Supreme Court. The application of conflict of laws rules is, as it is with any other Venezuelan laws, subject to appeal to higher courts including the Supreme Court. This is acknowledged in Article 4 of the GRPIL Convention, Article 412 of the Bustamante Code and in Article 61 of the Statute on Private International Law. Thus, the control of the correct application of Venezuelan conflict of laws rules will be allowed in the same cases and under the same circumstances as in respect of any other provisions of Venezuelan law. The control of the application of Venezuelan conflict of laws rules is a condition necessary to the control of foreign laws[21].

The main driver of the Venezuelan solution appears to be the notion that conflict of laws rules are rules of law, and thus their correct application is subject to judicial control.

2. *Foreign Law*

Exactly as in respect of the erroneous application of domestic conflict of laws rules, the erroneous application of foreign law is subject to appeals before higher courts, including before the Supreme Court of Venezuela. Thus, the control of the correct application of foreign laws will be allowed in the same cases and under the same circumstances as in respect of any provisions of Venezuelan law.

The main driver of the Venezuelan solution appears to be the principle of equality of procedural treatment of domestic and foreign laws[22].

IV. FOREIGN LAW IN OTHER INSTANCES

Administrative and other non-judicial authorities, including notaries, seldom apply and ascertain foreign law. It may be that such authorities consider that they are not bound to apply and ascertain foreign law. However, Article 2 of the GRPIL Convention and Article 2 of the Statute on Private International Law are clear enough as to impose a duty to apply foreign law *ex officio* on any and all Venezuelan authorities regardless of

---

[21]   See File 000871, Foreign Credit Insurance Association v. Naviera Rassi C.A. et al., 20 December 2001, http://www.tsj.gov.ve/decisiones/scc/Diciembre/RC-0451-201201-00871.htm.

[22]   See de Maekelt, Tatiana B. "Recursos, Artículo 61", Maekelt, Tatiana B. et al. (Coordinación), *Ley de Derecho Internacional* Privado *Comentada*, T. II, Universidad Central de Venezuela, Caracas, 2005, at p. 1233 et seq.

whether they are part of the judiciary. Probably tax authorities are better trained and, therefore, are better suit to research *ex officio* issues of foreign law, and in practice do apply it. However, we are not aware of situations where those authorities have relied on treaties on international judicial cooperation in order to obtain information on foreign law.

In international arbitration proceedings, parties relying on foreign law usually resort to expert witness testimony as a means to provide information on and/or proof of foreign law. Although arbitrators are subject to the duty of applying foreign law *ex officio*, they do very little research on their own regarding foreign law. They tend to expect that the parties provide the bulk of allegations and proof of applicable foreign law. The question about the ascertainment and proof of foreign law rarely or never arises in cases of mediation or other alternative dispute resolution mechanism. This is because in most, if not in all, arbitration cases in Venezuela, the merits of the dispute are subject to Venezuelan law.

In advisory work by attorneys, notaries, etc. in contractual negotiations, estate planning or family arrangements, the ascertainment of foreign law is a difficult task. Attorneys engaged in advisory work when faced with issues of foreign law commonly research those issues on the Internet. The results so obtained will provide a first conceptual approach that will help them in determining the necessary further steps in order to deepen a possible research of the issues. This assumes a certain command of the relevant languages and a prior understanding of the conflict of laws queries that are relevant for the case at stake. Although this practice may sound as routine, it cannot be taken as determinative of the issues and may cause the Venezuelan attorney to face issues of professional responsibility, because he/she may not be sufficiently qualified to provide legal advice on those foreign law issues. In several instances after the Venezuelan lawyer has gained an insight of the particularities of the relevant foreign legal system it is that he/she then contacts lawyers admitted to practice in the relevant foreign jurisdiction for more formal advice. To this effect, legal networks provide a very useful tool.

Resorting to Comparative law, and thus to foreign law, is quite frequent in the drafting of laws and regulations by domestic authorities. The same applies to the preparation of research papers at the academic level.

V. ACCESS TO FOREIGN LAW: STATUS QUO

Venezuelan State agencies do provide legal information through their official website[23]. However, the information found in those webpages is limited to the text of laws, decrees and regulations, in most of the cases taken directly from the *Official Gazette*, and not always timely updated. It is not frequent to find explanations on the law or guidance on Venezuelan law, because those webpages are not meant to provide any type of legal advice. It must be pointed out that the web page of the Supreme Court of Venezuela[24] is a repository of all the decisions rendered by the Court since its inception in 1999, and contains decisions of other lower courts.

As far as judicial network is concerned, Venezuelan courts, particularly the Supreme Court of Justice, have resorted directly to the information provided by the European Judicial Network in order to ascertain the contents of foreign laws, as mentioned above (See *supra* II(C)(2)(b)). It may be reasonable to expect that other Venezuelan courts will research foreign laws in similar databases.

As mentioned, Venezuela is a party to the Montevideo Convention so that its mechanism can be used to collect information on foreign law. In addition, Venezuela is a party to the Bustamante Code, which also provides for mechanisms to facilitate access to foreign law among the contracting parties (Articles 410-411). There are no official figures available evidencing the application of either the Bustamante Code or the Montevideo Convention. In respect of the Montevideo Convention though, some commentators manifest certain satisfactory results[25], while others consider it a failure similar to its European counterpart[26]. It is, thus, difficult to assess the practical results of the Montevideo Conven-

---

[23]   See for example http://www.pgr.gob.ve/.

[24]   http://www.tsj.gob.ve.

[25]   Tellechea Bergman, Eduardo. "Aplicación e información del derecho extranjero en el actual ámbito interamericano y regional, con especial referencia al derecho uruguayo", Fernández Arroyo, Diego P./ González Martín, Nuria (coordinadores), *Tendencias y Relaciones Derecho Internacional Privado Americano Actual (Jornadas de la ASADIP 2008)*, Universidad Nacional Autónoma de México, Editorial Porrúa, ASADIP, Mexico, 2010, p. 95 et seq., at p. 113.

[26]   Nyota Lamm, Martin. *Die Interamerikanischen Spezialkonferenzen für Internationales Privatrecht*, Ergon Verlag, Wuerzburg, 2000, at p. 135

tion. Sarcastic as it can be, no one can say for sure whether or not the Montevideo Convention is "half dead"[27].

In our experience, these international instruments do not work well to ascertain foreign law. Several factors can be considered as impairing the success of the Montevideo Convention, namely (i) lack of knowledge of the Convention and its mechanisms, (ii) lack of well-provided law libraries and research centers, and (iii) lack of sensibility vis-à-vis the requests for information in light of petitions for international judicial cooperation among Latin American countries. In addition to the foregoing, time constraints and a heavy workload also influence the judges attitude to escape from the examination of issues of conflict of laws, and, accordingly, are determinative of their decision to avoid resorting to the mechanisms of international judicial cooperation for the gathering of information on foreign laws. Only teaching and State awareness of its international commitments will help to overcome the aforementioned deficit.

VI. ACCESS TO FOREIGN LAW: FURTHER DEVELOPMENTS

1. *Practical Need*

Unquestionably, there is need to improve access to foreign law. It particularly applies to judicial authorities and other non-judicial authorities, which are faced with the largest amount of cases involving foreign laws. As far as the circumstances in which access to foreign law is most needed, we believe that it is in the course of litigation. This does not mean that access to foreign law is not important for all remaining instances. In the latter cases, the parties may anticipate together with legal counsel a number of legal issues that may be consulted or verified with foreign counsel as appropriate. The same may be true for litigation matters. This would ease the tasks of judicial authorities and the parties.

Without hesitation, we consider that family law is the area where access to foreign law is more crucial, this is because parties involved in these situations are very rarely sophisticated and knowledgeable enough about legal issues, and may not have the financial resources to retain the services of competent legal counsel.

---

[27]   Christian von Bar and Mankowski, Peter. *Internationales Privatrecht, Band I. Allgemeine Lehren*, Verlag C.H. Beck, Munich, 2003, at p. 375 referring to the European Convention on Information on Foreign Law: "*Sarkastisch, aber treffend ist die Bezeichnung des Übereinkommens als halbtot*".

Access to foreign laws is a deficit of the Venezuelan system of private international law, which requires immediate correction. It would not be exaggerated to affirm that lack of easy and affordable access to foreign law is one of the main reasons that causes judicial authorities to refrain from ascertaining foreign laws, and which makes litigators reluctant to plead the applicability of choice of laws rules. The consequence of the foregoing is the scarce application of foreign laws by Venezuelan judicial authorities.

2. *Conflict of Laws Solutions*

The modification of Venezuelan conflict of laws rules does not appear as the most desirable way to solve the foregoing situation. We do not think that Venezuelan conflict of laws rules must be amended *de lege ferenda* to reduce the number of cases in which foreign law is applied. We believe that these rules are well balanced.

Neither should the treatment of foreign law in Venezuela be changed *de lege ferenda*. We do not think that any changes are necessary in respect of the current status of Venezuelan laws regarding the treatment of foreign laws by judicial and non-judicial authorities. The *ex officio* application of foreign laws should be kept for all areas of law.

Unfortunately, as explained above (see *supra* V(5), so far regional instruments in Latin America have proven unsuccessful.

3. *Methods of Facilitating Access to Foreign Law*

Theoretically, we think international or regional instruments that establish administrative and/or judicial cooperation to exchange information on participating States' law are useful tools to facilitate access to foreign law. But in practice lack of commitment of the member states lead to very poor results.

Any instrument facilitating access to foreign law should be flexible enough to allow adaptations to future needs. It should also make affordable the access to the information and should not impose unnecessary formalities, such as legalizations or apostilles. The timing for answering the request should be kept to a minimum. Such international instruments should be open to not only judicial authorities, but also to individuals and/or any other authorities. However, the treatment of each case must be different, particularly in respect of costs.

Using intermediaries to send a request to foreign competent authorities or designated experts should be kept to a minimum. Transmission of the requests and the corresponding results should allowed by means similar to those allowed by The Hague Convention of 15 November 1965 on the Service Abroad of Judicial and Extrajudicial Documents in Civil or Commercial Matters.

The answer provided by the requested should not be binding. The assessment of the information provide should be left to the authorities of the requesting state, otherwise, according to Venezuelan law, it could be understood that the authority to adjudicate the matter has been delegated to a third party in violation of the right to an ordinary judge or to a non-authorized official.

As far as the costs for the provision of services on legal information are concerned, a differentiated treatment should be given. In the situations where the judicial or non-judicial authorities request the information, the legal information should be provided without costs. On the contrary, if the interested parties request the information then they should bear the costs. In the case of Venezuela, the foregoing approaches would be consistent with constitutional and legal rules (See *supra* II(C)(6) above).

It is to be noted that reliability and certainty of the information should be guaranteed at all times and in all cases.

Any method for accessing information on foreign laws would be a plus. We could think about enhancing direct communication of judges, establishing networks for other legal professionals (e.g., law firms), identifying qualified experts or expert institutes (e.g., creating a list of experts), or providing information on national laws on the Internet.

- *LA CORRUPTION DANS LES CON-TRATS COMMERCIAUX INTERNATIO-NAUX ET SES EFFETS EN DROIT PRIVE / THE CIVIL LAW EFFECTS OF COR-RUPTION IN INTERNATIONAL COM-MERCIAL CONTRACTS*

THE CIVIL LAW EFFECTS OF CORRUPTION IN INTERNATIONAL COMMERCIAL CONTRACTS

Eugenio Hernández-Bretón and Claudia Madrid Martínez
PROFESSORS, CENTRAL UNIVERSITY OF VENEZUELA

I. THE CIVIL LAW CONSEQUENCES OF CORRUPTION IN GENERAL

1. *Is corruption a criminal offence in your country, and if so, how is it defined?*

The fight against corruption has been the subject of many efforts and different laws throughout the history of Venezuela. Notably, the first special law on the matter was enacted in 1982 (Organic Law for the Safeguard of the Public Patrimony, published in the *Official Gazette* N° 3.777 of 23 December 1982). Previously corruption was punished by the relevant provisions of the different Criminal Codes in force since the XIXth century. Corruption is in fact a criminal offence under Venezuelan law. Currently anti-corruption legislation is contained in in the Law against Corruption (*Ley contra la Corrupción*), published in the Special *Official Gazette* N° 5.637 of 7 April 2003 ("Anti-Corruption Law"). There are several provisions of the Anti-Corruption Law that establish criminal offences that fall under the common meaning of corruption. Following herein you will find a description of the contents of those provisions.

Pursuant to the Anti-Corruption Law, there are at least six crimes that, pursuant to the circumstances of each specific case, may be applicable. To wit:

1. Inducement to give or promise benefits (Article 60 of the Anti-Corruption Law): This crime is committed when a public official, abusing his functions, induces someone to give or promise, for himself or for another person, a sum of money or any other undue benefit or gift.

2. Improper passive corruption (Article 61 of the Anti-Corruption Law): This crime is committed when a public official who, because of a certain act related to his functions, receives or accepts a promise, for himself or for others, of retribution or other benefits not due to him. The person giving or promising the retribution or benefit shall also be subject to criminal liability.

3. Proper passive corruption (Article 62 of the Anti-Corruption Law): This crime is committed when a public official, with the purpose of delaying or omitting an act corresponding to his functions or performing an act contrary to his functions, receives or accepts money, a promise or other benefits, directly or indirectly. In this case, the penalties corresponding to this crime will also be imposed on (i) the intermediary of the public official or person who received the money, promise or other benefits on behalf of the public official; and (ii) the person giving or promising the money or other benefits.

Article 62 of the Anti-Corruption Law also provides that the crime of proper passive corruption shall be aggravated in the following circumstances:

a) When the object of the act of corruption is to confer public employment, subsidies, pensions or honors or to cause the public official to agree to sign contracts related to the administration to which the official belongs;

b) When the object of the act of corruption is to favor or cause any harm or damage to any of the parties in an administrative, criminal, civil or any other kind of procedure or lawsuit; and/or

c) When the act of corruption is committed by a judge who renders a judgment of deprivation of freedom exceeding 6 months.

4. Incitement to corruption (Article 63 of the Anti-Corruption Law): This crime is committed by a person who, without achieving his objective, insists on persuading or inducing any public official to commit any of the crimes of corruption.

5. Collusion (Article 70 of the Anti-Corruption Law): A conspiracy or concert of action between a public official and persons or intermediaries

in order to obtain a specific result from a given contract. This offence is aggravated if the public official receives moneys, gifts or undue earnings.

6. Representation of relationships with public officials (Article 79 of the Anti-Corruption Law): This crime is committed by a person that representing that he/she has relationships with public officials is capable of influencing their decision making, and for such reason receives or is promised moneys or any other benefit for his intermediation or in order to remunerate the granting of favors from public officials. The same offence is committed by the person giving or promising those moneys or benefits, unless the payer has denounced the situation to the authorities before the initiation of the criminal judicial proceedings.

For purposes of the foregoing, the following persons do qualify as public officials (Articles 2 and 3 of the Anti-Corruption Law):

1. Those invested with public functions, permanent or transitory, remunerated or *ad honorem*, whether by election, appointment or contract granted by competent authorities, serving at Agencies of the Republic, of the states, territories and federal dependencies, district, metropolitan districts or municipalities, national, state, district and municipal autonomous institutes, public universities, Central Bank of Venezuela or of any entities that exercise Public Powers.

2. Directors and administrators of civil and commercial companies, foundations, civil associations and other institutions crested with public funds or managed by any of the State entities mentioned in Article 4 of the Anti-Corruption Law, or when the aggregate of contributions in a year, from one or several of these entities, represents 50% or more of its budget or net worth; and the directors appointed to represent such bodies and entities, even if the participation of the Venezuelan government is less than 50% of the capital or net worth of such civil and commercial companies, foundations, civil associations or institutions.

3. Any other person in the cases provided for in the Anti-Corruption Law.

Generally, the following are considered to be part of the public sector: (i) Bodies and entities in charge of exercising the national public power; (ii) Bodies and entities in charge of exercising the public power of the states; (iii) Bodies and entities in charge of exercising the public power in the districts and metropolitan districts; (iv) Bodies in charge of exercising the municipal public power and the rest of the local entities established in the Organic Law of the Municipal Regime; (v) Bodies and entities in charge of exercising the public power in the federal territories and dependencies; (vi) National, state, district and municipal autonomous institutes; (vii) the Central Bank of Venezuela; (viii) Public universities; (viii) other national, state, district and municipal public law person; (ix) Any other public law entities, whether national, state, district or municipal; (x) Partnerships of any nature in which the above mentioned persons have participation in their capital, as well as those partnerships incorporated with the participation of such persons; and (xi) Foundations and civil associations and other institutions created with public funds or that are directed by the persons mentioned in the above numbers or in which said persons appoint their authorities or when the budget contributions in a year by one or several or the persons mentioned in the above numbers represent at least 50% or more of its budget (Article 4 of the Anti-Corruption Law).

A. *Is corruption a criminal offence only in the public sector or also in the private sector?*

Under Venezuelan law, corruption has been treated as an offence in the public sector only. However, under Article 17.3 of the Law to Protect and Promote Free Competition (*Ley para Promover y Proteger el Ejercicio de la Libre Competencia*), published in the *Official Gazette* N° 34.880 of 13 January 1992, commercial bribery (*soborno comercial*) is considered to be an act of unlawful competition (*competencia desleal*), thus prohibited and sanctioned by that Law. This would lead to the imposition of fines. In order for commercial bribery to constitute unlawful competition it must be aimed to "eliminating competition". Additionally, the recently approved Decree with Rank, Value and Force of Organic Law on Fair Prices (*Decreto con Rango, Valor y Fuerza de Ley Orgánica de Precios Justos*), published in the *Official Gazette* N° 40.340 of 23 January 2014) expressly punishes a type of corruption between/among individuals (*corrupción entre particulares)*. Indeed, Article 64 penalizes the conduct of anyone who personally or through an intermediary promises, offers or grants to officers, directors, employees or business partners, companies, associations, foundations or organizations, a benefit or advantage of any kind, in order to favor him/her or a third person against another, in breach of their obligations, in the purchase or sale of goods or the provision of services. The officer, director, employee or partner, who by him/herself or through another person, receives, solicits or accepts such benefit or advantage shall also be subject to the same criminal sanctions, i.e., Imprisonment from two to six years.

B. *Is corruption a criminal offence also if committed by a national*
of your country in a foreign country?

The basic rule of Venezuelan law is that criminal laws are of a territorial nature, and are applicable to crimes committed on Venezuelan soil regardless of the nationality of the persons involved (Article 3 of the Criminal Code, published in the Special *Official Gazette* N° 5.768 of 13 April 2005). Exceptionally they apply, e.g., to persons irrespectively of their nationality for offences committed abroad in violation of Venezuelan criminal laws, and to Venezuelans for crimes committed against Venezuelans in violation of Venezuelan criminal laws (Article 4 of the Criminal Code). The Anti-Corruption Law prescribes its extraterritorial application in respect of nationals or foreigners for criminal offences involving Venezuelan public officers abroad (Article 3 of the Anti Corruption Law).

2. Is your country party to any of the abovementioned international conventions, or to any other international instrument, on corruption?

Venezuela is a party to the Inter-American Convention on Corruption (approbatory law published in *Official Gazette* N° 36.211 of 22 May 1997) and to the United Nations Convention against Corruption (approbatory law published in *Official Gazette* N° 38.192 of 23 May 2005).

3. Is there any statutory regulation in your country dealing specifically with the civil law consequences of corruption?
If so, please describe its content

Although the Anti-Corruption Law refers to the civil liability arising from the criminal offences regulated therein in several provisions (e.g., Articles 21, 33, 42, 48, 87, 88, 90, 97), there is no express statutory regulation in that Law or in any other Venezuelan law dealing specifically with the civil law consequences of corruption. Therefore, the general rules on civil liability arising from criminal offences contained in the Criminal Code will apply (Articles 113 et seq.). Those provisions deal fore mostly with the civil liability of the offender vis-à-vis the victim and the Venezuelan State. Under Article 120 of the Criminal Code, civil liability derived from criminal offences comprises (i) restitution, (ii) reparation, and (iii) indemnification of damages. Accordingly, the civil consequences of corruption shall be determined pursuant to the general rules on contract and tort liability, as applicable under the circumstances, which are contained in the Civil Code.

4. *Are there any court decisions/arbitral awards rendered in you country dealing with the civil law consequences of corruption? If so, please provide an overview of them*

Although there is a considerable amount of court decisions dealing with the application of the Anti-Corruption Law, we have been unable to locate a single court decision/arbitral award dealing with the civil law consequences of corruption. Similarly, domestic commentators are silent on the subject matter.

5. *In the absence of a specific statutory regulation in your country on the civil law consequences of corruption, what principles of general contract law would be relevant in this respect:*

A. *Those concerning "illegal" or "immoral" contracts?*

In Venezuela, commentators prefer to use the notion of "unlawfulness" (*ilicitud*) rather than "illegality" (*ilegalidad*) when referring to the violation of (i) the law, (ii) the public policy (*orden público*) or (iii) the bones mores (*buenas costumbres*). In this latter case, commentators also use the term "immorality" (*inmoralidad*). The general rule is contained in Article 6 of the Civil Code according to which "Laws of public policy or affecting bones mores cannot be waived or modified by private agreements." (*No pueden renunciarse ni relajarse por convenios particulares las leyes en cuya observancia están interesados el orden público o las buenas costumbres*). The foregoing provision, however, does not expressly establish the effects of such a waiver. Nonetheless, commentators and case law generally admit that an agreement in violation of the law, public policy or bones mores is null and void, and it triggers civil liability. Furthermore, the Anti-Corruption Law can be considered as a set of mandatory rules, which also reflects high moral standards (bones mores) to be respected in the course of dealings with the Public Administration, the violation of which shall cause the contract to be not only illegal but unlawful as well, because it would be contrary to bones mores, and thus null and void.

Additionally, there are two provisions on contracts contained in the Civil Code dealing with the notion of unlawfulness which are worth mentioning. Under Article 1.155 of the Civil Code the object (*objeto*) of a contract must be lawful (*lícito*). The cause (*causa*) of the contract must be lawful (*lícita*) as well (Article 1.157 of the Civil Code). In general terms, the dealings, negotiations, agreements and/or payments preceding the execution of an agreement, which are made in violation of the Anti-Corruption

Law, shall be illegal and, as such, null and void. If any of the foregoing actions can be considered as the cause of a subsequent agreement executed with the Public Administration, in the sense that any of those actions constituted the motive or reason that lead the parties to execute the agreement, then the cause can be treated as unlawful, and the agreement will be null and void. In this connection, from a comparative law standpoint it is worth noticing that Article 1.157 of the Venezuelan Civil Code was drafted after Articles 27 and 29 of the French-Italian Draft on Obligations and Contracts of 1927. Article 1.157 provides as follows: "The obligation without a cause, or based on a false cause or unlawful, shall have no effect. The cause is unlawful when it is contrary to the law, the bones mores or the public policy. Whoever has paid an obligation against bones mores cannot claim restitution, except if on his/her part there was no violation of the latter".

B. *Those concerning the authority of agents?*

The rules and principles concerning the authority of agents (*representación*) will also apply. The acts performed by the agent in the name of the principal within the limits of his/her powers directly develop their effects in respect of the latter (Article 1.169 of the Civil Code). The agent shall not exceed the limits of his/her powers (Article 1.689 of the Civil Code). If the agent acts beyond the scope of his/her powers, then the agent is liable not only for willful misconduct (*dolo*) but for negligence (*culpa*) (Article 1.693 of the Civil Code). The principal will not be bound by the acts of the agent except if he/she expressly or tacitly ratifies the acts of the agent (Article 1.968 of the Civil Code).

C. *Others?*

It could be possible that the general rules on civil liability apply, either in contract or in tort.

6. *In applying the principles concerning "illegal" or "immoral" contracts in general and/or the principles concerning the authority of agents to contracts affected by corruption, what would the consequences be with respect to*

(a) The bribery contract, i.e. the agreement between the bribe-giver and the bribe-taker (normally an independent intermediary or an employee/public official of a principal-prospective counterpart to the main contract) whereby the bribe-taker undertakes, against payment of a "commission", to have the principal assign the main contract to the bribe-giver?

The bribery contract should be null and void because of the illegality of its object. The subject matter of the obligation of the bribe-taker would be a violation of the law (Article 1.155 of the Civil Code and Article 79 of the Anti-Corruption Law), and the cause of the contract would be illegal because the contract is in violation of the law, and also unlawful because it is against bones mores and violates Venezuelan public policy. Because the contract is against bones mores the bribery-giver and the bribery-taker shall be precluded from claiming restitution (*actio de in rem verso*) against each other (Article 1.157 of the Civil Code). The last paragraph of Article 1.157 of the Civil Code is inspired by the different formulations of the principle of *nemo auditur,* namely (i) *nemo auditur propriam turpitudinem allegans,* (ii) *in pari causa turpitudinis melior est condictio possidentis,* and (iii) *in pari causa turpitudinis cessat repetitio.* Some commentators go even beyond the text of the last paragraph of Article 1.157 and state that the same consequence shall apply to contracts which cause (*causa*) violates public policy or the law. When in the foregoing cases the Civil Code prohibits the filing of an *actio de in rem verso* it allows an unjust enrichment (*enriquecimiento sin causa*). This decision can be justified by the legislature's desire of sparing courts the embarrassment of deciding claims regarding contracts executed and performed by dishonest persons. In sum, it would be absurd to grant legal protection to the very same person that purports to violate the law.

(b) The main contract concluded between the bribe-giver and the principal?

The main contract would be null and void because it is executed in violation of an imperative rule. The cause of the contract would be illicit (Article 1.157 of the Civil Code), and therefore it cannot be ratified by the principal.

II. THE CIVIL LAW CONSEQUENCES OF CORRUPTION IN INTERNATIONAL COMMERCIAL CONTRACTS

Supposing the law governing the respective contracts is the law of your country, what in your view would be the answer to the questions posed in connection with the following cases?

Case N° 1.

Contractor A of country X enters into an agreement with agent B ("the Commission Agreement") under which B, for a commission fee of USD 1,000,000 would pay, on behalf of A, USD 10,000,000 to C, a high-ranking procurement advisor of D, the Minister of Economics

and Development of country Y, in order to induce D to award A the contract for the construction of a new power plant in country Y ("the Contract"). B pays C the USD 10,000,000 bribe and D awards the Contract to A.

Ques. 1.1: Can A refuse to pay B the agreed commission fee invoking the illegality of the Commission Agreement?

Yes. The Commission Agreement would be in violation of an imperative rule, and therefore null and void because of an illegal object and an illicit cause (Articles 1.155 and 1.157 of the Civil Code). Additionally, it would be against bones mores and public policy (Article 6 of the Civil Code) to allow B to collect the commission fee.

Ques. 1.2: In the case that, although B has paid C the bribe, D does not award A the Contract, can B request the payment of the agreed commission fee from A, and can A recover from B the bribe B has paid to C?

B cannot request the payment of the agreed commission fee from A because it would be in violation of an imperative rule, and therefore null and void because of an unlawful object and an unlawful cause (Articles 1.155 and 1.157 of the Civil Code). Additionally, it would be against bones mores and public policy (Article 6 of the Civil Code) to allow B to collect the commission fee.

A cannot recover from B the bribe B has paid to C. The payment of a bribe is not only a violation of an imperative rule but it is also against bones mores and public policy. According to the facts, A was aware of the illicit payment made by B to C. The payor of an obligation which is in violation of bones mores is prohibited from filing an *actio de in rem verso* unless the payor was unaware of the violation (last paragraph of Article 1.157 of the Civil Code). In the case at stake A appears to be fully aware of the destination of the payment made by B to C. Thus, A cannot recover from B the bribe B has paid to C.

Ques. 1.3: Supposing that D, when awarding the Contract to A, did not know nor ought to have known of the bribe paid to C, can D choose to treat the Contract as effective, with the consequence that A would be obliged to perform and D to pay the price, subject to an appropriate adjustment taking into consideration the payment of the bribe?

N° Under Article 88 of the Law on Public Contracts (*Ley de Contrataciones Públicas*) (published in the *Official Gazette* N° 39.503 of 6 September 2010) when a contract is awarded by a governmental entity based on false data or in violation of legal provisions, the contracting entity shall declare the nullity of the award by way of a duly motivated decision. Additionally, it may seek restitution and the reparation and indemnification of damages suffered as a result of the declaration of nullity pursuant to general tort provisions contained in the Civil Code (Articles 1.185 et seq.)

Ques. 1.4: Still supposing that D, when awarding the Contract to A, did not know nor ought to have known of the bribe paid to C, can D choose instead to treat the Contract as being of no effect, with the consequence that neither of the parties has a remedy under the Contract?

Yes. See answer to Ques. 1.4. In this case, D may seek restitution and damages pursuant to the general tort provisions contained in the Civil Code (Articles 1.185 et seq. of the Civil Code). A will not have a remedy under the Contract or at law (last paragraph of Article 1.157 of the Civil Code).

Ques. 1.5: Supposing that A, after having been awarded the Contract, has almost completed construction of the power plant when in country Y a new Government comes to power which claims that the Contract is invalid because of corruption and refuses to pay the outstanding 50% of the price, would the parties be left where they are or would they be granted restitutionary remedies, i.e. A be granted an allowance in money for the work done corresponding to the value that the almost completed power plant has for D, and D restitution of any payment it has made exceeding this amount?

Because of the same reasons mentioned above, the Contract would be null and void. D may seek restitution and damages pursuant to the general tort provisions contained in the Civil Code (Articles 1.185 et seq. of the Civil Code). A will not have restitutionary remedies or any other remedy under the Contract or at law (last paragraph of Article 1.157 of the Civil Code).

Case N° 2.

A, an aircraft manufacturer in country X, knowing that C, the Ministry of Defence of country Y, intends to purchase a number of military aircraft, enters into an agreement with B, a consultancy firm located in country Y, by which B, for a commission fee, is to negotiate the possible purchase by C of the aircraft manufactured by A ("the Agency Agreement").

Ques. 2.1: Supposing that C, despite B's efforts, does not buy the aircraft from A, can A refuse to pay B the agreed commission fee, invoking a statutory regulation of country Y prohibiting the em-

ployment of intermediaries in the negotiation and conclusion of contracts with governmental agencies?

Regardless of the application of Venezuelan law to the Contract, a Venezuelan court would examine the legal nature of the regulation of country Y prohibiting the employment of intermediaries in the negotiation and conclusion of contracts with governmental agencies in order to determine whether such a regulation qualifies as mandatory laws or *lois d'application immédiate ou nécessaire*, protecting general interests of country Y for economic, political or social reasons. Assuming that the regulation satisfies the test, then the Venezuelan Court, because country Y has close ties with the Contract, may discretionarily apply that regulation to the Contract based on Article 1 of the Venezuelan Act on Private International Law and on the last paragraph of Article 11 of the Inter American Convention on the Law Applicable to International Contracts, Mexico City, 1994 ("It shall be up to the forum to decide when it applies the mandatory provisions of the law of another State with which the contract has close ties."), being the latter applied as a generally accepted principle of Private International Law. In this case, the Venezuelan court may void the Contract because of an illegal object and an illicit cause, as it was explained above.

Case N° 3.

A, an aircraft manufacturer in country X, knowing that C, the Ministry of Defence of country Z, intends to purchase a number of military aircraft, enters into an agreement with B, an intermediary located in country Z, by which B, for a "fee" of 5% of the contract price, is to "negotiate" the purchase by C of the aircraft manufactured by A ("the Agreement"), on the understanding that B will pay half of the "fee" to a high ranking procurement advisor of C.

Ques. 3.1: Supposing that A, after C has purchased the aircraft from A, refuses to pay the agreed "fee" invoking the illegality of the Agreement, can B require payment on the ground that in Country Z not only is there no statutory regulation prohibiting the employment of intermediaries in the negotiation and conclusion of contracts with governmental agencies, but it is a generally accepted practice that intermediaries "share" their "fees" with their contact persons in the governmental agencies concerned?

Regardless of the fact that there is no statutory regulation in Country Z prohibiting the employment of intermediaries in the negotiation and conclusion of contracts with governmental agencies, and that in Country Z it is a generally accepted practice that intermediaries "share" their "fees" with their contact persons in the governmental agencies concerned, under

Venezuelan standards that payment would be against bones mores and public policy. Thus the Contract would have an illegal object and an illicit cause (Articles 1.155 and 1.157 of the Civil Code). Additionally, it would be against bones mores and public policy (Article 6 of the Civil Code) to allow B to collect the agreed fee.

III.A. DROIT COMMERCIAL / COMMERCIAL LAW

CURRENT CHALLENGES FACED BY COMPANIES (*SOCIEDADES ANÓNIMAS*) IN VENEZUELA.
-SPECIAL REFERENCE TO THEIR REGULATION UNDER BUSINESS LAW-

*Andrea I. Rondón García**

PROFESSOR, ANDRES BELLO CATHOLIC UNIVERSITY

INTRODUCTION

Even if due to the trend of moving away from Codes, that is also observed in Venezuela, many provisions regulating business corporations are found in special laws, the general statute is still preserved in the Commercial Code. The Commercial Code maintains formally the basic premises that serve as grounds for Liberalism, a philosophical and political doctrine characterized by limiting the powers of the State and ensuring greater autonomy and freedom of the individual, and for which, one must have a State with well-defined powers and competence to prevent the abuse of rights and freedoms by some to the detriment of the rights and freedoms of others.

In our Commercial Code we find the following:

- Predominance of the principle of party autonomy in the regulation of relationships (for example, Article 200 of the Commercial Code[1]).

---

* Juris Doctor, *magna cum laude* (2002); Procedural Law Specialist, *honors* (2006); Attending Program for LLM degree (2007-thesis preparation) from Universidad Central de Venezuela. Legal Argumentation Teacher, Andrés Bello Catholic University (2006-to date). Collaborator, *Centro de Divulgación del Conocimiento Económico* (CEDICE).

- Recognition of State intervention to verify that joint merchants comply with incorporation requirements, which benefits both shareholders and third parties (for example, Article 200, sole paragraph, of the Commercial Code).

- Public policy rules are the exception. Several of them are intended to facilitate control of merchant activities by tax inspection and collection agencies, without involving any arbitrary interference (functionalizing) with the activity of the merchant (for example, business accounting regulation, Articles 32, 33 et seq[2]).

- Regulation of private property is rare. The existing regulation is intended to protect third parties and shareholders in the case of joint merchants (for instance, Articles 244 and 264[3]).

---

[1]   "Article 200

Business companies or partnerships are those whose object is to carry out one or more acts of trade. Without prejudice to the provisions of special laws, companies and limited liability partnerships will always be commercial in nature, regardless of their object, unless they are exclusively engaged in agriculture and livestock exploitation.

Business companies are ruled by the agreements of the parties and by the provisions of this Code and the Civil Code.

Sole Paragraph: Through competent administrative agencies the State shall see to the compliance with the formal requirements established for the incorporation and operation of Companies and Limited Liability Partnerships."

[2]   "Article 32. Every merchant must keep its accounting the Spanish language, comprising mandatorily the Journal, Ledger, and Inventory books.

He may also keep such auxiliary books as he may deem advisable for a better order and clarity of his transactions."

"Article 33. The Journal and Inventory books cannot be used without having been previously submitted to the Court, or to the Commercial Registrar, in such places where the latter are available, and where not, to the ordinary Judge of highest category, in order that a note about the folios which the book has can be placed on its first page, dated and signed by the Judge and his Secretary or by the Commercial Registrar. All other pages will be stamped with the seal of the office."

[3]   "Article 244. Managers must deposit in the corporate treasury a number of shares prescribed by the by-laws.

These shares are fully pledged to secure all acts of management, even exclusively personal acts for a manager; shall be nontransferable and shall be marked with a special stamp indicating their non-transferability. Upon the approval of the account of the managers, a note signed by the Directors shall be placed on those shares to indicate that they have become transferable."

"Article 264. When the managers shall recognize that the capital stock according to inventories and balance sheet has decreased by one third, they shall call the shareholders

Regarding autonomy of the parties, even if it is a principle of Law manifesting the freedom of the individual to exercise his faculties in the contracting area, submitting his behavior to certain rules in his relationship with others, this principle has lost its effectiveness in Venezuela in most fields where it should be applied with preference.

In practice, it does not matter that no reform has been made to the Civil Code and Commercial Code, wherein the principle of autonomy of the parties is the rule and public policy provisions–those which cannot be relaxed by the parties- are the exception, because, in fact, there is not much left of that principle.

For instance, if one wishes to sell a used car, a significant number of previous controls must be passed and many formalities must be completed before a Notary Public –controls and formalities not contemplated by law– to be finally able to obtain the title deed under the name of the buyer.

Another example, and a case of interest in this report, is that in order to register shareholder meeting minutes it is no longer sufficient to comply with the provisions of the company's by-laws –i.e., the rules that were freely agreed by the stockholders- or, in the absence of regulation, to meet the requirements set forth in the Commercial Code, but it shall be necessary to comply in addition with the demands –not set forth in the law- of Registry officials.

We could go on and on with examples (house leasing, selling of land, etc.) in which the autonomy of the parties has been in some cases frankly diminished and in others eliminated by senseless limitations, restrictions, and controls.

It has been deemed essential to draw attention to the above because, even if our report will focus mainly on company related regulations such as the Commercial Code, the Public Registry and Notaries Law and the opinion of Commercial Registries, there is another type of regulation that also affects companies in a significant manner, especially in their operation, such as the Law for Defending People's Access to Goods and Services[4], the Decree with status of Law on Fair Costs and Prices[5], the De-

---

and ask them whether they elect to refund the capital, or limit it to the remaining amount, or liquidate the company.

When the capital has decreased by two thirds the company will be necessarily liquidated, if the shareholders do not choose to refund the capital or limit the corporate fund to the existing capital."

[4]   Published in Official Gazette N° 39.358 of February 1st, 2010.

cree with status of Organic Law on Agro-Food Security and Sovereignty[6], the Foreign Exchange Crimes Law[7], the Organic Law on Work and Workers[8], among others. These regulations constitute an important limitation to the principle of autonomy of private parties.

Lastly, although we will not deal in depth with this additional regulation, as it escapes the objectives of this report, in the analysis of the general aspects of companies in Venezuela we will touch on certain current practices that drastically detract from the autonomy of shareholders and give rise to confusion, and that in overcoming the same or in operating with them pose a real challenge to companies in Venezuela today.

I. PRINCIPAL REGULATION

With the aforesaid phenomenon of moving away from Codes, many provisions that regulate the activity of businessmen are contained in special laws. However, it is evident that the general statute is still contained in the Commercial Code and, therefore, we are obliged to its analysis.

It is worth noting that our first Commercial Code is from February 15, 1862[9] and the current one dates back to 1919, with successive reforms in 1938, 1942, 1945 y 1955[10]. We would wish to say that the influence of

---

[5]   Published in Official Gazette N° 39.715 of July 18, 2011.

[6]   Published in Official Gazette N° 5.889, extraordinary issue of July 31, 2008.

[7]   This law was published for the first time in Official Gazette N° 38.272 of September 14, 2005 and its most recent reform was published in Official Gazette N° 5.975, extraordinary issue of May 17, 2010.

[8]   Published in Official Gazette N° 6.076, extraordinary issue of May 7, 2012.

[9]   Main legislative compilations omit reference to this Commercial Code and refer to the Code of August 29, 1862 as the first Commercial Code. This has caused some confusion mentioned by scholars. The changes are insignificant and as of today there is no explanation for the approval of this second Code. On this matter, see Grisanti Luciani, Héctor, *Antecedentes de nuestra legislación civil y mercantil*, [Background of our civil and commercial law], Caracas, 2002, pp. 18-20, Morles Hernández, Alfredo, "Evolución Histórica y tendencias mercantil venezolana" [Historical Evolution and mercantile trends in Venezuela] (pp. 273-306), in: *Centenario del Código de Comercio*, México, Universidad Autónoma de México, 1991.

[10]   Morles Hernández, Alfredo: *Evolución Histórica y tendencias mercantil venezolana...*, p. 288.

the liberal ideas of the XVIII and XIX centuries was present in our Commercial Codes, but such influence was inconsistent.

For example, the Codes of 1862 provided that the incorporation of companies could only take place with the previous authorization of the Head of State and that amendments to the by-laws required government authorization. The Code of 1873 eliminated the requisite of previous authorization in order to organize a company but established that the provisions of the incorporation papers were governed by the Commercial Code, the Civil Code, and in last instance, by the agreement between the parties. For authors such as Morles Hernández, this could be interpreted as assigning imperative rules[11].

If we keep in mind that the last reform to this Code was made in 1955 and several areas of the Code were not then modified, we could say that this Code has straggled, and this fact has not been completely remedied by the special laws. An example of such straggling is Article 244 of the Commercial Code, which provides that in order to guarantee their performance, managers must deposit or cause to be deposited a share of stock in the corporate treasury. Clearly the purpose of this provision is not accomplished in practice, taking into account the face value of a share of stock in comparison to the damages that improper manager performance could cause to the shareholders.

The above situation has led to various efforts seeking to update this legislation. For instance, there was a total reform draft completed in 1962 by a commission whose reporter was Roberto Goldschmidt, and which was sent to but not considered by Congress in 1963; a draft Securities Act, from a commission presided by René De Sola in 1978, which the National Executive never sent to Congress; a draft General Securities Act from the commission presided by Alfredo Morles Hernández in 1984, sent to the National Executive and forwarded by the latter to Congress who never discussed it. Also, in 1988, that same commission sent to the Ministry of Justice a draft Business Corporation Act which the National Executive never sent to Congress; in that same year 1988, Leopoldo Borjas prepared the draft Venezuelan Bankruptcy Act, which was handed over to the

---

[11]   Morles Hernández, Alfredo, "Tendencias de la reforma mercantil en materia de sociedades" [Trends of mercantile reform in the matter of corporations] (pp. 169-182), in: *Boletín de la Academia de Ciencias Políticas y Sociales*, volume 38, Caracas, Academy of Political and Social Sciences, 1981, especially pp. 172-173.

Economy Committee of the Chamber of Deputies of Congress, but was never introduced to the Chambers[12].

Besides the use of special laws, such as the Insurance Activity Law, Banking Sector Institutions Law, etc., there has been an attempt to regulate some aspects of companies through the Public Registry and Notaries Law.

For instance, under Article 56 number 1 the Commercial Registrar can deny the registration of a company if such Registrar considers that the capital is insufficient to carry on the corporate object. In the matter of this provision we express our disagreement, not only because of the arbitrariness –non-discretion- which it has brought in respect of the performance of Commercial Registries, but also because it interferes with the autonomy of private persons, who are in a better position to know what capital would be congruent and sufficient to accomplish their corporate object.

Though this provision has been defended by a respected sector of academic writers[13], we still observe that it opens the door to inappropriate interference with the autonomy of shareholders (and might end up directing the same), and that it is a regulation that could be interpreted to originate from the bad faith of shareholders and is rather aimed at regulating a pathology, such as corporations with insufficient capital, which are characteristic of our private sector.

In fact, in a publication from the 80's, Moisés Naím points out that the Venezuelan private enterprise was characterized -even then- for being very young, not greatly competitive, domestic, and in debt "…having insufficient capital for the volume and diversity of the activities in which it was engaged"[14]. By the time when the commented provision was introduced through the Public Registry and Notaries Law of 2000, and its last reform of 2007, the situation was not very different from that described in the 80's.

---

[12]   Morles Hernández, Alfredo, *La reforma de 2007 del Código de Comercio*. [The 2007 reform to the Commercial Code], at http://acienpol.org.ve/cmacienpol/Re sources/ArchivosCIJ/0003. pdf, accessed on 2/10/2013.

[13]   Morles Hernández, Alfredo, "Responsabilidad del Registrador Mercantil respecto a la capitalización de las sociedades y a la transmisión de las acciones nominativas" [Responsibility of the Commercial Registrar in respect of the capitalization of companies and the transmission of registered shares] (pp. 203-236), in: *Cuestiones de Derecho Societario*, Caracas, Academy of Political and Social Sciences, 2006.

[14]   Naím, Moisés, "La empresa privada en Venezuela: ¿Qué pasa cuando se crece en medio de la riqueza y la confusión?" [Private enterprise in Venezuela: What happens when it grows amidst richness and confusion?] (pp. 152-182), in: *El caso Venezuela: una ilusión de armonía*, Ediciones IESA, Caracas, 2nd edition, 1985, p. 164.

However, we insist that if the intention is to adopt legislation that promotes a productive and competitive economy, it is not possible to legislate from pathologies, as the only result from it will be to attack the effects instead of the causes of the problem.

In sum, even if our Commercial Code reflects the influence of the liberal thought of the XVIII and XIX centuries, it does not favor the establishment of the conditions required in order to exercise fully the liberties and ownership rights in the entrepreneurial area.

A reform of the Commercial Code is necessary; not only to update it to current trends of Comparative Law, but also to constitute one of the measures required to be adopted in order to create the necessary conditions to achieve an independent, competitive, and strong private sector.

II. PRINCIPAL LEGAL FORMS OF PRIVATELY-HELD COMPANIES

The Venezuelan Commercial Code provides for different types of companies that can be used in order to do business in Venezuela. These include, among others, (i) the company (*compañía anónima*), which is the most commonly used corporate form in Venezuela, (ii) the limited liability company (*sociedad de responsabilidad limitada*), (iii) the general partnership (*sociedad en nombre colectivo*), and (iv) the limited partnership (*sociedad en comandita*). These last three forms are seldom used in practice.

The company (*compañía anónima*) is the most regularly utilized. In a company, the shareholders are liable for the amount of their subscribed capital only and, contrary to what happens with the membership interest in limited liability companies, are not subject to any share transfer restrictions.

One of the reasons why *compañías anónimas* were so frequently used was that they were not restricted to a minimum or maximum capital stock, while limited liability companies were[15]. Nevertheless, as we have mentioned, this has changed with Article 56, number 1, of the Public Registry and Notaries Law[16], which provides as follows:

---

[15]   Article 315 of the Commercial Code.

[16]   Published in Official Gazette N° 5.833, extraordinary issue of December 22, 2006.

"It is the duty of the Commercial Registrar to monitor compliance with the legal requirements established for the incorporation and operation of companies and limited liability partnerships pursuant to the Sole Paragraph of Article 200 of the Commercial Code. For this purpose, the Commercial Registrar shall comply with, among others, the following obligations:

1. Reject the registration of companies with insufficient capital, by applying reasonableness criteria related to the corporate object ..."

In practice, Registries do not make an analysis of the case so as to decide on the basis of reasonableness criteria related to the corporate object. For example, when a Registry Office objects the amount of the capital stock, it only states in most cases that such capital is insufficient, without indicating the motives of such objection.

Furthermore, it would seem to derive from the above provision that the requirement of sufficient capital applies in respect of the incorporation of the company. However, if a corporate object is modified, or if an integral restatement of the articles of incorporation is intended, Commercial Registries demand in some cases, and based on that provision, a capital stock increase[17].

III. INTERNAL STRUCTURE OF COMPANIES

In order to organize a company (*compañía anónima*) and, in general, any business corporation, the presence of at least two stockholders is required (Article 200 of the Commercial Code and 1649 of the Civil Code). However, after the company has been organized it is not mandatory to keep a minimum number of shareholders and, consequently, it is frequent to find companies organized with two shareholders -one of them with insignificant participation- where immediately after the incorporation only one shareholder remains[18].

---

[17] In this report we will not elaborate on the various problems that the Special Law on Fiscal Stamps of the Capital District has brought in recent years. In matters including, among other things, the subscription of capital stock, increase of capital stock or sale of goodwill, this Law provides for taxes significantly higher than those set in the Public Registry and Notaries Law that applies to companies registered in Commercial Registries located outside the Capital District. But certainly this is an aspect that is necessarily taken into account at the time of evaluating strategies to carry out the operations mentioned above.

[18] This has not been recently analyzed, but has been a topic of scholarly discussion. In this respect, see: Goldschmidt, Roberto, "La sociedad mercantil unipersonal

Despite the lack of official statistics, it could be said that in practice the structure of Venezuelan companies is very diverse, having from one shareholder (an individual or corporation) to several shareholders, who can be either corporations organized in the country or foreign corporations.

In connection with foreign investment, it should be pointed out that it is possible provided that it does not contravene any provisions of domestic law; i.e., the foreign investment must be made respecting the limits set for the various sectors that have been reserved, and must not contravene the legal rules of general or particular application in Venezuela.

Regarding the sectors of the economy in which to invest, the proportion of foreign direct investment in a company that is in the process of being organized or in existence depends on the economic activity of that company. The sectors reserved for local and mixed companies are limited to some specific activities[19] and, therefore, foreign capital participation in Venezuela is authorized within a still wide range of business, industry or service activities. The legal conditions to which such activities would be subject constitutes another topic worth examination.

Companies operating in any other sector can be formed with a foreign participation of up to 100% of the company's capital. These companies may continue to have a majority or entire foreign participation indefinitely.

On the other hand, no official statistics exist in respect of the proportion between privately-owned and State-owned corporations. Nevertheless, in recent years the presence of the State in the national economy -not only to implement development policies or in the capacity of regulator- has con-

---

con particular consideración al Derecho Venezolano" [The sole member business corporation with particular consideration of Venezuelan Law], in: *Ponencias Venezolanas al VII Congreso Internacional de Derecho Comparado*, Caracas, Imprenta Universitaria-UCV, 1966.

[19]   Article 26 of Decree 2095, published in Official Gazette N° 34.930 dated March 25, 1992 provides as follows: "The following sectors of the economic activity are reserved [for] domestic companies: a) television and radio broadcasting; newspapers in the Spanish language. b) Professional services whose exercise is regulated by domestic law..." In addition, it must be stated that in the last years the number of activities reserved for the State by law or organic decree-law have increased significantly, such reservation including since 2007 to date the production of cement, steel bars, fuel distribution and sale, imports of raw materials and essential goods, among others. In this regard, see: http://www.empresate.org/economia/el-socialismo-del-siglo-xxi-podra-sostenerse-con-un-tamano-del-estado-crecido-a-50-del-pib/, accessed in March, 2013.

siderably increased. In this regard, the participation of the State through the formation of new companies is not the only manner in which it takes part in the national economy.

In relation to the above, one must consider the statement made on June 17, 2013 by the Chairman of the Confederation of Venezuelan Industrialists (CONINDUSTRIA), Carlos Larrazábal), to the effect that in the 4 years in which he has presided over said organization more than 1,190 private companies[20] have been seized. This figure, added to the number of state companies that are frequently created in direct form through decrees published in the Official Gazette of the National Government, will give an approximate idea of the exorbitant number of corporations directly owned by or in the possession of the State.

Unfortunately, far from encouraging sustained and constant economic growth, this participation of the State has proved how inadvisable it is that the State participates so actively in the economy.

In this regard, studies have been conducted on the evolution of the most representative cases of private companies that were later expropriated. In his article entitled "Are socialist state-owned companies productive in Venezuela?," author Albinson Linares highlights the following information: 23,000 million dollars were invested between year 2007 and 2010 by the Venezuelan State for the expropriation, acquisition, start-up, and creation of companies under the socialist development paradigm[21].

The aforementioned article also singles out "The Management book in Red", authored by Richard Obuchi, Bárbara Lira and Anabella Abadí, published by Instituto de Estudios Superiores de Administración (IESA), in which 16 cases of the socialist productive model implemented by the present government are evaluated. We quote next some of the cases of this study:

-   Venepal C.A., a company expropriated in year 2005 after having been declared bankrupt in 2004. Later, Invepal is born under a model of joint management sharing between the State and workers represented by the Venezuelan Pulp and Paper Cooperative

---

[20]   http://www.el-nacional.com/economia/Conindustria-reporta-empresas-in tervenidas-an os_0_ 210578956.html, accessed in June, 2013.

[21]   Linares, Albinson: ¿Son productivas las empresas estatales socialistas en Venezuela? [Are socialist state-owned companies productive in Venezuela?] Prodavinci, consulted at http:// prodavinci.com/2011/06/22/economia-y-negocios/%C2%BFson-productivas-las-empresas-estatales-socialistas-en-venezuela-por-albinson-linares/, in June, 2011.

(Covinpa), with an initial capital of 13.2 million bolivars. In 2009, the President of the cooperative informed that production continued to be very low.

-   Ruedas de Aluminio C.A. (Rualca), a company expropriated in year 2008 after paralyzing its business since 2007. By year 2009 it was completely inactive and in April 2010 it was transferred to CVG Industria Venezolana de Aluminio.

-   Venirauto Industrias C.A., a company arising from a cooperation and technology transfer agreement between Iran (51%) and Vene-zuela (49%). The initial investment was 118 million bolivars in domestic capital and 123 millions in Iranian capital. The initial goal was to produce 8000 vehicles in 2007 and begin the assembly of light duty vehicles by the end of that year. According to statements from Alcibíades Molina, Vice President of the company, 804 units had been assembled by the closing of 2006.

IV. COMPANY FORMATION

In order to organize a company (*compañía anónima*) in the country it is necessary to register the articles of incorporation in the Commercial Registry and subsequently publish the registered articles in a newspaper of the Commercial Registry's jurisdiction or in absence of such newspaper, in the most public medium existing at the place where the company has its corporate domicile.

Such articles of incorporation must contain the following information:

1. Name of the company.
2. Corporate object. A complete and detailed description of the corporate object of the company.
3. Domicile of the company. The exact address where the offices of the company will be located must be stated in accordance with Article 56, number 3, of the Public Registry and Notaries Law[22].
4. Capital stock[23].

---

[22]   "It is the duty of the Commercial Registrar to monitor compliance with the legal requirements established for the incorporation and operation of companies and limited liability partnerships pursuant to the Sole Paragraph of Article 200 of the Commercial Code. For this purpose, the Commercial Registrar shall comply with, among others, the following obligations: (...) Demand that the address where the company is headquartered, which shall be considered its domicile for all legal purposes, ...is indicated".

5. Duration, pursuant to Article 56, number 4, of the Public Registry and Notaries Law[24].

6. Financial year, and time when the Annual Meeting of Shareholders shall be held.

7. Management of the corporation.

In relation to these minimum contents, we would like to draw your attention to two of the above points. The first point involves capital stock because, in addition to the recent demands for sufficient capital stock, there is the novelty of a discussion regarding bearer shares.

Bearer shares were prohibited in Venezuela based on Decision N° 291 of the Andean Community of Nations. However, with the withdrawal of Venezuela from said economic integration system, there seems to remain our Code, lastly reformed in 1955, to refer to this matter, and this Code does not prohibit bearer shares.

An authoritative sector of academic writers[25] sustains that bearer shares could be issued. So far in practice there have been no such cases, but is to be noticed that there are no legal grounds for the prohibition.

Regarding this point, the withdrawal of Venezuela from the Andean Community of Nations involved a significant setback in various areas due to the fact that *"a community legislation, having qualities of permanence, agreement, technical quality, and pre-eminence, has been replaced by a*

---

[23] In addition to considering the provisions contained in the Public Registry and Notaries Law, the stipulation contained in Article 249 of the Commercial Code should be kept in mind: "For the final incorporation of the company it is necessary that the entire capital stock is subscribed and that at least one fifth of the amount of the shares subscribed by each shareholder is delivered by same to the treasury, provided that the incorporation papers do not require a greater delivery. However, if contributions are made in other than cash or if there is provision for advantages benefiting a shareholder or shareholders in particular, there must be compliance, in addition, with the provisions of Article 253".

[24] "It is the duty of the Commercial Registrar to monitor compliance with the legal requirements established for the incorporation and operation of companies and limited liability partnerships pursuant to the Sole Paragraph of Article 200 of the Commercial Code. For this purpose, the Commercial Registrar shall comply with, among others, the following obligations: (...) 4. Homologate or reject the term of duration of the company, respecting the statement of intention of the shareholders, unless the duration is deemed excessive."

[25] Morles Hernández, Alfredo, "El retiro de Venezuela de la Comunidad Andina de Naciones y sus efectos en la legislación mercantil" [The withdrawal of Venezuela from the Andean Community of Nations and its effects on business law] (pp. 279-304), in: *Revista de la Facultad de Ciencias Jurídicas y Políticas de la Universidad Central de Venezuela N° 127*, Caracas, Universidad Central de Venezuela, 2007, especially p. 293.

domestic legislation of unknown or uncertain stability and whose rank or hierarchy may vary ... "[26] Add to this, that in most cases this domestic legislation dates back to the middle of the last century.

In connection with the company's management, which is the second point we wish to comment on, it should be noticed that in Venezuela the managing body is not required to have specific characteristics such as, for instance, being a Board of Directors with a maximum or minimum number of directors. The company can be managed by a Board of Directors or a Sole Administrator. Most companies entrust their management to a Board of Directors composed of three (3) to five members and their respective alternates.

However, in respect of the conditions required to be met by directors, administrators, managers or designees[27] to manage and conduct a company, we should mention the demands from Commercial Registries in the last few years.

In fact, in the last three years Commercial Registries have demanded that such persons be Venezuelans or foreigners with a visa, or at least, a business visa. Although this demand is recent, the Registries base it on the visa issuance Rules of Procedure of year 2000[28].

The application of this requirement by Commercial Registries was very confusing at first, because said regulation of year 2000 was not being invoked nor was it being applied consistently by all Registries[29].

---

[26]   Morles Hernández, Alfredo, "El retiro de Venezuela de la Comunidad Andina de Naciones y sus efectos en la legislación mercantil", p. 287.

[27]   In companies (*compañías anónimas*), they are elected by the shareholders meeting, may be either shareholders or not, are temporary, and are revocable by the same shareholders meeting (Article 242 of the Commercial Code). If no term of office is specified, the provision of Article 267 of the Commercial Code is applied instead, and it provides for a term of 2 years. Regarding the term of office, it must be noticed that in the last years Commercial Registries used to prohibit terms of office longer than 5 years. Neither the Commercial Code nor the Public Registry and Notaries Law provide anything in this respect.

[28]   Published in Official Gazette N° 5.427, extraordinary issue of January 5, 2000.

[29]   The lack of uniformity of opinion is one of the problems attributed to present Commercial Registries. Also pointed out in this respect is the lack of qualification of the officials and the absence of administrative studies (see Chavero Gazdik, Rafael J., Purga registral, in: EL UNIVERSAL, on June 19, 2013, consulted at http://www.eluniversal.com/opinion/130619/purga-registral, in December, 2012).

Lastly, regarding directors and managers, another item to which we would like to draw your attention is tenure. Scholarly opinions have agreed in admitting that unless replaced at the expiration of the term for which they were appointed, directors or managers continue in office until they are either ratified or substituted[30]. It is not even deemed indispensable to include a provision of this type in the articles of incorporation.

However, practice has compelled to pay great attention to the date of expiration of director and manager positions because the failure to appoint them or ratify them at the expiration of their term is an obstacle for continuing the procedures before various public agencies, such as the National Register of Contractors[31], and even with private entities such as banks. This requirement applies regardless of whether or not the articles of incorporation provide that directors or managers will remain in office until they are ratified or until their substitutes are appointed.

V. SHAREHOLDER PROTECTION MECHANISM

Another point evidencing how our legislation has lagged in the area of corporations involves the rights of shareholders.

For instance, few defense mechanisms are available to a minority shareholder, who is entitled to participate in the management of the company through his vote at shareholder meeting deliberations, and to be informed of matters that will be submitted to such meeting; to review the share register and shareholder meeting minutes book (Article 261 of the Commercial Code); to examine the inventory, shareholder list, general balance sheet of the company and examiner's report (Article 284 of the Commercial Code), and to report management irregularities to the examiner (Article 310 of the Commercial Code).

However, facing these mechanisms, we have the following questions:

How effective is the right to participate in management decisions through vote when you are a minority? Certainly, the Commercial Code provides for a qualified majority of three fourths of the capital stock plus the affirmative vote of those representing one half, in order to decide in respect of early dissolution, extension of the company's duration, merger

---

[30] Hung, Francisco, *Sociedades*, Caracas, Hermanos Vadell Editores, 6th edition, 2002, p. 246 and next.

[31] A Register in which those who contract with public entities must be entered.

into another company, sale of corporate assets, refund or increase of capital stock, reduction of capital stock, change in the corporate object and amendment to the by-laws (Article 280 of the Commercial Code). A qualified majority would offer certain protection to the minority shareholder, but this provision is not a matter of public policy and the articles of incorporation/by-laws can provide for other rules for quorum.

How effective will it be to report management irregularities to the examiner, when examiners have a certain dependence or connection with managers? It should be noted that examiners are officers in charge of supervising the management of the company, but in contrast with special laws, such as the Capital Markets Law, the Commercial Code does not establish a minimum qualification (technical knowledge or no relationship to managers) for individuals designated as examiners.

Admittedly, our legislation does not forbid to grant a right of veto to a certain share or class of shares and, in fact, this may have ground in Article 292 of the Commercial Code which provides that "shares shall be of equal value and give their holders equal rights, if the by-laws to not provide otherwise". But again, in the case of minorities, the exercise of this right will have little influence at a shareholders meeting.

Contrary to what happens with other bodies of law, in the matter of corporations Venezuela has been left mainly with a Commercial Code whose last reform dates back to the middle of the last century, and, problems such as shareholder protection, as regards privately held companies not subject to supervision or control of a regulator, such as banks and insurance companies, have not been resolved by laws like the Public Registry and Notaries Law.

VI. SHAREHOLDER AGREEMENTS

Another aspect that has raised debate or at least confusion has to do with shareholder agreements, which are perfectly valid in our body of laws, based on the principle of autonomy of the parties.

The confusion centers around the formalities that must be completed in order that said agreements may become effective.

In this respect, decision N° 157 of February 13, 2008 from the Political-Administrative Chamber should be recalled which established the following:

"On the other hand, the *Joint Partnership Agreement (Acuerdo de Sociedad Mancomunada)* entered into on December 30, 1996 by PDV-IFT, Science Applications International Corporation and SAIC (Bermuda) LTD in order to lay down the matters related to the organization and management of INTESA, includes the following provision concerning the shareholder meetings of the latter:

(…)

A slight change in respect of the articles of incorporation/by-laws of INTESA is introduced with this rule, as such articles of incorporation/by-laws do not provide for any regulation regarding the notices of convocation after the second notice and the percentage of capital stock required in order to deem validly constituted the shareholders meeting, in which case, the rules provided to that effect in the Commercial Code would apply.

As to the manner in which decisions are to be made at such meeting, the legal transaction commented herein reproduces the same terms contained in the corporate by-laws of INTESA.

The *Joint Partnership Agreement* also provided the rules that were to govern the Board of Directors of INTESA.

(…)

As can be noticed, another amendment to the by-laws of INTESA is inferred from the text of this rule, specifically in respect of the composition of the Board of Directors, since, according to the registry record, *"two Principal Directors appointed by the majority of Class B Shares or two Alternates appointed by those holders"* should be part of the meetings of such Board, while in accordance with the agreement entered into on December 30, 1996, only one of them (or an alternate) is required.

Ultimately, with the foregoing opinions the Court wishes to observe that through said agreement PDV-IFT, Science Applications International Corporation, and SAIC (Bermuda) LTD intended to modify the stipulations that ruled the business activity of INTESA. Situations like the one previously described are regulated by Article 221 of the Commercial Code, which provides that:

> *"Amendments to articles of incorporation and by-laws of companies, regardless of their kind, will not produce any effects until registered and published according to the provisions of this Section."*

Therefore, the event contemplated in the above copied rule, in which the circumstance that the *Joint Partnership Agreement* has established changes to the incorporation papers of INTESA falls, plus, the fact that no recording of such changes is reflected in the commercial file, results in denial, in the field of law, of the effects of any provision other than those in the by-laws of the company, and this is the conclusion arrived at by the Court in connection with that legal transaction. Consequently, notwithstanding the evaluation of the latter in the preceding chapter of this decision, no value should be given to any provisions that contradict any rule established by the mutual agreement of the shareholders of INTESA through a document executed before the respective registration authority. It is so decided."[32]

In the last paragraph quoted above, the decision compares the Agreement to an invalid amendment of the by-laws, and does not specify whether the ineffectiveness of the Agreement applies only in regard to third parties, without including the parties to the Agreement. It could not have been the intention of the Political-Administrative Chambers to exclude from the effectiveness of the Agreement the parties who took part in it, as this would be contrary to the principle of autonomy of the parties will[33].

On the other hand, it has also been argued that even if registered in the Commercial Registry under Article 51 number 1 of the Public Registry and Notaries Law, a Shareholder Agreement does not become effective as against the company, due to the principle of relativity of contracts and because the shareholders meeting is still the maximum body of formation of the company's will[34]. This position would qualify to the extent that the Agreement regulates aspects directly affecting the shareholder who is a party to the Agreement, such as, for instance, the preferred right in favor of the shareholders who are parties to the Agreement.

VII. SHARE TRANSFERS

Lastly, another point we would like to consider refers to transfer of shares as, until recently, such transfer only needed to be recorded pursuant to Article 296 of the Commercial Code, which provides as follows:

---

[32]   Consulted at http://www.tsj.gov.ve/decisiones/spa/febrero/00157-13208-2008-2004-0183. HTML

[33]   Morles Hernández, Alfredo, "Las alteraciones de la regla de la proporcionalidad ("una acción, un voto") [Alterations to the rule of proportionality ("one share, one vote")] (pp. 113-139), in: *Breves estudios de Derecho Mercantil*, Caracas, Academy of Political and Social Sciences, 2008.

[34]   El Arigie, Raif: "Los Convenios Accionarios en el marco de la legislación venezolana" [Share agreements within the framework of Venezuelan law] (pp. 103-135), in: *Trabajos Jurídicos*, Caracas, Venamcham, 2005.

"The ownership of registered shares is proved by its recording in the books of the company, and the transfer of such shares is made by a statement in those books, signed by the transferor and transferee or their attorneys in fact …"

The above was interpreted as aforesaid by most Venezuelan scholars and case law.[35]

However, by its decision N° 383 of March 25, 2009, the Political-Administrative Chamber determined the following:

"In order to clarify the matters regarding the evidentiary value of said proof, this Court deems advisable to transcribe the provisions contained in our Commercial Code. Some of them refer to the obligations of merchants with respect to the documents that must be registered and published (Articles 19, ordinal 9th, and 25), and others relate to the form of the incorporation papers (Articles 212, 215, 217 and 221). They literally state:

"Article 19. - The following are the documents that must be recorded in the Registry of Commerce under Article 17:

(…)

9th An extract of such documents in which a company is formed or extended or altered in a way of interest to third parties, or dissolved, and of those in which liquidators are appointed.

Article 25. – The documents mentioned under 1st, 2nd, 3rd, 7th, 8th, ..9th,.. 10, 11, 12 and 13 of Article 19, ..are not effective until they are registered and set.

However, no failure to timely register and set can be enforced against third parties in good faith by the parties interested in the documents mentioned under those numbers.

Article 212. – An extract of the general partnership or limited partnership agreement __shall be registered__ in the Commercial Court of the jurisdiction and __published in a newspaper edited in the jurisdiction of that Court.__ If no newspaper is published in the jurisdiction of the Court, then the publication shall be made by placing posters at the most public places of the registered address. The publication shall be proved by either an issue of the newspaper or one of the removed posters, certified by the Clerk of the Commercial Court. (…)

---

[35] On the evolution of this discussion and a detailed description of scholarly opinions and case law, see Morles Hernández, Alfredo, "El sistema registral de la transferencia de acciones nominativas de la sociedad anónima" [The recording system of registered share transfers of a company](pp. 29-52), in: *Cuestiones de Derecho Societario*, Caracas, Academy of Political and Social Sciences, 2006.

Article 215. – (...)

*Within fifteen days after the execution of the incorporation papers of a company, limited partnership, or limited liability company, the appointed manager(s) will submit such papers to the Commercial Judge of the jurisdiction where the Company is to have its seat or to the Commercial Registrar of that jurisdiction, along with a copy of the by-laws, if any. **The respective official shall, prior verification that in forming the company the legal requirements have been met, order the <u>registration and publication</u> of the incorporation papers and order the filing of the by-laws.***

*Article 217. – **Any agreements or resolutions having as purpose** the continuation of the company after the expiration of its term, **the amendment of incorporation papers as to <u>clauses that must be registered and published,</u>** the reduction or extension of the term of its duration, the exclusion of any of its members, the admission of others or the change of the corporate name, the merger of the company into another, and the dissolution of the company, even in accordance with such papers, **<u>will be subject to registration and publication as set forth in the preceding Articles.</u>***

Article 221. – "*Amendments to articles of incorporation and by-laws of companies, regardless of their kind, will not produce any effects until registered and published according to the provisions of this Section*". (Emphasis by the Court)

From the previously quoted rule it derives that the intention of the Lawmaker was among other things to render unavoidable both to leave proper record in the respective Commercial Registry of any such actions that involve changes or alterations that *may be of interest to third parties* in respect of the articles of incorporation/by-laws of the diverse forms of corporations regulated by the Commercial Codes, as well as the publication of those changes, considering that it will be through that publication that third parties will become aware of the modifications that may have occurred in the corporations involved i.e., in their shareholding or partnership formation and, consequently, in respect of those who are capable of binding such company.

In the case of the evidence put forth by the taxpayers, that concerns the transfer of shares as of November 20, 1991 so as to show who were its shareholders by such date, this Court of Appeals must state that such records demonstrate the ownership of the shares as between the shareholder and the company itself but not as against third parties. Therefore, such document is not effective as against the National Treasury in order to prove the recorded transfer of shares, until it has been registered and published under the abovementioned provisions. For this reason, this Court must reject the purported evidentiary value of the records made in said share register submitted by the taxpayer. It is so declared."[36]

---

[36]   Decision consulted at www.tsj.gob.ve, on December 2, 2010.

The decision is clear in establishing that the records of transfers in the share register will be effective only in respect of the other shareholders and the company but not in respect of third parties.

In light of this opinion, Commercial Registries started to demand the recording of transfers or assignments of shares in duly registered documents. It could also be said that this position is based on Article 51, number 1, of the Public Registry and Notaries Law which provides as follows:

"The purpose of the Commercial Registry is:

1. The registration of individual and corporate merchants and other subjects specified by law, and the registration of acts and contracts related to same, in accordance with the law..."

This decision from the Political-Administrative Chamber was subject to a motion to reopen, which was granted by the Constitutional Chamber in decision N° 107 of February 25, 2014.

In said recent decision, acknowledging a violation of the principle of legitimate trust for not having respected the criteria set by the very Political-Administrative Chamber's decision N° 336 of March 6, 2003, case: *Eduardo Leañez, and the Constitutional Chamber's* decision N° 1577 of October 21, 2008, case: *Iván Gómez Millan*, the following was established:

"In view of the foregoing considerations, this Court believes that the criterion sustained by the Political-Administrative Chamber was not according to law. This is so because in this specific case there was a violation of the petitioner's constitutional rights to due process of law and defense, and of the principle of legitimate trust, all of them being contemplated in the Constitution, as, in the decision submitted for reopening, the consolidated case law criterion sustained by this Chamber and the Political Administrative Chamber in connection with Article 296 of the Commercial Code was not observed, when resolving the matter submitted for consideration, after having verified that in the present case the sale of shares of the company Agropecuaria Flora, C.A. was carried out in accordance with the rule set forth in the Commercial Code. It is so decided.

In this respect, this Chamber deems it necessary to specify that the transfer of the shares, with its record in the respective Share Register –under the provisions of the aforesaid Article 295 *eiusdem* in tax matters- is, for tax purposes of the State, the sufficient constitutive element and, therefore, the dividends originated from the transfer of said shares -as established in the 1999 Income Tax Law- must be directly demanded from the company Flor de Mayo, C.A. and not from the company Agropecuaria Flor, C.A. ...."

We hope this criterion will be replicated by the Commercial and other similar Registries and that it will not relegated to tax matters.

CURRENT CHALLENGES FACED BY COMPANIES (SOCIEDADES ANÓNIMAS) IN VENEZUELA.

It is our belief that retrieving the criteria set by the Political Administrative Chamber in 2003, by the Constitutional Chamber in 2008, and in so many other cases, would in fact involve respecting, at least insofar as the transfer of shares, the spirit of the Commercial Code maker and with that, respecting the principle of autonomy of the parties that, in this case, is reflected by admitting as sufficient evidence of assignment the record on the share register and not requiring the declaration of a public official such as the Commercial Registrar.

FINAL CONSIDERATIONS

In contrast with Public Law, for which practically a whole new legislation has been issued in the last 15 years, the basic legislation of Private Law has not been reformed or modified. However, this does not mean that Private Law has not been affected in recent years.

We could say that in the last years Private Law has been displaced and almost abolished in some areas by the excessive regulation issued by the National Assembly and National Executive Power through their regulatory power. In addition, Private Law has suffered an important setback with the withdrawal of the Venezuelan State from the Andean Community of Nations. Reacting to this disquieting trend there have been dissident voices[37].

---

[37] See: Alfredo Morles Hernández has been one of the few authoritative voices that has reported this situation with knowledge and strength through various works including among others "El nuevo modelo económico del socialismo del siglo XXI y su reflejo en el contrato de adhesión" [The new economic model of XXI century socialism and its reflection on the adhesion contract] (*Revista de Derecho Público* N° 115); "La total desaparición del contenido dispositivo del contrato en los contratos de adhesión" [The total disappearance of contractual provision content in adhesion contracts] (Revista de la Facultad de Ciencias Jurídicas y Políticas de la Universidad Central de Venezuela N° 132); "El retiro de Venezuela de la Comunidad Andina de las Naciones y sus efectos en la legislación mercantil" [The withdrawal of Venezuela from the Andean Community of Nations and its effects on business law] (*Revista de la Facultad de Ciencias Jurídicas y Políticas de la Universidad Central de Venezuela* N° 127); "El nuevo modelo económico para el Socialismo del Siglo XXI" [The new economic model of XXI Century Socialism] (*Revista de Derecho Público* N° 112); and "El intento inacabado por establecer un modelo económico socialista" [The unfinished attempt to establish a socialist economic model] (*Anuario de Derecho Público de la Universidad Monteávila*).

Certain aspects of companies which we have discussed in this report evidence this displacement of Private Law. In the specific case of companies (*compañías anónimas*) such displacement is due to (i) an absence of a modern regulation in pace with the trends of Comparative Law, (ii) recent regulations that deny the principle of autonomy of the parties, and (iii) a dismal performance by present Commercial Registries who act based on excessively discretional rules and without providing an adequate reasoning for their decisions.

IV.B. DROIT CONSTITUTIONNEL / CONS-TITUTIONAL LAW

- LE RECOURS AUX PRÉCÉDENTS ÉTRAN-GERS PAR LE JUGE CONSTITUTIONNEL / FOREIGN PRECEDENTS IN CONSTITU-TIONAL LITIGATION

LE RECOURS AUX PRÉCÉDENTS ÉTRANGERS PAR LE JUGE CONSTITUTIONNEL : LE CAS VÉNÉZUELIEN

Claudia Nikken
PROFESSEURE, UNIVERSITÉ CENTRALE DU VENEZUELA

INTRODUCTION

Du point de vue scientifique, le droit constitutionnel vénézuélien est méconnu ailleurs et peu reconnu à l'intérieur. Pourtant il peut être surprenant.

Le Venezuela est le premier État de l'Amérique latine -et le troisième au monde- à s'être doté d'une *constitution* écrite au sens moderne et d'une déclaration de droits (1811). C'est aussi l'un des premiers pays au monde à concevoir en droit le contrôle par le juge de la constitutionnalité des lois.

Il est dit, en fait, que le contrôle judiciaire de la constitutionnalité des lois est institué au Venezuela depuis l'entrée en vigueur de la première constitution en 1811 ; ceci, parce que ce texte déclarait que les lois qui en serait en contradiction étaient dépourvues de toute valeur, compte tenu en plus de la décision Marbury v. Madison (1803), vue la ressemblance de cette première constitution vénézuélienne et de celle des États-Unis[1].

Or, la véritable originalité se trouve dans ce que c'est dans la Constitution vénézuélienne de 1858 que pour la première fois, en droit positif, l'on adopte le contrôle judiciaire concentré de constitutionnalité[2], opposé au contrôle diffus exercé par les juges aux États-Unis[3]. Cette Constitution a conféré à la Cour Suprême le pouvoir de déclarer la nullité des lois provinciales (des états fédérés) contraires à la Constitution, sous demande de tout citoyen.

À partir de là, avant même le développement théorique -et pratique- sous l'influence de Kelsen de la justice constitutionnelle et, plus précisément, du contrôle concentré de constitutionnalité, le Venezuela fait preuve d'une longue habitude du contrôle de constitutionnalité.

D'ailleurs, après une évolution assez articulée[4], la Cour Suprême instituée en 1961 admet progressivement que le contrôle de constitutionnalité doit être exercé sur les actes de toute nature, même sur les actes dits politiques et, quoique timidement, sur les lois de révision constitutionnelle. C'est d'ailleurs le principe qui fonde le système de justice constitutionnelle dessiné par l'actuelle Constitution du 30 décembre 1999, qui a instituée une Chambre constitutionnelle au sein du dénommé désormais Tribunal Suprême de justice, tout en gardant les institutions bâties au cours

---

[1] Voir Brewer-Carías, A.R. *Instituciones políticas y constitucionales*, 3ᵉ éd., T.VI, EJV –UCAT, Caracas-San Cristóbal, 1996, p. 122

[2] *Cfr.* M. Fromont, *La justice constitutionnelle dans le monde*, Col. Connaissance du droit – Droit public, Dalloz, Paris, 1996, p. 12-15. Voir aussi Brewer-Carías, A.R. *Instituciones políticas y constitucionales*, T. VI, *cit.*, p. 131; Wolf, E., *Tratado de derecho constitucional venezolano*, T. II, Tipografía Americana, Caracas, 1945, p. 167.

[3] Et aussi au contrôle politique envisagé en France dès les jours de la Révolution de 1789 suivant les idées Montesquieu et de Sieyès, et de celui pratiqué par le Sénat conservateur institué par la Constitution de l'an VIII.

[4] Pour plus de détails quant à l'évolution de la « juridiction constitutionnelle » au Venezuela, voir J. G. Andueza, *La jurisdicción constitucional en Venezuela*, Facultad de derecho de la Universidad Central de Venezuela, Caracas, 1955, p. 31-35 ; Ayala Corao, C., *Origen y evolución del control constitucional en Venezuela*, Anuario de Derecho Constitucional Latinoamericano, I, 1996, p. 247-257 ; Brewer-Carías, A. R. *Instituciones políticas y constitucionales*, T. VI, *cit.*, p. 131-134. Voir aussi, Nikken, C., *La Cour Suprême de justice et la Constitution vénézuélienne du 23 janvier 1961*, Thèse, Université Panthéon-Assas (Paris II), Paris, 2001, p. 47-56.

de l'histoire constitutionnelle vénézuélienne, même le contrôle diffus, aujourd'hui constitutionnalisé[5].

La Chambre constitutionnelle, parmi d'autres attributions, est chargée de contrôler la constitutionnalité des lois (nationales, des états fédérés et municipales), ainsi que celle des autres actes des pouvoirs publics "édictés en exécution directe de la Constitution" qui en seraient contraires.

En dépit de tout ce qui vient d'être dit, l'étude systématique de la justice constitutionnelle n'est pas des plus développées au Venezuela. La doctrine estime que le pays possède probablement le plus complet -et le plus complexe- des systèmes de contrôle de constitutionnalité d'Amérique, voire du monde ; mais très peu recherchent véritablement à expliquer la dynamique de ce système[6]. De ceci découle la difficulté de l'analyse à laquelle je me suis engagée depuis quelques mois, et que j'ai essayé d'accomplir de la meilleure façon possible[7].

En ce qui concerne notre sujet d'analyse, le recours aux précédents étrangers par le juge, particulièrement par le juge constitutionnel, n'est pas une question nouvelle au Venezuela. Ce qui est nouveau c'est d'en faire l'analyse : si aux facultés de droit il semble *naturel* de faire appel à la doctrine étrangère, le recours à la jurisprudence constitutionnelle, même nationale, est une pratique assez récente.

En 1936, en effet, l'ainsi dénommée par ce temps Cour Fédérale et de Cassation, saisie d'un recours en inconstitutionnalité qui visait l'annulation de l'article 32-6, résultant d'un amendement de la Constitution de 1914, fît appel à la jurisprudence de la Cour Suprême des Etats-Unis sur deux questions, traitées dans cet ordre : la régularité des dispositions constitutionnelles et légales dont l'objet serait de bannir le communisme et l'anarchisme ; et la compétence du juge constitutionnel pour prononcer l'annulation des révisions constitutionnelles.

---

[5] Le contrôle diffus de constitutionnalité fut institué au Venezuela au moyen du Code des procédures civiles en 1894.

[6] D'ailleurs, dans les pays industrialisés, l'originalité du modèle latino-américain de justice constitutionnelle, apparu bien avant le modèle européen, ne semble pas attirer l'attention des chercheurs, car « le contrôle de constitutionnalité dans ces pays remplit des fonctions autres » que celles qu'il remplit dans les démocraties occidentales (A. von Brünneck, *Le contrôle de constitutionnalité et le législateur dans les démocraties occidentales*, Annuaire International de Justice Constitutionnelle IJC, 1988, IV, p. 15).

[7] Je me suis servie en bonne partie, il faut le dire, de ma thèse doctorale, *La Cour Suprême de justice et la Constitution vénézuélienne* du 23 janvier 1961, *cit.*

La disposition constitutionnelle attaquée autorisait le Président de la République à empêcher l'entrée sur le territoire de la République ou à en expulser les individus affiliés aux doctrines communistes ou anarchistes. Dans la décision, il a été établi que, étant donné que les doctrines communistes et anarchistes tendent au bannissement des libertés individuelles « essentielles et immanentes à la personnalité », aboutissant à des « diverses formes d'oligarchie et d'absolutisme », empêcher que ces tendances prennent des racines au pays « constitue la sauvegarde », dans un État « normalement constitué » de la propriété, la liberté personnelle, la liberté de travail, la liberté d'industrie, la sécurité individuelle[8].

À l'époque, la politique judiciaire de la Cour Suprême des États-Unis tenait à une idée « issue en partie du profond sentiment d'horreur qu'un mot comme "socialisme" faisait naître dans le cœur des juges » [9]. Il est donc possible de dire que, même sans citation, cette politique s'est reproduite au Venezuela.

En ce qui concerne le contrôle de la constitutionnalité des lois de révision constitutionnelle, il fut établi que, même si les facultés accordées au Président de la République étaient « excessives », il n'était pas dans les attributions de la Cour Fédérale et de Cassation de corriger l'œuvre du pouvoir constituant[10]. Pour arriver à une telle conclusion, la Cour a eu recours expressément à la position de la Cour Suprême états-unienne, renvoyant certainement aux décisions National Prohibition Cases[11] et United States v. Sprague[12].

Sur cet exemple de 1936 commence notre rapport au sujet du recours aux précédents étrangers par le juge constitutionnel vénézuélien. Or, avant de poursuivre, je tiens à avertir le lecteur –surtout à celui qui a eu la chance de lire « The use of foreign precedents by constitutional judges »,

---

[8]   CFC-SPA, 6/8/1936, Memoria de la Corte Federal de Casación, 1937, p. 177-178.

[9]   McCloskey, Robert G. *La Cour Suprême des États-Unis*, Vent d'Ouest, Paris, 1965, p. 175

[10]   CFC-SPA, 6/8/1936, Memoria de la Corte Federal de Casación 1937, p. 175-176. Dans le même sens, CFC-SPA, 17/4/1941, M Memoria de la Corte Federal de Casación 1942, p. 180-185.

[11]   253 US 350 (1920)

[12]   282 US 716 (1931). En 1939, dans la décision *Coleman v. Miller* [307 US 433 (1939)], la Cour Suprême établit que « les allégations d'une prétendue inconstitutionnalité d'un amendement à la Constitution fédérale étaient des "question politiques" dont il n'appartenait pas au juge constitutionnel de connaître ».

édité par Mmes. Tania Groppi et Marie-Claire Ponthoreau[13] : à la différence des travaux publiés dans cet ouvrage là, celui-ci n'est certainement
pas le produit de plusieurs années de recherche, mais le point de départ
d'une étude qui peut s'avérer richissime en résultats.

Cela étant, rigueur exige, de suite seront exposés les trois volets définis
dans la méthodologie choisie pour le développement de ce travail : le contexte national (I) ; la recherche empirique (II) et l'analyse du recours aux
précédents étrangers (III).

I. LE CONTEXTE NATIONAL

Suivant la méthodologie choisie pour développer ce rapport, et puis,
pour accomplir la recherche sur le recours aux précédents étrangers par les
juges constitutionnels en général, il faut établir d'abord chaque contexte
national. Cette même méthodologie indique que, pour ce faire, il faut définir le contexte relatif à la constitution et le système juridique (1) ; le contexte relatif au juge constitutionnel, donc au Tribunal Suprême de justice
et sa Chambre constitutionnelle (2) ; et finalement le contexte relatif à la
doctrine. Le tout, suivant des paramètres assez bien fixés (3).

1. Le contexte relatif à la constitution et le système juridique

D'après la méthodologie impartie, la définition du contexte national
passe en prime abord par la définition du contexte relatif à la Constitution
vénézuélienne dite *de 1999* et le système juridique, en particulier par la
définition du rôle joué par les emprunts juridiques au moment de
l'élaboration de la Constitution et de sa révision (A) ; par la détermination
du lien entre les sources constitutionnelles étrangères et l'interprétation
des dispositions constitutionnelles sur la base de dispositions constitutionnelles étrangères ou/et de précédents étrangers (B) ; et par l'exposition du
lien entre la tradition juridique et l'utilisation de sources étrangères (C).

---

[13]   Groppi, T. et Ponthoreau, M-C (éd.), *The use of foreign precedents by constitutional judges*, Hart Studies in Comparative Law, Hart Publishing, Oxford-Portland
(Oregon), 2013.

A. *Le rôle joué par les emprunts juridiques au moment de l'élaboration de la constitution et de sa révision*

L'élaboration (1999) et la révision (2007-2009) de l'actuelle Constitution vénézuélienne sont clairement marquées par des emprunts juridiques. Ceci ne devrait représenter aucune particularité en Amérique Latine, dont les conceptions de Droit et d'État sont, elles-mêmes, des emprunts. Or, c'est le rôle des emprunts ce qui intéresse de souligner ici.

En premier lieu, il se trouve que l'emprunt de la *Théorie de la Constitution* de Carl Schmitt fut à la base du processus constituant mené pendant l'année 1999[14] ; et fonde aussi le régime de manifestation de la souveraineté populaire. Il y a même une vingtaine de décisions dans lesquelles il est directement cité.

Sur cette question du régime de la manifestation de la souveraineté populaire, je veut au juste transcrire l'article 70 de la Constitution vénézuélienne : « Les moyens de participation et protagonisme du peuple pour l'exercice de sa souveraineté, dans le domaine politique, sont : l'élection aux postes publiques[15], le référendum[16], la consultation populaire[17], la révocation du mandat[18], les initiatives législative, constitutionnelle et constituante, le « cabildo » ouvert, l'assemblée de citoyens et citoyennes dont les décisions seront obligatoires, parmi d'autres ; et dans le domaine social et économique : les instances d'attention citoyenne, l'autogestion, la cogestion, les coopératives de toutes formes y comprises celles à caractère financier, les caisses d'épargne, l'entreprise communautaire et d'autres formes associatives guidées par les valeurs de la coopération mutuelle et la solidarité ».

---

[14] Nikken, C., *La Cour Suprême de justice et la Constitution vénézuélienne du 23 janvier 1961, op.cit.*, p. 357-408.

[15] Président de la République, députés à l'Assemblée Nationale ; gouverneurs et législateurs des états fédérés ; maires et conseillers municipaux.

[16] La Constitution prévoit un référendum consultatif, et plusieurs référendums décisoires : pour révoquer le mandat des autorités élues ; pour approuver des lois; pour abroger des lois ; pour approuver les amendements et réformes à la Constitution ; pour convoquer une assemblée nationale constituante.

[17] On soutient que cette « consultation populaire » ne peut être que le référendum consultatif, or comme il s'est passé illégitimement avec d'autres institutions, une forme différente de consultation pourrait bel et bien être instituée.

[18] Il est dit que cette « révocation du mandat » ne peut être que le référendum révocatoire ; mais, comme il s'est passé illégitimement avec d'autres institutions, une forme différente de révocation pourrait être instituée.

On voit mal comment tous ces mécanismes peuvent faire ressortir l'exercice de la souveraineté, sauf si l'on suit Schmitt, précisément.

En second lieu, nous trouvons plusieurs emprunts dans le texte de l'actuelle constitution, parmi lesquels la création d'une Chambre constitutionnelle au sein du Tribunal Suprême de justice, dont la dénomination est elle-même un emprunt ; ainsi que la dénomination et l'organisation du pouvoir législatif national en *Assemblée Nationale.*

L'on pourrait croire, à ce sujet, que changer de la *Cour* historique à un *Tribunal* « moderne » est l'effet (révolutionnaire) de la participation de professeurs espagnols ou des juristes avec une formation espagnole dans le processus constituant ; et que passer du *depuis-toujours-existant Congrès* bicaméral à une *Assemblée Nationale* unicamérale est un clin d'œil à la « Révolution française ». Or, en France l'Assemblée Nationale est l'un des organes du pouvoir législatif et se réunit en *congrès* avec le Sénat. N'aurait-on pas pensé plutôt à l'Assemblée Nationale (unicamérale) du Pouvoir Populaire et au Tribunal Suprême non pas de justice, mais « Populaire » cubains?

En fait, la source essentielle de la révision constitutionnelle proposée par la Président de la République en 2007 est la « constitution » cubaine. Il prétendait en somme l'institution d'un « pouvoir populaire » non démocratique dans le contexte d'une société socialiste.

Cette révision constitutionnelle a certes échouée lorsque soumise à référendum[19] ; cependant sa *source* essentielle est aujourd'hui la plus importante source de législation *contre* la Constitution[20]. Nous avons même une « Loi organique du pouvoir populaire » ; nos ministères sont des ministères « du pouvoir populaire ». Le plan de développement pour la période 2013-2019 cherche à institutionnaliser le « pouvoir populaire » et, par là, à instaurer un régime socialiste[21].

---

[19]   Voir en: http://www.lefigaro.fr/international/2007/12/04/01003-20071204 ARTFIG00 431-lavertissement-des-venezueliens-a-hugo-chavez.php; http://www.lepoint. fr/actualites-monde/2007-12-03/premiere-defaite-dans-les-urnes-pour-hugo-chavez /924/ 0/212799; http://www.lemonde.fr/cgi-bin/ACHATS/acheter.cgi?offre=ARCHIVES &type _item=ART_ARCH_30J&objet_id=1015327&xtm c =hugo_chavez&xtcr=12

[20]   Sur la législation relative au pouvoir populaire durant et après la discussion de la révision constitutionnelle faillie de 2007, voir Nikken, C., « La Ley Orgánica de los Consejos Comunales y el derecho a la participación ciudadana en los asuntos públicos », in *Leyes orgánicas sobre el poder popular y el Estado comunal*, Col. Textos Legislativos N° 50, EJV, Caracas 2011, p. 183-358.

[21]   Pour consulter le "Plan de la Patria 2013-2019", http://cdnun.ultimasnoti cias.com. ve/unfotos/planpatriadoc2013.pdf

Il faut souligner, avant de continuer, que la Constitution vénézuélienne de 1999 incorpora –et non pas emprunta-, malheureusement par des termes généraux et abstraits, les systèmes de droits humains auxquels l'État était partie (ONU–OEA) et le système d'intégration andine. Aujourd'hui, après « simple » dénonciation des traités visés, le Venezuela est en dehors du système de protection des droits de l'homme établi par la Convention américaine relative aux droits de l'homme, ainsi que de la Communauté Andine de Nations. Il demeure attaché au système de protection des droits humains des Nations Unies, et s'est incorporé au *Mercosur*, non sans difficultés.

B. *Le lien entre les sources constitutionnelles étrangères et l'interprétation des dispositions constitutionnelles sur la base de normes constitutionnelles étrangères ou/et de précédents étrangers*

Il peut être affirmé que les sources constitutionnelles étrangères que l'on vient d'identifier ne sont pas liées à l'interprétation des dispositions constitutionnelles sur la base de normes constitutionnelles et/ou des précédents étrangers. Ces sources spécifiques sont certainement liées à l'interprétation de la Constitution mais actuellement le recours à d'autres dispositions constitutionnelles et à des précédents étrangers n'est qu'un outil pour justifier ce qui, la plupart du temps, demeure injustifiable, c'est une forme de *cherry-picking*.

Les sources constitutionnelles étrangères dont le poids est le plus évident sont celles qui se rapportent à la manifestation *directe* de la souveraineté populaire, quoique ces sources sont rarement citées : on ne trouvera pas une décision du juge constitutionnel par laquelle il soit dit que *l'acclamation* est un moyen valable d'exercice de la souveraineté populaire comme l'affirmait Schmitt, mais il fera en sorte que l'opinion publique puisse se mesurer par un référendum consultatif et, par là, exprimer la *volonté souveraine du peuple*[22] (sauf si cela ne convient pas au pouvoir[23]).

---

[22]   Voir   http://www.tsj.gov.ve/decisiones/scon/diciembre/1490-011200-00-3071.htm

[23]   Voir http://www.tsj.gov.ve/decisiones/scon/enero/03-0017.htm

La question du *pouvoir populaire* emprunté au Cuba est, à ce jour, une nouvelle donne dans l'interprétation constitutionnelle. Or, le Cuba n'est jamais mentionné dans les décisions du Tribunal Suprême, comme n'est pas développée l'idée de *pouvoir populaire*, pour l'instant[24].

C. *Le lien entre la tradition juridique et l'utilisation de sources étrangères*

La *légèreté* avec laquelle le juge s'est servi au Venezuela des sources étrangères en matière d'interprétation constitutionnelle se fonde, à mon avis, sur la conception locale du système juridique de droit continental.

En effet, il semblerait que c'est à peine en 1999 quand les juristes vénézuéliens se sont rendus compte du fait que le juge constitutionnel *interprète* la Constitution par un acte de volonté que l'on désigne comme « interprétation authentique »[25]. Ceci car le projet de constitution en discussion contenait deux innovations : la déclaration suivant laquelle le Tribunal Suprême, comme garant de la suprématie et de l'effectivité des normes et principes constitutionnels, est « le plus haut et dernier interprète de [la] Constitution et [veille] à son interprétation et application uniforme », et puis celle d'après laquelle las interprétations de la Chambre constitutionnelle sur les normes et principes constitutionnelles lie les autres chambres du Tribunal Suprême ainsi que le restant des tribunaux de la République[26].

Jusque là, toute référence à la jurisprudence était sans importance car considérée comme purement complémentaire. Après, des positions contradictoires s'opposent. Au milieu, la Chambre constitutionnelle a déformé le principe expressément institué dans l'article 335 de la Constitution, en exercice la nouvelle compétence qui lui fut octroyée consistant au pouvoir de réviser les décisions définitivement firmes d'*amparo* constitutionnel et de contrôle de la constitutionnalité des lois et d'autres actes normatifs issues des tribunaux inférieurs.

---

[24] Le pouvoir populaire a une définition légale, c'est « le plein exercice de la souveraineté par le peuple dans les domaines politique, économique, social, culturel, de l'environnement, international, et dans tout domaine dont le déploiement et développement est déterminé par les niveaux de conscience politique et l'organisation du peuple » (article 2 de la Loi organique du pouvoir populaire). Qu'est-ce que cela peut bien vouloir dire? Personne n'en est certain.

[25] Voir, avant cette nouvelle donne, Nikken, C., *La Cour Suprême de justice et la Constitution vénézuélienne* du 23 janvier 1961, *op.cit.*, p. 251-292.

[26] Article 335 de la Constitution de 1999.

Cette compétence de révision fut *interprétée* par la Chambre constitutionnelle, puis par la législation, comme permettant la révision des décisions des autres chambres du Tribunal Suprême. De plus, il est établi que les décisions à réviser sont toutes celles contenant des interprétations constitutionnelles, même si elles ne sont pas rendues au cours d'un procès d'*amparo* ou si le juge n'a pas contrôlé la constitutionnalité d'une loi ou d'un autre acte normatif, comme prévu par le constituant[27].

Maintenant l'on parle même d'une « juridiction normative » dont la titularité appartiendrait à la Chambre constitutionnelle[28]. Or, on ne parle pas sur le recours aux précédents étrangers.

2. Le contexte relatif au Tribunal Suprême de justice et sa Chambre constitutionnelle

Pour développer le recours aux précédents étrangers par le juge constitutionnel, il a été demandé d'esquisser le contexte relatif au juge constitutionnel, dans le cas vénézuélien, au Tribunal Suprême de justice et sa Chambre constitutionnelle.

À cet égard, suivant la méthodologie impartie, référence est faite aux techniques du raisonnement judiciaire utilisées (A) ; aux raisons et proportions de la citation de jurisprudence internationale (B) ; à l'importance donnée aux discours prononcés par les juges sur le recours aux précédents étrangers (C) ; et aux caractéristiques de la carrière des juges (D).

A. *Les techniques du raisonnement judiciaire utilisées*

Le Tribunal Suprême de justice vénézuélien est organisé en six chambres (constitutionnelle, politico-administrative, électorale, cassation civile, cassation pénale, cassation sociale), chacune desquelles statue indépendamment des autres ; il décide aussi en assemblée plénière, consistant celle-ci logiquement à la réunion de tous les magistrats, en exercice d'attributions spécifiquement désignées par la Constitution et la loi à cette assemblée, qui ne sont pas du ressort de la compétence des autres

---

[27] Voir, à ce sujet, Pesci Feltri, F., *La revisión constitucional de sentencias definitivamente firmes*, Col. Cuadernos de Derecho Público N° 7, FUNEDA, Caracas, 2011.

[28] Voir M., Pesci Feltri, *La* Constitución *y el proceso*, 2 éd., Col. Estudios Jurídicos N° 82, EJV, Caracas 2011, p. 91-126.

chambres[29]. La chambre constitutionnelle compte avec sept magistrats, et les autres avec cinq ; il y a alors trente-deux magistrats au Tribunal Suprême.

Les décisions de toutes les formations du Tribunal Suprême peuvent être prises à l'unanimité ou à la majorité des voix. Dans ce dernier cas sont admises les opinions dissidentes et aussi les opinions concurrentes.

Les précédents étrangers apparaissent de façon assez homogène dans le corps des décisions judiciaires, et des opinions dissidentes et concurrentes. Il n'st donc pas utile de faire le point sur le recours à cet outil par la majorité ou des minorités. Ceci dit, d'une étude plus approfondie, j'en suis certaine, pourraient ressortir des questions assez intéressantes au même sujet.

B. *La citation de jurisprudence internationale : raisons et proportions*

La seule jurisprudence *internationale* citée par la Chambre constitutionnelle du Tribunal Suprême vénézuélien est celle de la Cour européenne des droits de l'homme[30]. Rien à célébrer, nonobstant.

---

[29] Il faut dire que la pratique fait que l'on appelle l'assemblée plénière du Tribunal Suprême « Chambre pleine » (*Sala Plena)*, ce qui est erronée puisque ce n'est pas une « chambre » *(sala)*, mais la réunion de toutes les chambres, en réalité de tous les magistrats. La nuance n'est pas sans importance, car cette pratique est le fondement qui s'est donné la chambre constitutionnelle pour réviser et annuler les décisions de l'assemblée plénière du Tribunal Suprême (voir http://www. tsj.gov.ve/decisiones/scon/Marzo/233-110305-04-3227.htm), ce qui est inacceptable. Non seulement la Constitution ne lui octroie pas la compétence pour réviser les décisions des autres formations du Tribunal, mais encore il ne peut pas être soutenu qu'une partie de l'organe décisoire (la chambre constitutionnelle par rapport à l'assemblée plénière) puisse renverser les décisions prises par la majorité.

Il faut ajouter que même si aujourd'hui –et depuis 2004- la Loi Organique du Tribunal Suprême de justice accorde à la chambre constitutionnelle le pouvoir de réviser les décisions prises para les autres *chambres,* c'est parce que ladite chambre l'avait ainsi établi dans sa jurisprudence préalablement (voir http://www.tsj.gov.ve/decisiones/scon/enero/33-250101-00-1712.HTM). Il faut dire aussi que la faculté de révision des décisions de l'assemblée plénière demeure sous-entendue, car la loi n'en parle pas directement. Il faut attendre des magistrats raisonnables pour renverser un tel critère.

[30] Jusqu'au 10 septembre 2013 le Venezuela était partie de la *Convention américaine relative aux Droits de l'Homme* et, dès lors, se trouvait sous la juridiction de la Cour interaméricaine des Droits de l'Homme. Par conséquent, au regard de ce travail, à partir de cette date toute citation de jurisprudence peut être tenue comme recours à la jurisprudence internationale. Or, il n'y a en pas encore (et je ne pense pas qu'il y en aura dans les jours à venir).

La Chambre constitutionnelle cite (mal) des soi-disant précédents trouvés dans la jurisprudence de la Cour européenne des années 80, pour fonder le rejet des recours judiciaires de toute nature, dont l'objet est de dénoncer la méconnaissance des droits de la défense en raison de la durée, extrêmement longue, des procès.

Le raisonnement consiste à dire que, pour déterminer si une procédure a eu une durée déraisonnable, il faut tenir compte d'une série d'éléments, tels la complexité de l'affaire[31], comme l'affirmerait la Cour européenne, et sur sa jurisprudence, le Tribunal constitutionnel espagnol. Par ce biais, la Chambre constitutionnelle détourne le raisonnement suivi plutôt au regard de la charge d'épuiser les recours internes avant de saisir une juridiction supranationale, pour déterminer s'il y a eu ou non violation ou méconnaissance des droits de la défense.

Il y a tout de même très peu de décisions –prés d'une dizaine- dans lesquelles la Chambre constitutionnelle se *sert* de la Cour européenne des droits de l'homme.

En ce qui concerne la jurisprudence de la Cour interaméricaine des Droits de l'Homme, si l'on cherche sur *Google* les décisions de la chambre constitutionnelle dans lesquelles est nommée la Cour Interaméricaine, l'on trouve environ une soixantaine. Or, si cette jurisprudence en principe lie les tribunaux vénézuéliens, la chambre constitutionnelle du Tribunal Suprême a soutenu que la même ne lui était pas *opposable*[32], étant donc considérée comme jurisprudence « étrangère ».

Dans une décision du 15 juillet 2003, *Rafael Chavero Gazdik*[33], la chambre a affirmé que, dans les termes de l'article 23 du texte constitutionnel[34], seuls atteignent le rang de la Constitution les traités ratifiés par la République portant sur les droits humains, tout en écartant les rapports et avis émis par la Commission Interaméricaine des Droits de l'Homme et

---

[31] Voir par exemple http://www.tsj.gov.ve/decisiones/scon/Junio/1565-110603-02-2112. htm

[32] Voir, par exemple, http://www.tsj.gov.ve/decisiones/scon/Marzo/272-9312-2012-11-0341.html

[33] Voir in http://www.tsj.gov.ve/decisiones/scon/julio/1942-150703-01-0415. htm

[34] *Article 23:* Les traités, pactes y conventions relatifs aux droits humains, suscrits et ratifiés par le Venezuela, jouissent de hiérarchie constitutionnelle et prévalent dans l'ordre juridique interne, dans la mesure où ils contiennent des normes sur leur jouissance ou exercice plus favorables que celles établies par cette Constitution et les lois de la République, étant aussi d'application immédiate et directe par les tribunaux et les autres organes du Pouvoir Public.

par la Cour même. Par rapport au contenu de l'article 31 constitutionnel[35], dirigé à garantir l'exécution des décisions rendues, parmi d'autres, par la Cour Interaméricaine, il a été dit, dans le même arrêt *Rafael Chavero Gazdik*, que l'obligation d'exécution de l'État demeure valable seulement si la décision à exécuter n'est pas contraire à la Constitution ou aux traités qui les régissent. De cette façon, la chambre fonde tout écart futur de la jurisprudence de la Cour interaméricaine des Droits de l'Homme, et on peut le constater.

Avant cette décision, il est possible de trouver des références à la jurisprudence de la Cour Interaméricaine, par rapport aux sujets sensibles, tels l'application du Traité de Rome instituant la Cour Pénale Internationale[36] et la disparition forcée des personnes[37], ou d'autres moins controversés comme l'action civile qui découle de la responsabilité pénale[38], ou même la durée du procès par rapport aux droits de la défense[39].

Après 2003, la chambre constitutionnelle a éventuellement suivi la jurisprudence Cour interaméricaine dans le domaine de la disparition forcée des personnes[40], mais les références à la jurisprudence *supranationale* ressort la plupart du temps des allégations des parties ou de l'argumentation des opinions dissidentes et concurrentes.

En fait, de plus près, il s'agit de décisions comme celles rendues le 18 décembre 2008 *(Corte Primera de la Contencioso Administrativo*[41]*)* et le

---

[35]   ***Article 31:*** Toute personne a droit, dans les termes des traités, pactes et conventions portant sur les droits humains ratifiés par la République, à diriger des pétitions ou plaintes devant les organes internationaux créés à de telles fin, dans le but de leur demander la protection de ses droit humains.

L'État adoptera, d'après les procédures établies dans cette Constitution et la loi, les mesures qui résultent nécessaires à l'exécution des décisions prises par les organes internationaux prévus dans cet article.

[36]   Voir http://www.tsj.gov.ve/decisiones/scon/diciembre/3167-091202-02-2154.htm

[37]   Voir http://www.tsj.gov.ve/decisiones/scon/Agosto/1043-140800-00-0648.htm

[38]   Voir http://www.tsj.gov.ve/decisiones/scon/abril/607-210404-03-2599.htm

[39]   Voir http://www.tsj.gov.ve/decisiones/scon/Agosto/2249-180803-02-2115.htm

[40]   Voir http://www.tsj.gov.ve/decisiones/scon/Noviembre/1674-91111-2011-11-1172.html

[41]   Voir http://www.tsj.gov.ve/decisiones/scon/diciembre/1939-181208-2008-08-1572.html

17 octobre 2011 *(Leopoldo López Mendoza[42])*, par lesquelles la chambre constitutionnelle non seulement exerça une sorte de « contrôle de la constitutionnalité » de deux décisions de la Cour interaméricaine après avoir déclarée comme « dépassée » la conception des *droits* versée dans la Convention Américaine des Droits de l'Homme, car il faut mettre les droits économiques, sociaux et culturels avant les droits individuels –ce qui ne ferait pas la Convention- ; de surcroît, la chambre constitutionnelle a "exhorté" le Président de la République à dénoncer la Convention, précisément car contraire à la Constitution[43]. Et c'est fait. Depuis le 10 septembre 2013, le Venezuela n'est plus partie à la Convention américaine relative aux Droits de l'Homme et donc du système international de protection des droits de l'homme qu'elle institue.

C. *L'importance donnée aux discours prononcés par les juges sur le recours aux précédents étrangers*

Aucune importance n'est donnée, en général, aux discours prononcés par les juges sur le recours aux précédents étrangers. Il n'y a, à vraiment parler, aucun discours à ce sujet.

D. *Les caractéristiques des carrières des juges*

Jusqu'à une époque assez récente, les *magistrats* en poste au plus haut tribunal de la République étaient soit des juges professionnels, soit des avocats, soit des juristes des administrations. Tous avaient en commun le fait d'être ou d'avoir été des professeurs aux écoles de droit nationales ou privées. Normalement, aussi, ils étaient des auteurs d'ouvrages juridiques et beaucoup avaient fait des études en Europe, notamment en France, en Italie ou en Allemagne puis en Espagne, ou bien aux Etats-Unis et plus rarement en Angleterre.

Depuis quelques années, particulièrement depuis l'entrée en vigueur en mai 2004 de la Loi Organique du Tribunal Suprême de Justice[44], les juges

---

[42]   Voir   http://www.tsj.gov.ve/decisiones/scon/octubre/1547-171011-2011-11-1130.html

[43]   Voir à cet égard Ayala Corao,C., *La « inejecución » de las sentencias internacionales en la jurisprudencia constitucional venezolana* (1999-2009), Col. Estudios, Fundación Manuel García-Pelayo, Caracas, 2009.

[44]   Parmi d'autres changements, cette loi augmenta le nombre de magistrats de 21 à 32 et, donc, obligea l'incorporation de 11 nouvelles personnes à ce corps.

sont plutôt des activistes que des juristes, avec une certaine expérience dans le judiciaire, l'administration ou bien dans le litige, comme en témoignent les *curricula vitae* publiés sur le site http://www.tsj.gov.ve/el tribunal/magistrados.shtml, mais avec pour mission de renforcer la révolution *bolivarienne* afin de accomplir la construction de *l'État communal,* fondé sur la philosophie « socialiste »[45]. Ceci en dépit que, par un référendum, fut rejetée la proposition de révision constitutionnelle présentée par le Président de la République qui avait pout but, précisément, de fonder les bases de cet *État communal,* « socialiste ».

Il faut dire de nouveau que le recours aux précédents *socialistes* n'apparaît pas de façon évidente, du moins pas encore, dans les décisions constitutionnelles ; c'est-à-dire, on ne fait pas référence au Tribunal Suprême Populaire cubain[46], parmi d'autres actuels ou anciens, ce qui n'empêche les rapports culturels entre les organes, comme l'évidence la visite rendue en novembre 2013 par des magistrats cubains au Tribunal Suprême vénézuélien[47].

Il faut ajouter que le texte constitutionnel interdit le militantisme politique au sein du pouvoir judiciaire, y compris le Tribunal Suprême de justice, afin de garantir notamment son indépendance[48]. Il a été constaté que cette règle n'est pas respectée au Venezuela[49].

3. *Le contexte relatif à la doctrine*

Pour finir avec le contexte national par rapport au recours aux précédents étrangers par le juge constitutionnel, il est demandé de faire référence au contexte relatif à la doctrine.

---

[45] On peut lire les discours pour l'installation de l'année judiciaire et le constater. Voir, par exemple : http://www.tsj.gov.ve/ informacion/miscelaneas/discurso MagYrisP.pdf ; http://www. tsj.gov.ve/informacion/miscelaneas/DiscursoMagMarrero.pdf; http://www.tsj.gov.ve/informacion/mis celaneas/DicursoMagVegasApertura2011.pdf ; http://www.tsj.gov.ve/informacion/miscelaneas/ Dis-   cursoMagADR.pdf ; http://www. tsj.gov.ve/informacion/miscelaneas/DiscursodOrden2013Mag IP.pdf

[46] Voir in http://www.tsp.cu/tribunal_supremo_popular_cuba

[47] Voir en http://www.tsj.gov.ve/informacion/ notasdeprensa/notasdeprensa. asp?codigo= 11545

[48] Article 256 de la Constitution de 1999.

[49] Cfr. A/HRC/DEC/19/110, 4 avril 2012; ONU, Rapport sur l'Examen Périodique Universel, Venezuela, disponible sur: http://www.onu.org.ve/CD_EPU_Vene zuela/MenuPrincipalCD2. htm.

À cet égard, on verra les liens entre la doctrine et les juges (A) ; ainsi que l'attention donnée par la doctrine à la question de l'influence des précédents étrangers (B)

A. *Les liens entre la doctrine et les juges*

Plus que citer des précédents étrangers –ou nationaux-, le juge vénézuélien, y compris le juge constitutionnel, fait recours à la doctrine nationale et étrangère pour fonder les choix d'interprétation qui sont à la base de ses décisions. Il s'agit d'une pratique qui demeure inchangée depuis environ près d'un siècle.

Il y a même plusieurs décisions qui ressemblent à des mémoires de recherche, telles que http://www.tsj.gov.ve/decisiones/scon/julio/1309-190701-01-1362.htm, dans laquelle son cités Kelsen, Dworkin, Hart, Ross, afin de construire une "théorie" de l'interprétation constitutionnelle. On trouve aussi des décisions comme http://www. tsj.gov.ve/decisio nes/scon/Marzo/379-070307-06-1488.htm, dans laquelle se dessine une théorie sur les principes et valeurs constitutionnels à partir de plusieurs notes de doctrine étrangère, notamment espagnole et états-unienne.

D'un autre côté, c'est à travers la doctrine étrangère que le juge constitutionnel arrive à connaître des précédents « utiles » pour résoudre les questions qui lui sont posées, comme le montre http://www.tsj.gov.ve/ decisiones/scon/Abril/565-150408-07-1108.htm.

Il faudrait faire une étude approfondie à ce sujet au Venezuela, tenant compte spécialement des *courants* juridiques et politiques doctrinaires suivis dans la jurisprudence.

B. *L'attention donnée par la doctrine à la question de l'influence des précédents étrangers (y-a-t-il ou non un débat relatif au recours aux précédents étrangers par les juges?)*

Á franchement parler, on ne donne au Venezuela aucune importance à la question de l'influence des précédents étrangers sur l'interprétation constitutionnelle. Il n'y a pas de débat en doctrine –ou autre- à ce sujet.

Il n'y a donc pas lieu, malheureusement, à rendre un rapport à ce sujet comme celui présenté par A. Sperti dans son étude sur le recours aux précédents étrangers par la Cour Suprême des États-Unis[50].

II. LA RECHERCHE EMPIRIQUE

La recherche empirique dont l'accomplissement est demandé dans le cadre de cette étude d'ensemble, suppose d'abord la définition de la période étudiée (1) ; le discernement des citations explicites de précédents étrangers (2), puis des influences implicites (3).

Avant de continuer, il faut avertir que depuis le 1er janvier 2000 jusqu'au 30 novembre 2013, la Chambre constitutionnelle a rendu approximativement 35.405 décisions[51]. Il y aurait, dans une première approche à travers *Google,* environ 300 décisions dans lesquelles référence expresse est faite à des précédents étrangers. Le chiffre ne représente même pas 1% des décisions, mais il n'est pas négligeable tout de même.

Cela étant, il n'a pas été matériellement possible de préparer en quelques mois et puis de présenter, une étude complète de toutes les décisions rendues par le Tribunal Suprême dans le domaine constitutionnel, même la limitant aux décisions de la Chambre constitutionnelle, pour montrer avec précision le recours aux précédents étrangers ; même si le moyen officiel de diffusion jurisprudentielle du Tribunal Suprême est un site web, www.tsj.gov.ve/decisiones, et que ce site est assez bien géré.

Cette étude porte ainsi sur la période susmentionnée, mais elle est approximative et non pas exhaustive.

1. *La période*

Il a été déjà dit que le recours aux précédents étrangers par le juge constitutionnel, au Venezuela, est une pratique assez ancienne même si elle est discrète. Or, cette étude ne porte pas sur toute la pratique vénézuélienne de justice constitutionnelle, mais sur celle instituée sur la base de l'actuelle Constitution.

---

[50]   Sperti, A. *United States of America: First Cautious Attempts of Judicial Use of Foreign Precedents in the Supreme Court's Jurisprudence*, in « The Use Of Foreign Precedents by Constitutional Judges », *cit*, p. 393-410, notamment p. 398-403.

[51]   Le chiffre est un calcul à partir des informations publiées sur le site www.tsj.gov.ve.

Cette actuelle constitution vénézuélienne est entrée en vigueur, formellement, le 30 décembre 1999 ; c'est aussi la date à laquelle fut instituée la Chambre constitutionnelle de l'actuel Tribunal Suprême de Justice. Ceci explique le choix de la période : janvier 2000 – novembre 2013.

2. *Les citations explicites de précédents étrangers si les juges les citent souvent*

Même si la pratique demeure discrète, la Chambre constitutionnelle du Tribunal Suprême de justice vénézuélien cite de façon explicite, assez souvent, des précédents étrangers (environ dans 1 sur 118 jugements). De ces références il est possible de discerner les indicateurs formels (A) et matériels (B) dont la définition est demandée dans le cadre de cette recherche.

A. *Indicateurs formels*

Les indicateurs formels à être établis à partir des références aux précédents étrangers sont, en premier lieu, la *source* du précédent ; deuxièmement, *l'objet* de la citation ; en troisième lieu, la place occupée par la citation dans le corps des décisions analysées ; et dernièrement, la façon dont s'exprime le précédent.

En ce qui concerne la *source* des précédents, d'une façon approximative il peut être affirmé que les parties présentent les précédents étrangers autant que le font les juges de manière spontanée. Or, dans plusieurs cas, lorsque ce sont les parties qui citent des précédents étrangers, la Chambre constitutionnelle n'en tient pas compte. Question de *souveraineté*?

Par rapport à l'objet de la citation, il est rarissime de trouver des citations ou références à une opinion dissidente ; ce sont les opinions unanimes ou majoritaires qui en font l'objet.

Pendant la préparation de ce rapport, il a pu être constaté en outre que dans la plupart de décisions observées, les citations et références aux précédents étrangers se trouvent dans l'opinion de la majorité, quoiqu'on en trouve aussi dans des opinions dissidentes et concurrentes.

Pour finir, il faut juste signaler que la Chambre constitutionnelle fait des simples –même trop simples- références à des précédents étrangers, en même temps qu'elle cite des paragraphes entiers. Je dirai que la pratique en ce sens est « équilibrée ».

Pour faire le point sur ces indicateurs formels, il faudrait certainement les comptabiliser et préparer les chartes qui montrent les résultats qui viennent d'être annoncés de façon approximative.

B. *Indicateurs matériels fondés sur l'analyse du raisonnement judiciaire*

Lorsqu'il est demandé d'établir les indicateurs matériels qui peuvent être discernés de l'analyse du raisonnement judiciaire, toujours en ce qui concerne le recours explicite aux précédents étrangers, l'on pointe vers l'établissement des fonctions de ces précédents ainsi que des raisons qui justifient la pratique. Dans le cas vénézuélien, il semblerait que l'on ne peut pas séparer ces deux aspects.

En effet, le juge constitutionnel vénézuélien ne cherche pas à justifier le recours aux précédents étrangers ; simplement il les cite textuellement ou en fait référence de façon plus ou moins concrète, comme ses paires de la tradition de droit civil[52]. Objectivement, il n'est donc possible de définir les raisons de ce recours que par rapport aux fonctions qu'il accomplit, étant entendu que jamais il n'est dit « on s'écarte de la position d'une telle cour », sauf peut être de manière générale par rapport à a Cour interaméricaine des Droits de l'Homme –et ceci pour dénier de son *pouvoir* sur l'État vénézuélien.

Quelles sont alors les *fonctions* du recours aux précédents étrangers par la Chambre constitutionnelle vénézuélienne.

Très rarement la Chambre fait appel aux précédents étrangers pour résoudre une affaire « nouvelle », un problème constitutionnel qui ne se soit pas posé auparavant, comme le ferait le juge constitutionnel de *common law*. C'est le cas, cependant, de la décision rendue le 14 aout 2008, dans l'affaire *Yolima Pérez Carreño*[53], par laquelle la Chambre constitutionnelle, s'appuyant sur un précédent espagnol et sur un autre colombien, statua sur le droit d'une fille de 12 ans en péril de mort à refuser un traitement médical sur la base de ses croyances religieuses. La Chambre décida que le droit à la vie devait faire l'objet de protection par l'État, même au détriment des libertés de conscience et de culte de la fille.

Cela étant, les références aux précédents étrangers apparaissent la plupart du temps dans des cas qui n'ont pas besoin de justification tellement la solution est *évidente* ; ou bien servent à justifier un choix d'interprétation qui demeure toutefois injustifiable.

On trouve, ainsi, comme étant superflue une référence à la jurisprudence de la Cour constitutionnelle fédérale allemande justifiant la constitution-

---

[52]   *Cfr*. T. Groppi et M-C Ponthoreau, *op.cit.*, p. 429.

[53]   Voir http://www.tsj.gov.ve/decisiones/scon/agosto/1431-140808-07-1121. htm

nalité des mandats d'arrêt préventifs[54], alors que la Constitution vénézuélienne, elle-même, autorise expressément ce genre de mesure[55]. La Chambre constitutionnelle cite, d'ailleurs, sa propre jurisprudence, donc les précédents qu'elle-même a posés à ce sujet.

Dans une affaire jugée le 4 aout 2011 (*Germán Mundaraín, Defensor del Pueblo*[56]), portant sur l'annulation de l'article 192 de la Loi générale de la banque et d'autres institutions financières, la Chambre constitutionnelle fut appelée à déterminer s'il existe au Venezuela un droit constitutionnel à la protection des données personnelles. Elle fît recours à deux précédents étrangers, l'un colombien et l'autre espagnol, pour déclarer qu'un tel droit est garanti aussi par la Constitution vénézuélienne. Or, quelques années auparavant, le 15 décembre 2005 (*G.A.N.B., INSPECTORES DE RIESGOS ASOCIADOS, S.A.*[57]), la même Chambre était arrivée à la même conclusion sans pour autant se fonder sur des précédents étrangers. Ce qui attire l'attention c'est que les deux décisions furent rédigées par le même rapporteur, Mme. Luisa Estella Morales, alors présidente de la Chambre constitutionnelle.

Il semblerait que, dans ces cas, les précédents étrangers jouent un rôle *d'illustration* ou, peut-être, de « preuve » d'illustration.

Dans le domaine de *l'injustifiable* on trouve, par exemple, la décision rendue par la Chambre constitutionnelle le 12 juin 2001 *(Elías Santana y Queremos Elegir)*[58], dans laquelle elle prétend fonder ses critères d'interprétation de l'article 58 de la Constitution sur la jurisprudence du Tribunal constitutionnel espagnol, la Cour Constitutionnelle fédérale allemande et la Cour Suprême des Etats-Unis. Or, les passages cités ou désignés par la Chambre constitutionnelle n'ont pas de rapport avec les conclusions qu'elle apporte[59].

---

[54]   Voir   http://www.tsj.gov.ve/decisiones/scon/Octubre/1381-301009-2009-08-0439.html

[55]   Article 44.1 de la Constitution vénézuélienne.

[56]   Voir   http://www.tsj.gov.ve/decisiones/scon/Agosto/1318-4811-2011-04-2395.html

[57]   Voir   http://www.tsj.gov.ve/decisiones/scon/diciembre/4975-151205-05-0952.htm

[58]   Voir http://www.tsj.gov.ve/decisiones/scon/junio/1013-120601-00-2760%20.HTM

[59]   Sur cette décision, Brewer-Carías, A.R., Faúndez Ledesma, H., Nikken, P., Ayala Corao, C., Chavero Gazdik,R., Linares Benzo,G., Olavarría,J., *La libertad de expresión amenazada* (Sentencia 1.013), IIDH-EJV, Caracas-San José, 2001.

La Chambre constitutionnelle fut saisie par M. Santana et l'association civile *Queremos Elegir* d'un *amparo* constitutionnel aux droits de réplique et de rectification, à cause de quelques déclarations du Chef de l'État par rapport aux requérants dans son émission radio dominicale *Aló Presidente*. La Chambre declara un *non-lieu* sans procès (ce qui est une de ses « inventions »), après avoir établi, sans procès j'insiste, « la doctrine obligatoire dans l'interprétation des articles 57 et 58 de la Constitution ».

En ce qui concerne l'interprétation de l'article 58 constitutionnel, la Chambre se fonde sur des précédents étrangers qui, eux, se rapportent à un sujet spécifique : la véracité des informations. Cette véracité – vraisemblance– serait l'une des exigences du droit à l'information, et les précédents cités par la Chambre constitutionnelle se chargent d'expliquer à quoi consiste une telle exigence, se référant toujours à des « faits », donc à des événements, dont la accomplissement est diffusé notamment par les médias. Nonobstant, la Chambre affirme, sans aucun rapport aux précédents (ni au recours formé devant elle) :

1. C'est un abus des médias, contraire à l'exigence de véracité, d'émettre des *concepts* négatifs ou *critiques* par rapport à des *idées, jugements* et d'autres, sans expliciter à quoi consiste ce qui fait l'objet de critique, car cela empêcherait le public de s'informer de ce qui résulte « frêle ».

2. C'est aussi abusif et contraire a l'exigence de véracité, de « frapper des phrases »[60] avec des lieux communs pour *critiquer* une « attitude » ou une « idée » sans exprimer ce qui est critiqué ; ainsi que d'isoler de son contexte une partie de ce qui a été dit ou s'est produit et en faire le *commentaire* sans tenir compte de ce contexte, car cela changerait le sens de ce qui a été isolé.

3. C'est un « attentat » à l'encontre de l'information « vérace et impartiale », d'avoir « un nombre majoritaire de rédacteurs d'une seule tendance idéologique, sauf si –et voici un non-sens- le média par ses éditoriaux o ses porte-parole, maintient et s'identifie avec une ligne d'opinion congruente avec celle des rédacteurs et collaborateurs ».

Il peut alors être conclu que les références aux précédents étrangers, dans ce cas comme dans d'autres, cherchent à donner une apparence de légitimité à ce qui ne l'a pas : les opinions ne peuvent pas être soumises à un test de véracité ; la tendance idéologique des journalistes ne peut pas

---

[60] On utilise ici le verbe « frapper » comme il est utilisé dans l'expression « frapper des monnaies », parce que c'est le sens donné par la Chambre constitutionnelle: « *acuñar frases* ».

servir comme critère pour établir la véracité des informations qu'ils expriment, du moins ce n'est pas ce qui est dit par les juges constitutionnels cités.

3. *Les influences implicites si les juges ne citent pas souvent les précédents étrangers*

L'influence étrangère sur le juge constitutionnel vénézuélien est indéniable. Relativement, il ne cite pas très souvent des précédents étrangers, mais, comme il a été dit, on trouve des références à la doctrine étrangère en bon nombre de décisions. Par ailleurs, dans une quantité non négligeable de jugements, la Chambre constitutionnelle fait aussi référence expresse à des textes constitutionnels et légaux étrangers. Beaucoup parmi les décisions citées plus haut en font preuve, mais malheureusement je n'ai pas pu accomplir, pour l'instant, la charge de comptabiliser les décisions pour en rendre compte précise. Je ne peux donc pas, dans cet exposé, faire le point sur la *conduite* des magistrats par rapport à la pratique du droit comparé ; ce que je peux avancer, c'est que l'analyse approximative ne permet pas d'affirmer qu'il y aurait un ou plusieurs magistrats qui se comporterait différemment par rapport aux autres au sujet du recours au droit comparé.

Il n'y a donc pas, à première vue, une influence « cachée » de la doctrine ou du droit étrangers sur la jurisprudence constitutionnelle vénézuélienne, car apparemment cette influence est belle et bien « publique ». C'est ainsi pour la doctrine et le droit espagnol, français, allemand, italien et d'autres pays européens, comme pour le droit et la doctrine colombienne, argentine, péruvienne, chilienne, costaricaine, et même états-unienne.

Or, à vraiment parler, la référence à la doctrine et au droit étrangers a pour fonction principale, comme c'est le cas de la référence aux précédents étrangers, de faire preuve de *l'illustration* des magistrats et, le plus important, de cacher l'illégitimité du choix de certains critères d'interprétation.

Ainsi, par exemple, dans une décision du 29 novembre 2007 *(Claudia Nikken et Flavia Pesci Feltri*[61]*)*, rendue à l'occasion d'un recours en *amparo* visant à empêcher la mise en référendum de la révision constitutionnelle proposée par le Président de la République en 2007, la Chambre

---

[61] Disponible en http://www.tsj.gov.ve/decisiones/scon/noviembre/2211-29 1107-07-1617.html

constitutionnelle, citant Rousseau, établit que la Constitution vénézué-lienne ayant adopté l'idée de « souveraineté populaire », cette souveraine-té est divisée entre tous les citoyens comme un droit « individualisée », « fractionné ». En raison de cela, aucune action en défense des droits et inté-rêts diffus ou collectifs comme celle instaurée par les requérantes ne peut prétendre la protection d'un droit du peuple vénézuélien à la reconnais-sance de sa souveraineté, car le « peuple » n'a pas ce droit, les titulaires étant les citoyens[62]. Sur ce fondement, le recours fut déclaré comme *irre-cevable*.

Cependant, après cette profondissime réflexion, le 14 février 2012, face à un recours en *amparo* exercé par un citoyen *(Rafael Antonio Velásquez Becerra[63])* en défense de ses droits individuels et politiques, dont le droit au suffrage, à l'encontre de la coalition d'opposition afin d'éviter que celle-ci ne détruise le matériel utilisé dans l'élection primaire de candidats tenue le 12 février 2012, la Chambre constitutionnelle décida qu'il s'agissait bel et bien d'une action en défense de droits collectifs (le droit au suffrage en l'occurrence), déclara l'action comme étant recevable et puis accorda une mesure préventive. Dans cette décision il n'y a aucune référence au droit ou à la doctrine étrangère...

---

[62]   La question fut ici traitée par la Chambre constitutionnelle comme étant simplement formelle. Or, le problème fondamental était sur la substance, sur le titre même de la souveraineté. On prétendait substituer le régime démocratique y républicain par un régime *socialiste*, écartant parmi d'autres principes le pluralisme; le régime fédéral était aussi visé; on annulerait le principe de séparation des pouvoirs; on modifierait le système de protection des droits humains, en particulier les principes de progressivité, égalité et liberté qui en sont le fondement.

Plus spécifiquement, il était établi que le peuple, « dépositaire » de la souveraineté, l'exercerait à travers le « pouvoir populaire »; lequel ne serait issu ni du suffrage ni d'une élection, mais de la condition des groupes humains organisés à la base de la population. Ce pouvoir populaire était conçu comme l'un des pouvoirs publics « territoriaux », à coté des pouvoirs national, étatique et municipal; dès lors, par mandat de l'article 5 constitutionnel, qui ne fut pas visé par la révision, il devait nécessairement être le résultat du suffrage (libre, universel, direct et secret).

Il s'écoulerait alors un changement dans la titularité et les moyens d'exercice de la souveraineté... Pas possible d'affirmer que l'on demandait la protection d'un droit indivi-dualisé.

La *Revista de Derecho Público* N° 112, publiée par l'Editorial Jurídica Venezolana est complétement dédiée à ce sujet.

[63]   Disponible en http://www.tsj.gov.ve/decisiones/scon/febrero/66-14212-20 12-12-0219. html

La question est de savoir si les droits et intérêts de quelqu'un participant –de tous ceux ayant participé– comme candidat à une élection primaire sont paisibles de protection, pour quoi ne l'est pas le « peuple souverain » lorsque sa souveraineté est menacée par une révision constitutionnelle illégitime? Rousseau n'avait rien à faire dans l'affaire, plus que rendre « légitime » un choix d'interprétation qui ne l'était pas[64].

Cette question de légitimité est d'autant plus importante que, comme on l'a déjà dit, le but poursuivi par le Tribunal Suprême et sa Chambre constitutionnelle, c'est de permettre la construction de l'État *communal* issu d'une société *socialiste*. Cependant, toute référence à la doctrine ou au droit cubains, chinois ou soviétiques, rendrait illégitime –nationalement et internationalement– toute décision prise, par exemple, au sujet de l'interprétation du droit de propriété ou de la liberté économique[65]. C'est pourquoi elle continue de citer la littérature juridique « libérale », même si elle s'y méprend.

Pour répondre à toutes les questions posées en ce qui concerne les influences implicites que la jurisprudence constitutionnelle vénézuélienne reçoit, il faut signaler que le Tribunal Suprême ne compte pas sur un bureau en charge des relations internationales, ni sur un bureau de recherche. Il y a au juste un centre d'information documentaire et une bibliothèque. Ce sont plutôt les assistants, beaucoup avec des études à l'étranger, notamment en Espagne, qui font la recherche.

III. ANALYSE DU RECOURS AUX PRÉCÉDENTS ÉTRANGERS

En guise de conclusion, il est demandé de présenter l'analyse du recours aux précédents étrangers, donnant des réponses à six questions précisément posées. On y va.

---

[64] Voir aussi, parmi d'autres décisions, http://www.tsj.gov.ve/decisiones/ scon/Febrero /52-3209-2009-08-1611.html; http://www.tsj.gov.ve/decisiones/ scon/Febrero/53-3209-2009-08-1610.html; http://www.tsj.gov.ve/decisiones/scon/Junio/864-21612-2012-11-1151.html

[65] Il faut dire que si c'est vrai que l'actuel régime politique est soutenu par la majorité des vénézuéliens depuis 1998, c'est vrai aussi que beaucoup de ses sympathisants considèrent que ce régime n'est pas « communiste »; que cette étiquette fait partie du discours de l'opposition.

1. *Sur la question de savoir s'il s'agit véritablement d'un dialogue entre les cours*

Un dialogue est une conversation entre deux ou plusieurs personnes. Pour qu'il existe, il faut donc que les intervenants s'entendent les uns aux autres, qu'ils *se répondent* –à moins qu'il ne s'agisse d'un monologue à plusieurs.

De ce point de vue, le recours aux précédents étrangers peut, certainement, se transformer dans un *dialogue* entre cours, particulièrement entre cours constitutionnelles. Or, à mon avis ce dialogue ne peut arriver que si les cours se voient comme "égales". Autrement, l'on trouve des cours qui citent la jurisprudence posée par d'autres qui, elles, ne se tournent même pas pour noter le phénomène. Là je parlerai plutôt de « fertilisation ».

Dans le cas vénézuélien, toutefois, il n'y a ni dialogue ni fertilisation.

2. *Quelles sont les cours les plus souvent citées?*

Sur la base d'une recherche « avancée » sur *Google*, même sans comptabilisation exhaustive, on peut dire que le Tribunal Constitutionnel espagnol est, de loin, le juge constitutionnel le plus cité ou mentionné par la Chambre constitutionnelle vénézuélienne. Après, c'est la Cour Constitutionnelle colombienne la plus mentionnée.

D'autres cours font l'objet de références : la Cour constitutionnelle italienne ; la Cour constitutionnelle fédérale allemande ; le Conseil constitutionnel français ; la Cour constitutionnelle autrichienne.

La Cour Suprême des Etats-Unis, même si elle servît auparavant de modèle d'interprétation constitutionnelle, apparemment n'est citée que trois fois depuis l'an 2000, deux fois dans la décision elle-même[66] ; la dernière dans une opinion dissidente[67].

Est aussi citée la jurisprudence de la Cour européenne des droits de l'homme, et nous savons dans quelles conditions l'est aussi la Cour interaméricaine des Droits de l'Homme.

---

[66]   Voir: http://www.tsj.gov.ve/decisiones/scon/octubre/1971-161001-00-00 24.htm; http:// tsj.gov.ve/decisiones/scon/Febrero/108-060201-00-2791.htm

[67]   Voir: http://www.tsj.gov.ve/decisiones/scon/Julio/1006-10712-2012-11-07 85.html

3. *Quels types d'affaires sont concernées par cette pratique?*

Certainement, la plupart des affaires dans lesquelles recours est fait aux précédents étrangers, cesont des affaires se rapportant aux droits constitutionnellement garantis, aux *droits humains.* Or, la Chambre constitutionnelle se sert aussi de cet outil, éventuellement, dans le domaine de l'organisation du pouvoir dans l'État.

4. *Pensez-vous que les juges justifient (suffisamment) la sélection des cas étrangers retenus?*

La Chambre constitutionnelle du Tribunal Suprême vénézuélien ne justifie pas la sélection des cas étrangers retenus. C'est une méthode qui rend efficace, à mon avis, le *cherry-picking.*

5. *Sur le « cherry-picking »*

Le recours aux précédents –et à la doctrine- étrangers par la Chambre constitutionnelle du Tribunal Suprême vénézuélien a certainement pour but de trouver ailleurs des arguments pour justifier ce qui, de toute façon, demeure injustifiable la plupart du temps.

Dans une décision rendue le 15 avril 2008 *(Interpretación del artículo 164.10 de la Constitución*[68]*)*, la Chambre constitutionnelle fît appel à la jurisprudence du Tribunal constitutionnel espagnol pour introduire dans le droit vénézuélien un principe jusqu'alors méconnu (en tout cas non reconnu) : le principe de *hiérarchie* entre les organes administratifs fédéraux (du « pouvoir national ») et ceux des états fédérés.

Or, si le précédent espagnol fait référence à la hiérarchie des normes "nationales" par rapport aux normes provinciales ou autonomiques, la Chambre constitutionnelle vénézuélienne va au-delà et, sur la supposée reconnaissance espagnole de la relation de hiérarchie entre la nation et les communautés autonomes, justifie non seulement l'existence d'une relation de hiérarchie entre l'administration fédérale et celle de l'état fédéré –ce qui est inconcevable dans notre système–, mais encore le pouvoir du législateur fédéral pour enlever aux états fédérés des compétences qui leur sont octroyées par la Constitution.

---

[68] Voir: http://www.tsj.gov.ve/decisiones/scon/Abril/565-150408-07-1108. htm. Elle se charge de citer un précédent de 2006, http://www.tsj.gov.ve/decisiones/scon/diciembre/2495-191206-02-0265.HTM

La disposition constitutionnelle visée –l'article 164.10- établit comme compétence « exclusive » des états fédérés « [l]a conservation, l'administration et la jouissance des routes et autoroutes nationales [fédérales], ainsi que des ports et aéroports à usage commercial, en coordination avec l'Exécutif National [fédéral] ».

De son côté, l'article 156.26 constitutionnel signale comme attribution du pouvoir fédéral, l'établissement du *régime législatif*, d'une part, de la navigation et transports aérien, maritime, fluvial, lacustre et terrestre ; et d'autre part, des ports et aéroports ainsi que de leur infrastructure.

Sur cela, la Chambre constitutionnelle soi-disant à partir du principe de coordination, affirma que si la prestation des services par les états fédérés est « déficiente ou inexistante », il résulte « inéludable » que le pouvoir fédéral intervienne directement, pour garantir leur continuité et efficacité ; en plus de son pouvoir pour *renverser* le « transfert » de compétences.

Car la Chambre constitutionnelle –et en cela n'ont rien à voir le maltraité Tribunal constitutionnel espagnol ou les auteurs cités[69]-, veut que, *sans texte*, l'article 164.10 constitutionnel soit une élongation de la Loi organique pour la décentralisation, délimitation et transfert de compétences du pouvoir public édictée en 1989 sous la Constitution de 1961 et que, sur sa base, avait valeur constitutionnelle. Cette loi établit, en effet, le transfert des compétences du pouvoir fédéral aux états fédérés et, dans le régime qu'elle définit conforme à la Constitution de 1961, prévit les *figures* de l'intervention et le renversement. Or, depuis 1999, surprise, il y a une nouvelle Constitution![70]

Comme cet exemple, on peut trouver plusieurs, chacun plus compliqué que l'autre, pour cacher le *cherry-picking* et puis l'arbitraire des décisions de la Chambre constitutionnelle[71].

---

[69]   Schmitt, Kelsen, puis Santamaría, Pastor.

[70]   À ce sujet, voir Brewer-Carías, A.R. « La Sala Constitucional como poder constituyente: la modificación de la forma federal del Estado y del sistema constitucional de división territorial del poder público », *Revista de Derecho Público* N° 114 (abril-junio 2008), p. 247-260.

[71]   Sur l'arbitraire des décisions de la Chambre constitutionnelle, voir Brewer-Carías, A.R. *Crónica sobre la « in » justicia constitucional. La Sala Constitucional y el autoritarismo en Venezuela.* Col. Instituto de Derecho Público Universidad Central de Venezuela, EJV, Caracas, 2007; Chavero Gazdik, R. *Justicia Revolucionaria, cit.;* Louza, L. *La revolución judicial en Venezuela*, FUNEDA, Caracas, 2011.

6. Pensez-vous qu'il y ait une convergence entre les traditions civiliste et de « common law » à propos du recours aux précédents étrangers?

Il semblerait, d'après l'étude dirigée par Mmes. Tania Groppi et Marie-Claire Ponthoreau, « *The use of foreign precedents by constitutional judges* », qu'il y a une corrélation presque parfaite entre la tradition légale et le recours aux précédents étrangers par le juge constitutionnel ; étant entendu que, exception faite de la Cour Suprême des Etats-Unis, les cours de *common law* ont tendance à cette pratique, tandis qu'elle est limitée voire inexistante dans la jurisprudence des cours de tradition civiliste[72].

Or, cette étude n'a pas pris en considération la particularité de l'Amérique latine, issue de son système de contrôle de constitutionnalité et puis de sa culture juridique, proche de la tradition civiliste, mais pour ainsi dire « tropicalisée ». En fait, seul le cas mexicain a fait l'objet d'une analyse dans cette étude[73], dont les trouvailles en principe ne sont pas trop éloignées de celles apportées aujourd'hui : d'une part, le juge constitutionnel fait appel aux précédents étrangers lorsqu'il lui semble utile ou nécessaire et les cite expressément ; d'autre part, la pratique ne pose pas de *scandale* au milieu académique ou doctrinaire. Certes, il y est établi que la pratique au Mexique est peu courante comme dans tous les pays de tradition civiliste, mais il est noté que les cas argentin, brésilien et colombien auraient certainement changé les résultats de la recherche et, pourquoi pas, la conclusion générale de l'ouvrage[74]. Il est certain qu'une étude approfondie du cas vénézuélien, au-delà en plus de la période considérée ici, en ferait autant.

La comparaison entre le cas mexicain par exemple et le cas vénézuélien montrerait l'énorme différence qui existe dans ces deux pays en ce qui concerne les buts poursuivis par le juge constitutionnel qui cite des précédents étrangers, malgré le rapprochement apparent des données objectives.

Il serait avantageux, à mon avis, de dépasser l'analyse quantitative, pour cerner la nature des affaires, les conditions et les buts du recours explicite aux précédents étrangers par un juge constitutionnel. Puis, il y faudrait aussi dévoiler les influences implicites et en faire autant.

---

[72] Groppi, T. et Ponthoreau, M-C *op.cit.*, p. 412-413.

[73] Ferrer Mac-Gregor. E. et Sánchez Gil, R., Mexico: « Struggling For an Open View In Constitutional Adjudication », in *The use of foreign precedents by constitutional judges, op.cit.*, p. 301-320.

[74] Groppi, T et Ponthoreau, M-C, *op.cit.*, p. 4.

Certainement on trouvera, comme dans la conclusion de l'étude susvisée, que des aspects tels l'habitude de fonder des décisions sur des interprétations préalables prises par autrui comme moyen de exhiber l'impartialité du jugement, ou bien la formation académique des juges, jouent un rôle qui peut être déterminant en ce qui concerne le recours aux précédents étrangers. Or, le besoin de rendre *légitime* une décision qui peut-être ne l'est pas, pourrait aussi faire un point.

Il faut distinguer en outre, comme il est fait dans l'étude « *The use of foreign precedents by constitutional judges* », entre les affaires se rapportant aux droits humains et ceux inhérents aux institutions étatiques. La *progressivité* des droits humains, naturellement *universalisante,* invite les cours constitutionnelles à un dialogue permanent, ce qui apparaît déjà assez clairement entre la Cour européenne des droits de l'homme et la Cour interaméricaine des Droits de l'Homme[75].

Pour les questions institutionnelles, qui normalement mettent en cause la souveraineté ou tout simplement la jouissance du pouvoir politique, le recours aux précédents étrangers sera certainement plus discret, en ce qu'il n'y aura pas des citations, il sera implicite, il sera peut-être *caché* derrière un autre précédent. C'est ainsi que l'on peut surmonter les « objections américaines » au recours aux précédents étrangers par le juge constitutionnel : les menaces à la démocratie et la souveraineté ; les difficultés techniques de la recherche ; le risque d'un usage incorrect du précédent du fait des différences sociales, économiques ou culturelles[76].

***

À la fin de ce travail, je me rends compte qu'il peut être décevant. D'une part, il ne contient pas des belles chartes et des chiffres montrant des résultats objectifs, « sérieux ». D'autre part, le recours aux précédents étrangers par le juge constitutionnel vénézuélien ne fait pas preuve d'un « dialogue jurisprudentiel » ou d'une « fertilisation transjudiciaire ».

---

[75]   Voir García Roca, J., Nogueira, H. y Bustos, R., *La comunicación entre los sistemas regionales americano y europeo de protección colectiva de los derechos humanos: el diálogo jurisdiccional entre la Corte Interamericana y el Tribunal Europeo,* disponible dans http://www. ijf.cjf.gob.mx/cursosesp/2013/Proteccion JurisdiccionalDH/Bustos%201.pdf; C. Ayala Corao, *Del diálogo jurisprudencial al control de convencionalidad,* EJV, Caracas, 2012.

[76]   Sperti, A. *United Sates of America: First Cautious Attempts of Judicial Use of Foreign Precedents in the Supreme Court's Jurisprudence, op.cit.*, p. 400.

Je pense, toutefois, que le résultat est aussi valable : le recours aux précédents (et à la doctrine ou au droit) étrangers sert aussi à *maquiller* les jugements ouvertement contraires à l'ordre juridique d'un État donné. Est-ce une pratique qui existe ailleurs?

IV.D. LIBERTÉS PUBLIQUES / HUMAN RIGHTS

- LES DROITS SOCIAUX ET ECONOMIQUES EN TANT QUE DROITS FONDAMENTAUX / SOCIAL AND ECONOMIC RIGHTS AS FUNDAMENTAL RIGHTS

SOCIAL RIGHTS AS FUNDAMENTAL RIGHTS AND ITS JUSTICIABILITY

Allan R. Brewer-Carías

PROFESSOR, CENTRAL UNIVERSITY OF VENEZUELA

Among the rights attributed to a person, there are those declared or recognized in the constitutions, as "constitutional rights," and among them there are the "human rights," referred to those attributed only to human beings. Within the latter it is also possible to distinguish the civil rights or civil liberties, that is, the individual rights of personal liberty or freedom guaranteed in the Constitution, such as freedom of speech, press, assembly, movement or religion. However, "civil rights" do not exhaust the list of constitutional rights, nor of human rights, which today also comprises social, economic, cultural and environmental rights. "Civil rights" were those first declared in the constitutions, what is called the first generation of rights, but at present time they are accompanied by a long list of other rights belonging to what has been called second and third "generations" of rights.

Another expression that must be kept in mind and mainly used in Europe, particularly in Germany and Spain, is that of "fundamental rights,"[1]

---

[1]   Article 93.1.4 a) German Constitution (1949); Article 53,2 Spanish Constitution. See Fernando Garrido Falla *et al*, *Comentarios a la Constitución*, Ed. Civitas, Madrid, 1980, p. 578.

used for the purpose of identifying certain constitutional rights that can be protected by a special judicial mean for protection also called *amparo* proceeding in Spain, which in general terms is equivalent to individual or civil rights.[2] This expression of "fundamental rights" is also used in the Colombian Constitution (Articles 11-41), to identify a category of constitutional rights, mainly individual rights, which are of immediate application and can be protected by the *acción de tutela* (Article 86). In the United States, the expression "fundamental rights" is also used when referring to civil rights that are protected in the Constitution, as "fundamental civil rights." As has been ruled by the Supreme Court in *United States v. Wong Kim Ark*, 169 U.S. 649; 18 S. Ct. 456; 42 L. Ed. 890 (1898), when referring to "fundamental civil rights for the security of which organized society was instituted, and which remain, with certain exceptions mentioned in the Federal Constitution..."

This expression "fundamental rights" has also been commonly used in Latin America with various meanings: First, from a formal point of view, they can be considered as the rights declared or numerated in the constitutions; second, from a substantive point of view, fundamental rights can also be considered as the most important rights that according to their own principles and value are recognized in each society[3]; and third, from a judicial point of view, as in Colombia, they are rights that can be judicially protected by special means such as the amparo.

---

[2]   According to these provisions, it is possible to distinguish among the constitutional rights those that can be considered as "justiciable rights" particularly by means of the specific judicial action or recourse of amparo, and constitutional rights not considered "fundamental rights." The latter group is left to be protected by means of the general or common judicial means. Constitutional rights can always be considered essentially justiciables, but their "justiciability" as the quality or state of being appropriate or suitable for reviewing by a court, will vary depending on the judicial means available in the legal system for such purpose. In some countries, all constitutional rights are justiciables by means of the general judicial means of protection, such as in the United States; in other countries all constitutional rights are justiciables by means of a specific judicial mean of protection like the habeas corpus or amparo action or recourse, such as in the case of Venezuela; and in other countries, the constitutional rights are protected by a special mean of protection if they are "fundamental rights," being the other constitutional rights justiciables through the common judicial means.

[3]   See Gairaud Brenes, Alfonso. "Los Mecanismos de interpretación e los derechos humanos: especial referencia a la jurisprudencia Peruana", in Palomino Manchego, José F. *El derecho procesal constitucional Peruano. Estudios en* Homenaje *a Domingo García Belaunde*, Editorial Jurídica Grijley, Lima, 2005, T. I, p. 124.

The main concern regarding constitutional or fundamental rights[4] in modern Constitutional States, is referred to their protection, which has been assured by declaring them in the text of the Constitution and in international treaties, thus out of the reach of the legislator, and by establishing the indispensable judicial guaranties in order to assure their exercise.

In this sense, social rights are without doubt "fundamental rights" in the sense that they are justiciable, that is, they can be protected by judicial means, in particular, those especially established to assure the protection of constitutional rights, as is the case of the action of *amparo*, so widely used in Latin America. This Report deals in particular with the situation of social rights as fundamental rights in Latin America.[5]

I. THE QUESTION OF THE JUSTICIABILITY OF SOCIAL RIGHTS

The most important question regarding the justiciability of constitutional rights in Latin America by means of the amparo action refers to the justiciability of economic, social and cultural rights. In some countries many of those rights are not declared in the constitutions, consequently lacking of constitutional judicial protection because not having constitutional rank. In other countries, as is the case of Colombia and Chile, many of those social rights are not considered as "fundamental rights" that are in general, the only ones that can be protected by means of the *tutela* and protection actions.

Yet even in countries that do not establish any distinction regarding the protected rights, the question of the justiciability of those economic, social and cultural rights continues to be an important issue, particularly because in some cases some sort of additional legislation is required for their full enforcement.

These rights, particularly the social rights, generally imply the obligation for the State to provide or render services or to accomplish activities,

---

[4]   The expression "constitutional rights" in this book is used as equivalent to "fundamental rights", among which are "human rights". In general terms, all of them are declared in the constitutions and can be protected by means of the amparo action.

[5]   See in general Brewer-Carías, Allan R., *Constitutional protection of Human Rights in Latin America. A Comparative Study of the Amparo Proceedings*, Cambridge University Press, New York, 2008. This Paper reproduces part of Chapter eleven of this book (pp. 240 ff.).

for which public expenses must be allocated regarding each service, depending on the political decisions of the government. Consequently, it has been sustained that the provisions establishing such rights can only be enforceable after the sanctioning by Congress of legislation providing the scope of their enjoyment as well as of the State's obligations, and after the adoption of specific public policies by the Executive. Yet such approach has been questioned particularly based in the principle of the connection that exists between social and civil rights, which implies the need to consider new principles deriving from the concept of the Social State and the functioning of the Welfare State.

For instance, in this regard, the Colombian Constitutional Court in its decision N° T-406 of June 5, 1992, established the principle that these rights have their *raison d'étre* in the fact that their minimal satisfaction is an indispensable condition for the enjoyment of the civil and political rights, that "without the respect of human dignity regarding the material conditions of existence, any aspiration of effectively enforcing the classical freedoms and egalitarian rights enshrined in the Constitution, would be just simple and useless formalism". That is why the Constitutional Court considered that "the judicial intervention in cases of economic, social and cultural rights is necessary when it is indispensable in order to assure the respect of other constitutional fundamental rights". Consequently, according to the Constitutional Court, the enforcement of social, economic and cultural rights cannot be confined to the political link existing between the Constituent and the Legislator, in the sense that the constitution's efficiency cannot only be in the hands of the Legislator. On the contrary, "the constitutional provisions would have no value, [if] the Constituent's will is subjected to the Legislator will."[6]

Nonetheless, based on these arguments, the Constitutional Court of Colombia concluded its ruling saying that due to the fact that "the application of social, economic and cultural rights gives rise to the political problem of deciding the allocation of public funds, the admission of *tutela* regarding social, economic and cultural rights can only be accepted in cases where a violation of a fundamental right exists."[7] From this ruling, the principle of the "connection" between social rights and fundamental rights regarding their justiciability, which has been developed in other countries

---

[6]   See decision T-406 of June 5, 1992, in Manuel José Cepeda, *Derecho Constitucional Jurisprudencial. Las grandes decisiones de la Corte Constitucional*, Legis, Bogotá, 2001, p. 61.

[7]   *Idem*. p. 61

like Mexico (right to life) and the United States (nondiscrimination), has also been applied in Colombia.[8]

Consequently, when no such connection between a fundamental right and a social one exists, the latter cannot in itself be protected by means of a *tutela* action, as for instance was the case of the constitutional right to have proper dwelling or housing, regarding which, the same Colombian Constitutional Court ruled that in that case, "as well as regarding other rights of social, economic and cultural contents, no subjective right is given to persons to ask the State in a direct and immediate way in its complete satisfaction".[9]

Those problems, related to the political conditions for the enforcement of some social, economic and cultural rights, have been the basis for the discussion in contemporary constitutional law, not on whether those rights, like education, health, social welfare or housing have or not constitutional rank, but on their justiciability, that is to say, the possibility of their enforcement by means of judicial actions against the State.

II. THE CASE OF THE RIGHT TO HEALTH AND THE STATE'S OBLIGATIONS

This discussion has been raised regarding many social rights, and particularly, regarding the right of the people to health, and consequently the obligation of the State in terms of providing public health services.

In almost all the Latin American constitutions, even if the constitutional fundamental character and rank of social, economic and cultural rights has been recognized, the courts have not always granted the amparo protection for their enforcement, particularly when brought against the State. The justiciability of the rights and the scope of the claimed protection, in many cases have been conditioned by the way the right is declared in the constitutions, particularly when the provisions are set forth as "programmatic" ones; an expression that refers to provisions having their contents conceived as a program directed to the Congress in order to legislate and which are not directly enforceable.

---

[8]   For instance, the Constitutional Court has protected the right to health of a military servicemen to be treated in a military hospital, even though he was not formally entitled to have such treatment because he had not given his military oath, considering that the right must be protected "when the health service is needed and is indispensable, in order to preserve the right to life, in which cases the State is obligated to render it to needy persons". See Decision T-534 of September 24, 1992, *Idem*, pp. 461 ff.

[9]   See Decision T-251 of June 5, 1995, *Idem*, p. 486.

On the other hand, regarding for instance the right to health, not all the Latin American constitutions have declared it at all, and when declared, it has not been expressed in the same way. Some constitutions refer to health as a public good, as is the case in El Salvador (Article 65) and Guatemala (Article 95), providing that not only the State but also the individuals have the duty to take care of its preservation and restoration.

In contrast, in other constitutions, like those of Bolivia (Article 7,a), Brazil (Articles 6 and 196); Ecuador (Article 46); Nicaragua (Article 59) and Venezuela (Article 84), it is provided for the "right to health" as a constitutional right and even as a "fundamental" constitutional right (Venezuela, Article 83), corresponding in equal terms to everybody, as it is also expressed in the Constitution of Nicaragua (Article 59). This principle of equal treatment is reaffirmed in the Constitution of Guatemala, by providing that "the enjoyment of health is a fundamental right of human beings, without any kind of discrimination" (Article 93).

In other constitutions the right to health derives from the recognition of constitutional rank to the International Covenant on Economic, Social and Cultural rights, as is the case in Argentina (Article 75).

Now, with this constitutional formula of the "right to health," what the constitutions have established is a constitutional right of everybody to have their health protected by the State, which conversely has the obligation, together with all Society, to care for the maintenance and recuperation of people's health.

That is why other Latin American constitutions, instead of providing for the "right to health," set forth in a more precise way for the right of persons "to have their health protected," as it is established in Honduras (Article 145), Chile (Article 19,9), Mexico (Article 4), Peru (Article 7), Cuba (Article 50) and Colombia (Article 49). This implies, in general terms, as it is provided in the Constitution of Panama, that this is a "right to the promotion, protection, maintenance, restitution and rehabilitation of health, and an obligation to maintain it; health understood as the complete physical, mental and social welfare" (Article 105) This right, as it is also declared in the Constitution of Paraguay, implies the obligation of the State "in the interest of community, to protect and promote health as a fundamental right of persons" (Article 68).

Consequently, this right to health, in the sense of a right to be protected by the State, eventually implies a right for all people to have equal access to the public services established for the purpose of taking care of people's health, as it is set forth in the Constitution of Chile, which provides that "the State protects free and equal access to the actions for promotion, protection and recovery of health and of rehabilitation of the individuals" (Article 19,9).

In order to guaranty the access to health services, the Latin American constitutions follow different approaches, from free general access to limited access regarding specific circumstances. Free access is for instance guaranteed in the Cuban Constitution, which sets forth that the State guaranties the rights of persons to have their health taken care of and protected by means of "rendering free public medical and hospital assistance" (Article 50).

In the case of Chile, a distinction is made between public programs and public services, providing that, on the one hand, "public health programs and actions are free for all"; and on the other, that "public services of medical attention will be free [only] for those who need them" (Article 43), stipulating that "in no case will emergency attention be denied neither in public nor private premises" (Article 43).

In general terms, the principle of free public health care, as a constitutional right is established in the constitutions in benefit of persons lacking financial support and in all cases, where the general public health needs to be protected. In this sense, the Constitution of El Salvador declares that the State must "give free assistance to sick persons lacking resources and in general to all inhabitants, when the treatment is an efficient mean to prevent the dissemination of a transmissible disease" (Article 66).

Regarding the former situation, for instance in Uruguay, the constitution sets forth that "the State must freely provide the means for protection and of assistance only to the needy and to those without enough resources" (Article 44); and in Panama, the constitution establishes that "these health services and medication will be freely rendered to whomever lacks economic resources" (Article 106).

Regarding the latter situation, for instance, the Constitution of Paraguay sets forth that "nobody will be deprived of public assistance in order to prevent or treat diseases, pests or plague, and of help in cases of catastrophes or accidents" (Article 68).

In other cases, the constitutions only express general principles referring to the regulations that must be established by statute. This is the case of the Colombian Constitution (Article 49), which requires the Legislator to "define the terms through which the basic attention for all the inhabitants will be free and obligatory"; and this is also the case of the Mexican Constitution, which indicates that "the rules and conditions for access to health services" must be established by statutes (Article 4).

From all these constitutional regulations, in addition to the general solidarity duties that are imposed on everyone in order to seek for preserving healthy conditions, a series of constitutional duties are also imposed on the State and public entities, which eventually are the ones that determine the scope of their justiciability.

For instance, the Panamanian Constitution provides that "it is an essential function of the State to care for the health of the population" (Article 105); and the Constitution of Guatemala, sets forth as an "obligation of the State" to take "care of the health and social assistance of all inhabitants" and to "develop," through its institutions, "actions for the prevention, promotion, recovery, rehabilitation and coordination in order to seek the most complete physical, mental and social welfare" (Article 94).

The Venezuelan Constitution, after declaring health as a fundamental right, also provides as an obligation of the State, the guaranty of health as part of the right to life (Article 83); and the Honduran Constitution sets forth that "the State must maintain an adequate environment for the protection of people's health" (Article 145).

In this matter of the State's obligations regarding health, other constitutions contain more detailed regulations, as is the case, for instance, of Cuba regarding hospital assistance (Article 50); Panama (Article 106) and Bolivia (Article 158,1) regarding general policies assigned to the State. In this same sense, for instance, the Constitution of Ecuador, establishes that the State guarantees the right to health, and the promotion and protection of health, "by means of the development of the alimentary safety, the provision of drinking water and basic sanitation, the promotion of family, labor and community healthy environment and the possibility to have permanent an uninterrupted access to health services, according the equity, universality, solidarity, quality and efficiency principles" (Article 42). In addition, in Ecuador, the State must promote "the culture for health and life, with emphasis in alimentary and nutrition education of mothers and child and in sexual and reproductive health, by means of societal participation and the social media collaboration" (Article 43). For such purpose, the State must formulate "a national health policy and will watch for its application; will control the functioning of sector entities; will recognize, respect and promote the development of traditional and alternative medicine, the exercise of which will be regulated by statute, and will promote the scientific and technological advancement in health care, subjected to bioethics principles. The State will also adopt programs tending to eradicate alcoholism and other toxic manias" (Article 44).

In a similar sense, the Constitution of Peru provides that "the State must establish the health policy" (Article 9); and the Constitution of El Salvador prescribes that "the State will determine the national health policy and will control and supervise its application" (Article 65). In Nicaragua, the constitution sets forth that the State must establish basic conditions for health promotion, protection, recovery and rehabilitation, and that it must direct and organize health programs, services and actions and promote popular participation in its defense" (Article 59).

186

In Brazil, the State has the constitutional duty to guaranty health as a right of everyone, "through social and economic policies tending to reduce the risk of sickness and providing a universal and equal access to actions and services for health promotion, protection and recovery" (Article 196).

According to all these expressed constitutional provisions, in some cases vague and in others with very detailed and precise expressions, the protection of health can be considered in general terms as a constitutional obligation of the State, which does not exclude the possibility for individuals to render health care services. So the services for the protection of health can be provided not only by the State, accomplishing an exclusive obligation, as is the case of Cuba, but also by individuals. That is, health services can be public or private; so the Chilean Constitution guaranties the right of "everyone to choose the health care system wanted to be received, whether public or private" (Article 19). This provision also implies the existence of another constitutional right of individuals to render health care services, as an economic right.

This is expressly set forth in the Brazilian Constitution where it is provided that "sanitary assistance is of free private initiative," but subject to express constitutional restrictions, like the possible participation of private institutions in the Unique Health Services (Article 199). Other Latin American constitutions also contain general principles regarding public and private health care services, integrated into a national or unique system (Chile, Article 45; Paraguay, Article 69; Venezuela, Article 84).

Except for the two mentioned cases of the Chilean (Article 19) and Brazilian (Article 197) constitutions, in the other Latin American constitutions references are made to private initiative to render health care services in an indirect way, when attributing to the State the express power to regulate all health care services, as it is provided in the Constitutions of Venezuela (Article 85), Uruguay (Article 44), Honduras (Article 149) and Colombia (Article 49).

The general consequence of all these provisions in the constitutions establishing State obligations to render health care services to satisfy people's constitutional right to be protected, is that such obligations are always materialized in the establishment of public health care services to render care to the people. This is expressly provided in the Colombian Constitution when it declares that "health care and environment sanitation are public services to be rendered by the care of the State" (Article 49); and in the Bolivian Constitution when providing that "social services are State functions", being the norms providing for public health, of "coactive and obligatory character" (Article 164).

In all these cases, the consequence of a constitutional provision establishing the obligation of the State to render a public service to take care of individual's health, is the existence of a constitutional right to use those services, which consequently implies that in principle, they can be judicially claimed and enforced against the State.

III. THE JUSTICIABILITY OF THE RIGHT TO HEALTH

Yet the fact is that the justiciability of the right to health has not had the same solution in all of Latin America.

It is clear, according to all the constitutional regulations that have been mentioned, that a person's constitutional right to health care is generally provided, particularly due to the obligations imposed on the States to render services for the maintenance and recovery of health. However, these provisions and the way they are conceived are, precisely, the ones that raise the question of the justiciability of such right to health, particularly by means of the amparo recourses or actions as specific judicial means for the protection of human rights.

This judicial enforceability of course depends on the way the specific regulations are established in the constitutions and in the statutes on the matter. For example, only in exceptional cases are such judicial protection for the enforceability of the right to health expressly provided for, as is the case in Peru, where the Constitutional Procedure Code expressly sets forth that the amparo recourse can be filed for the defense of the right "to health" (Article 37,24). In the case of Chile, the constitution only refers to the recourse for protection regarding the "right to choose the system of health care" (Article 19,9).

Apart from these two provisions, no other express constitutional or legal regulation exists in Latin America regarding the amparo proceeding for the protection of the right to health, which of course does not exclude such possible judicial protection. On the contrary, the jurisprudence in many countries has shown that as a matter of principle, amparo actions can be brought before the courts for the protection of the people's right to health, although not in a uniform way.

In this regard, from decisions issued by the Constitutional Courts or Constitutional Chambers of Supreme Courts, for instance, in Argentina, Peru, Colombia, Costa Rica, Chile and Venezuela, or by lower courts in Argentina, it is possible to distinguish at least four general tendencies.

The first tendency can be identified with the protection of health as a collective right, based in collective interest. The second tendency is characterized by granting a wide protection to the right to health in specific cases in connection with the right to life and when a particular legal relationship is established or exists between the plaintiff and the public entity acting as the defendant party, like the one derived from the Social Security programs to which the individual contributes. In this case because of the intimate "connection" with other fundamental rights, like the right to life, the courts have also rejected the "programmatic" character attributed to the right to health. The third tendency is the granting of a limited judicial protection to the right to health, subjected to the existing State policy on the matter, particularly regarding the allocation and availability of public funds. Finally, a fourth tendency can be identified when the protection is denied in cases of abstract claims.

1. *The protection to the right to health as a collective right*

The first tendency of the justiciability of the right to health is based in its consideration as a collective right, as it is established in the International Covenant on Economic, Social and Cultural Rights, where Article 12,1 provides that the States Parties "recognize the right of everyone to the enjoyment of the highest attainable standard of physical and mental health", and consequently, according to Article 12,2,c, it is prescribe that the steps to be taken by the States Parties to achieve the full realization of this right shall include those necessary for "the prevention, treatment and control of epidemic, endemic, occupational and other diseases".

In Argentina, the constitution (Article 75,22) has given constitutional rank to the International Covenant, and as a consequence of this, the collective right to health has been enforced by the courts. It was the case of an amparo action decided by the Federal Administrative Court of Appeals on June 2, 1998 (*Viceconte, Mariela c. Estado Nacional (Ministerio de Salud y Ministerio de Economía de la Nación) s/ Acción de Amparo* case), that was filed as a collective amparo by Mariela Viceconte seeking to force the State to produce the *Candid 1* vaccine, based on her own right to health and that of other few millions of persons exposed to contracting "Argentine Hemorrhagic Fever." The plaintiff specifically alleged a violation of the obligation to prevent, treat and fight epidemic and endemic diseases arising from Article 12.2.c of the International Covenant on Economic, Social and Cultural Rights, and the Court of Appeals concluded that the State's failure to arrange the production of the vaccine was a violation of the right to health under such article of the Covenant. Therefore, the Court ruled that the State had the obligation to manufacture the vaccine and ordered it to comply strictly and without delays with a schedule that had already been designed for such purposes by the Ministry of Health. The Court also asked the National Ombudsman to follow up on the schedule.[10]

2. *The protection to the right to health in connection to the right to life and the social security obligations*

The second tendency regarding the justiciability of the right to health by means of amparo refers to its protection in particular situations, derived from the specific social security obligations regarding specific insured persons.

As an example, the decision of the Constitutional Chamber of the Supreme Tribunal of Justice of Venezuela decision N° 487 of April 6, 2001, (*Glenda López y otros vs. Instituto Venezolano de los Seguros Sociales* case) can be mentioned, through which an HIV/AIDS infected person who filed an action against the Institute for Social Security was protected, compelling the Institute to provide medical attention to the plaintiff. In its decision, the Court pointed out that the right to health or to the protection of health is "an integral part of the right to life, set forth in the Constitution as a fundamental social right (and not simply as an assignment of State purposes) whose satisfaction mainly belongs to the State and its institutions, through activities intended to progressively raise the quality of life of citizens and the collective welfare." This implies, according to the Court's decision that "the right to health is not to be exhausted with the simple physical care of a person, but must be extended to the appropriate treatment in order to safeguard the mental, social, environmental integrity of persons, including the community".

In this particular case decided by the Court, the violation of the right to health and the threats to the right to life was alleged as caused by the Venezuelan Institute for Social Security, which the plaintiff considered was due to "give complete medical care to its affiliates." The Constitutional Chamber ruled that because of the omission of the Institute "to provide to the plaintiffs, in a regular and permanent way, the drugs for the treatment of HIV/AIDS prescribed by the specialist attached to a specific Hospital…, and to practice the specialized medical exams directed to help the

---

[10]   See the reference in Caputi, M. Claudia. "Reseña jurisprudencial. La tutela judicial de la salud y su reivindicación contra los entes estatales", in *Revista Iberoamericana de Estudios Autonómicos*, N° 2, Goberna & Derecho, Guayaquil, 2006, pp. 145–164.

efficient treatment of HIV/AIDS"; the right to health and even the right to life of the plaintiff were put in danger.[11]

This connection between the right to health and other fundamental rights, such as the right to life, which can immediately be protected by means of amparo, has also been the tendency followed by the courts in Argentina, Colombia, Costa Rica and Peru.

As aforementioned, in Colombia, the constitution does not include the right to health or to the protection of health within the list of the "fundamental rights," which are the only ones protected by means of the action of *tutela*. Nonetheless, the Constitutional Court, in order to assure its judicial protection, has applied the principle of the connection of the right to health with the right to life. It was the case in decision N° T-484/92 of August 11, 1992, issued when reviewing a lower court's *tutela* decision that was filed against the Institute of Social Security. The plaintiff in the case, also infected with HIV/AIDS, claimed that he was infected while covered by the Social Security program. The claimant had a favorable decision from the first instance Court that ordered the Institute to continue to render the health care services that the plaintiff had been receiving, and the Constitutional Court, when reviewing the case, affirmed that "health is one of those assets that because of its inherent character to the dignified existence of man, is protected, especially regarding persons that because of their economic, physical or mental conditions are in a manifest weakened condition" (Article 13, Constitution). Considering the right to health as being a right that "seeks the assurance of the fundamental right to life" (Article 11, Constitution), the Court ruled that due to its assistance nature, it implies the need for health care to be rendered by public entities, in order for its effective protection."[12]

In addition, the Court developed two sorts of arguments when connecting the right to health with the right to life. First, those that identify the right to health as an immediate condition for the right of life, in which case the harm to a person's health would be equivalent to a threat to his life. Consequently, for instance, actions harming the safe environment (Article 49,1) are to be treated in a concurrent way regarding health prob-

---

[11]   See in *Revista de Derecho Público*, N° 85-88, Editorial Jurídica Venezolana, Caracas, 2001, pp. 139-141.

[12]   File N° 2130, Muñoz Ceballos, Alonso, case. See in the same sense, Decision T-534, September 24, 1992, in Cepeda, Manuel José. *Derecho Constitucional Jurisprudencial. Las grandes decisiones de la Corte Constitucional*, Legis, Bogotá, 2001, pp. 461 ff.

lems, resulting in a fundamental right. The second argument tends to connect the right to health to the assistance character of the concept of the Welfare State, in the sense that its recognition in the constitution imposes concrete public actions that must be developed through legislation in order to render public services not only for medical assistance, but also for hospital, pharmaceutical and laboratory rights. The link between the right to health and the right to be assisted, although imprecise and subject to the circumstances of each case (Article 13, Constitution), always allows the Court to construct the existence of the right to health considering "that the right to health is fundamental when related to the protection of life".

Based on these argument, the Court, regarding the particular case of the petitioner infected with HIV/AIDS who received treatment from the health care services of the Institute for Social Security, ratified the lower court's *tutela* decision, bearing in mind that in the particular circumstance, the protection of the right to health, was the condition for the protection of his fundamental right to life.

In a similar case, the Constitutional Chamber of the Supreme Court of Justice of Costa Rica, N° 2003-8377 of August 8, 2003,[13] when deciding an amparo recourse filed by the People's Defendant on behalf of an aggrieved child (*Tania González Valle*) against the Costa Rican Institute for Social Security because of the denial of the requested treatment for a specific disease (known as Gaucher type 1) argued that such denial "harmed the right to life and health of the minor" who required the prescribed drug for "maintaining her life."

The Constitutional Chamber, after referring to the right to life protected in previous decisions that were based on the provision of the constitution (Article 21) establishing the inviolability of human life, concluded by deriving "the right that every citizen has to his health, thus corresponding to the State's responsibility to ensure public health... (N° 5130-94 of 17:33 hrs on 7 September 1994)". The Chamber also referred to "the preeminence of life and health as superior values of society [which] must be protected by the State [being] present not only in the Constitution, but also in the various international instruments ratified by the country".[14]

---

[13] File. 03-007020-0007-CO, *González Valle, Tania,* case.

[14] In particular, the decision made reference to Article 3 of the Universal Declaration on Human Rights, Article 4 of the American Convention on Human Rights; Article 1 of the American Declaration on Rights and Duties of Man; Article 6 of the International Covenant on Civil and Political Rights; Article 12 of the International Covenant on Economic, Social and Cultural Rights; and Articles 14 and 26 of the Convention on Children Rights (Law 7184 of July 18, 1990).

Consequently, due to the responsibilities of the State derived from these provisions, when analyzing the mission and functions of the Costa Rican Institute of Social Security, the Chamber considered, as it was declared in a previous decision (n° 1997-05934 of September 23, 1997), "that the denial by the Costa Rican Institute of Social Security to provide adequate therapy to patients infected with HIV/AIDS harms their fundamental rights." Departing from this assertion, when analyzing the particular case of the child with Gaucher disease, the Chamber found that she was not receiving the prescribed treatment due to the limited financial resources of the Social Security Institute and it concluded that although the cost of the prescribed drugs were undoubtedly onerous, nonetheless, due to the exceptional lethal characteristics of the illness and the impossibility for her parents to cover the costs of the prescriptions, it confirmed the recourse and ordered the Social Security Institute to immediately provide the specific drug in the conditions prescribed by her doctor.[15]

In Peru, the Constitutional Tribunal in a decision of April 20, 2004, also protected the right to health when deciding an extraordinary revision recourse filed against an amparo decision issued by the Superior Court of Justice of Lima. The latter had partially granted the amparo protection filed against the Peruvian State (Ministry of Health), ordering to render to the plaintiff, also an HIV/AIDS infected person, "integral health care by means of the constant provision of drugs needed to treat HIV/AIDS, as well as the performance of periodical exams and tests that the doctor orders".[16]

The Constitutional Tribunal, referring to the rights that are protected by means of the action for amparo, although admitting that "the right to

---

[15] The Court argued as follows: "This Court is conscientious regarding the scattered financial resources of the social security system, nonetheless it considers that the principal challenge the Costa Rican Institution of Social Security faces in this stage of its institutional development, –where Costa Rica has achieved life standards qualities similar to those of developed countries–, is to optimize the management of available resources of the system of health insurance and reduce the administrative costs in order to efficiently invest these resources. The Chamber considers that the prescribed drugs are undoubtedly onerous, nonetheless, due to the exceptional characteristics of the illness suffered, which is lethal, and due to the impossibility for her parents to contribute for the acquisition of the drugs, based on Articles 21 and 173 of the Constitution, and 24 and 26 of the Convention on the Child's Rights, it proceeds to confirm the recourse. The acceptance of the recourse implies that the Costa Rican Institution on Social Security must immediately provide Gonzalez Valle, Tania with the drug "*Cerezyme*" (Imuglucerase) in the conditions prescribed by her doctor". File 03-007020-0007-CO, *Tania González Valle* case.

[16] File N° 2945-2003-AA/TC, *Meza García, Azanca Alhelí* case.

health is not among the "fundamental rights" set forth in the Constitution, but is recognized in the Chapter related to social and economic rights[17]; concluded –referring to the Colombian Court doctrine– that in a "similar way as was decided by the Colombian Constitutional Court, when the violation of the right to health compromises other fundamental rights, like the right to life, the right to physical integrity and the right to the free development of one's personality, such right acquires fundamental right characteristics and, therefore, must be protected by means of amparo action (STC N° T-499 *Corte Constitucional de Colombia*)".[18]

The Peruvian Constitutional Tribunal also ruled that these rights were not to be considered as "programmatic rights" with limited effects, because without dignified education, health and quality of life, it would be difficult to talk about freedom and social equality. This implies that both the Legislator and the Judiciary have to act jointly and interdependently in the recognition of such rights, the satisfaction of which requires a minimum action from the State, by establishing public services to render health care for all the population.[19]

---

[17] Since 2004, the right to health is established in the Constitutional Procedure Code, as one of the rights expressly protected by means of the amparo action (Article 37,24).

[18] Considering the nature of the economic and social rights, as is the case of the right to health, which always originates State obligations directed to provide social assistance, the Perúvian Constitutional Tribunal in the same decision argued that the right to health, as all the so-called *"prestacionales"* (which implies to render something), like social security, public health, housing, education and other public services, constitutes "one of the social goals of the State through which individuals can achieve their complete development." Individuals can then "demand" the accomplishment of State duties by "asking the State to adopt adequate measures in order to achieve the social goals." However, the Tribunal recognized that "not in all cases are the social rights legally enforceable by themselves, due to the need of a budget support for its accomplishment." File N° 2945-2003-AA/TC, *Meza García, Azanca Alhelí* case.

[19] In this regard, the Tribunal also ruled that for the enforcement of these rights their traditional programmatic conception needed to be surpassed, so that with this criteria "this new vision of the social rights allows to recognize in their essential content, principles like solidarity and human dignity as funding of the Welfare State based on the rule of Law." After analyzing these principles, the Tribunal considered "erroneous the argument of the State defendant that being the national policy of health based on programmatic provisions, it only signifies a plan of action to be followed by the State"; adding that it would be naïve to sustain that the social rights are reduced to be just a matter of political relation between the Constituent and the legislator, which would be "an evident distortion regarding the Constitution's sense and coherence." But insisting on the right to health and its inseparable relation with the right to life, the Tribunal ruled that according to the Constitution "the defense of human beings and the respect of their dignity... pre-

The Tribunal concluded by affirming that "to judicially file an action claiming the protection of social rights will depend on various factors, such as the seriousness and reasonability of the case, its relation to other rights and the State's budget resources, provided that particular actions for social policies can be accomplished". Regarding the public policies in matters of public health, the Tribunal considered that if it is true that the accomplishment of the State obligations depends on the State's financial resources allocations, "in no way can it justify a prolonged [public] inaction, because it would result in an unconstitutional omission". The conclusion in the case was to grant the claimed protection to a social right as the right to health, due to the fact that in the particular case the conditions justifying it were fulfilled" not only "due to the potential damage to the right to life", but also because of the motives governing the existing legislation, providing the means for maximum protection to the HIV/AIDS infected persons.

Also in Argentina, the Supreme Court of the Nation in a decision of December 12, 2003 (*Asociación Esclerosis Múltiple de Salta* case), has recognized the amparo action as the most effective judicial mean to exercised in an unavoidable way "in order to safeguard the fundamental right to life and to health".[20]

---

supposes the unrestricted enforcement of the right to life"; because "the exercise of any right, privilege, faculty or power has no sense or results useless in cases of the inexistence of physical life of somebody in favor of which it can be recognized." The Tribunal continued its ruling saying that "28. Health is a fundamental right due to its inseparable relation with the right to life, which is irresoluble, due to the fact that an illness can provoke death or in any case, the deterioration of life conditions. Thus the need to materialize actions tending to take care of life (health care) is evident, oriented to attack the illness signs..." Then, after affirming that the right of people, to "be assigned sanitary and social measures for nourishment, clothing, dwelling and medical assistance, depending on what is allowed by public funds and social solidarity", the Tribunal considered the question of the justiciability of social rights, like the right to health, ruling that "they cannot be requested in the same way in all cases, due to the fact that it is not a matter of specific rendering, because it depends on budget allocations. The contrary, would suppose that each individual could judicially ask at any moment for an employment or for a specific dwelling or for health." *Idem.*

[20]   See Fallos: 326: 4931. See the reference in Caputi, M. Claudia. "Reseña jurisprudencial. La tutela judicial de la salud y su reivindicación contra los entes estatales," in *Revista Iberoamericana de Estudios Autonómicos*, N° 2, Goberna & Derecho, Guayaquil, 2006, pp. 145-164.

3. The limited protection of the right to health and the State's financial resources

The third tendency regarding the protection of social rights is a restricted or limited one in which the justiciability of the right to health, also regarding HIV/AIDS treatment, has been completely subordinated to the effective disposal of enough financial resources, as was the case of some 2000/2001 Chilean courts' decisions.

In one case, the action for protection was filed against the Ministry of Health for failing to provide medical treatment to a group of HIV/AIDS patients, arguing that it was a violation to the right to life and the right to equal protection. The plaintiff demanded to be treated with the same therapy that was given to other HIV/AIDS patients, which the Ministry denied arguing that it lacked enough economic resources to provide it to all Chilean HIV/AIDS patients.

The Court of Appeals of Santiago ruled that the obligation of the Ministry of Health, according to the Law regulating health care provisions (Law N° 2763/1979), was to provide health care in accordance with the resources that were available, and it considered the Ministry's explanation reasonable, that there was a lack of economic resources to provide the best available treatment to the plaintiffs. The decision was later confirmed by the Supreme Court.[21]

In another 2001 case, the same Ministry of Health was sued for the same reasons by HIV patients in more critical conditions, and even though the Court of Appeals of Santiago ruled in favor of the petitioners and ordered the Ministry to immediately provide them with the best available treatment, the Supreme Court reversed the ruling, arguing that the Ministry had acted in accordance to the law.[22]

4. The rejection of the amparo protection when argued in an abstract way

Finally, a forth tendency can be identified related to this limitative tendency to protect the right to health when claimed in an abstract way. In this regard, mention can be made to a 2004 decision of the Venezuelan Constitutional Chamber of the Supreme Tribunal, which ruled that when

---

[21]   See the reference in Courso, Javier A. "Judicialization of Chilean Politics," in Sieder, Rachel, Schjolden, Line and Angeli, Alan (Ed.), *The Judicializacion of Politics in Latin America*, Palgrave Macmillan, New York, 2005, pp. 11,9-120.

[22]   *Idem*, p. 120.

claimed in an abstract way, the right to health could not be protected by means of amparo actions, but only through political mechanisms of control regarding public policies.

The Chamber, in effect, in decision N° 1002 of May 26, 2004 (*Federación Médica Venezolana* case),[23] rejected an amparo action filed by the Venezuelan Medical Federation "defending diffuse social rights and interests, and in particular those of the physicians" seeking the protection of health against the "omissive" conduct of the Ministry of Health and Social Development and the Venezuelan Institute for Social Security, because failing to "provide efficient services of health to the population in the country, by means of promptly providing the necessary equipment and resources".

The Constitutional Chamber recognized that in the 1999 Venezuelan Constitution, all economic, social and cultural rights are considered "fundamental rights," ruling that this "implies specific consequences, among them, –in principle– the applicability of the protection by means of amparo", particularly "because the Constitution, in contrast to what is established in other legal orders, does not exclude certain rights from that guaranty, nor its immediate applicability, being the constitutional order of an immediate normative value and application, rejecting what are known as programmatic rights." Yet even admitting that because such economic, social and cultural rights have a fundamental character (not just being moral values aspirations) and that "they are undoubtedly judicially protected," nonetheless, the Constitutional Chamber concluded its ruling, constructing the denial of such justiciability regarding social right, stating that "the point is to determine when one is asking for the enforcement of an economic, social or cultural right, and when one is asking that the Public Administration performs the Welfare State based on the Rule of Law State clause, given that in both cases, the ways to sue or demand differ."[24]

---

[23] See in *Revista de Derecho Público*, N° 97-98, Editorial Jurídica Venezolana, Caracas, 2004, p. 143 ff.

[24] The Chamber said: "Policies are, in principle, outside the scope of judicial review, but not for that reason can they escape control; only that this applicable control is the political one also set forth in the Constitution. The State organs act under their own responsibility, which can be challenged in the political level, but it is not possible to challenge their political management before the Judiciary, unless when determining an administrative liability for damages caused by the political activity and putting aside that a fundamental right be affected by the decision, in which case, eventually, the control will not be regarding the political elements of the act and turn to be a control regarding its juridical elements..." The Chamber concluded that "a) The economic, social and cultural rights have, as all rights, judicial protection; b) In order to know if one is facing one of such rights, there must exist a perfectly defined juridical relation where the harm to them de-

Regarding the particular amparo action, the Constitutional Chamber concluded by affirming that being "of a reestablishing nature, the possibility to judicially control economic, social and cultural policies is not included in this constitutional guaranty". In the claim of the *Federación Médica Venezolana*, the court was asked to order the government to allocate enough funds to the hospitals, and to budget provisions for the acquisition of medical equipment and hospital materials. The claim was rejected by the Chamber considering that those were very evidently political activities and abstract in nature, which made them "impossible to be the object of an amparo action directed to restore particular juridical situations"; concluding that "the enforcement of the Third Generations of rights is not possible, and political control is the only way to verify its accomplishment, that is, to vote to change the government",[25] thus rejecting the actions brought before the courts by doctors' associations.

In contrast, in a country without the express constitutional provisions regarding the right to health as is the case of Argentina, the courts have developed a very progressive protective case law, granting amparo protection to the right to health deciding actions filed by various associations of doctors, for instance, ordering public entities to provide economic recourses in order to allow the functioning of hospitals.[26]

---

rives from a change of the legal sphere of a citizen or of collectivity; c) The State activity directed to satisfy the people's existence needs is an activity with political contents; d) That such activity can manifest itself by acts or through policies; e) That such acts can be the object of judicial control in their juridical elements, not in the political; f) That the policies, in principle, cannot be the object of judicial control but of political control; g) That such judicial impossibility cannot be understood as the rejection of the citizens' right to action." *Idem,* p. 143 ff.

[25]   The Court said: "Facing this evident incapacity of Public Administration to efficiently plan its activities, the citizens will withdraw the confidence given to their representatives by means of suffrage, as demonstration of the de-legitimating of the actors". *Idem,* p. 143.

[26]   See decision of the Appellate Chamber on Judicial Review of Administrative Actions (*Asociación de Médicos Municipales de la C.A.B.A vs. C.A.B.A.* case), of August 2002, regarding the functioning of the histopathology of the General Hospital of Agudos, *Teodoro Alvarez*; and decision of the Second Chamber of the Appellate Criminal Court of August 7, 2002, granting an amparo action filed by the *Doctors Association of the Buenos Aires Province v. IX District*, in order to improve the administration of the public hospital of Mar del Plata. See the reference in M. Claudia Caputi, "Reseña jurisprudencial. La tutela judicial de la salud y su reivindicación contra los entes estatales," in *Revista Iberoamericana de Estudios Autonómicos*, N° 2, Goberna & Derecho, Guayaquil, 2006, pp. 145-164.

IV.E. DROIT FISCAL / TAX LAW

- LA FISCALITÉ ET LE DÉVELOPPMENT / TAXATION AND DEVELOPMENT

TAXATION AND DEVELOPMENT
Case study: VENEZUELA

Serviliano Abache Carvajal[*]

PROFESSOR, CENTRAL UNIVERSITY OF VENEZUELA

I. INTRODUCTION. INTERNATIONAL TAX REGIME IN FORCE IN VENEZUELA

The principal institutions of the tax international regime now in force in Venezuela are found –for the most part– in the Income Tax Law[1], which

---

[*] Juris Doctor, Magna Cum Laude, Universidad Central de Venezuela. LLM in Tax Law with Honors, Universidad Central de Venezuela. LLM in Legal Reasoning, Outstanding, Universidad de Alicante, Spain. Undergraduate Studies (Introduction to Law) and Graduate Studies (Municipal Taxation) Professor, Universidad Central de Venezuela. Undergraduate Studies (Legal Reasoning) and Graduate Studies (Tax Assessment, Municipal Tax Law and Constitutional Tax Law) Professor, Universidad Católica Andrés Bello. Graduate Studies (State and Municipal Taxation) Professor, Universidad Metropolitana. Graduate Studies (International Taxation and International Business) Professor, Universidad Católica del Táchira. Visiting Professor (Tax Assessment), Instituto de Estudios Constitucionales. Visiting Professor (Income Tax), Universidad Nacional Autónoma de México. Winner of "Premio Academia de Ciencias Políticas y Sociales" award, 2012-2013 edition. Fellow, Venezuelan Association of Tax Law. Member and former Secretary, Procedural Tax Law Committee, Venezuelan Association of Tax Law. Member and former Secretary, Criminal Tax Law Committee, Venezuelan Association of Tax Law. Former Member of the Academic Commission, Venezuelan Association of Tax Law. Member of the Board of Directors, Venezuelan Association of Tax Law. Coordinator, Editorial Committee of Tax Law Journal (Revista de Derecho Tributario), Venezuelan Association of Tax Law. Member in Charge of Venezuelan Section of "Reseña de Fiscalidad Sudamericana" (South America Taxation Review), of Diritto e Pratica Tributaria Internazionale Journal directed by Prof. Víctor Uckmar. Coordinator, Venezuela Section of Doxa Observatory of Legal Reasoning, Universidad de Alicante, Spain, directed by Prof. Manuel Atienza.

[1] *Official Gazette of the Republic of Venezuela* N° 38.628, February 16, 2007.

provides in its Article 1 the essential foundations on which that *regime*[2] is built.

An outline of said Law will be provided in this work, following the guidelines set by the general reporter on the topic, from the viewpoint of the tax regime and its regulated institutions, which are of particular interest and efficacy from the perspective of international tax law.

The purpose of this research is to describe and comment on the Venezuelan international tax regime with its strengths and weaknesses and facilitate gaining an insight as to how it works, the tendency, benefits and principal regulations it presents, and its utility in developing the country provided it supplies incentives to attract foreign investment and, in that case, on what terms it does so or otherwise creates economic distortions and favors investors directly and their countries of residence indirectly.[3]

Notwithstanding the above, it can be said that –given the present reality of the country- there are other aspects (such as political, fiscal, regulatory and economic measures) not always advantageous to the conduct or setting up of business[4] by foreign investors and which, in the end, affect the free operation of companies, entrepreneurs, and individuals.

In sum, a review will be made of, on the one hand, the Venezuelan tax regime institutions which are most relevant from the viewpoint of international tax law and, on the other hand, the domestic regulations, policies and measures, –both tax as well as administrative– describing the scenario of rules currently in force, so that the reader can reach his own conclu-

---

[2]   An explanation of the difference between tax *system* and tax *regime* seems appropriate here as it will prove useful later on in this report. A tax *system* is understood as the integrated and coordinated set of taxes (imposts, fees and special contributions) forming part of the laws and regulations and ruled by the constitutional principles of taxation, becoming a rational and reasonable whole. Meanwhile, a tax *regime* refers to a group of overimposed taxes that do not constitute an organized, logical and integrated set and do not abide by the constitutional principles of taxation as a fundamental piece of a country's tax order. In this respect, *vid.* Abache Carvajal, Serviliano and Burgos-Irazábal, Ramón, "Parafiscalidad, sistema tributario y Libertad", in Herrera Orellana, Luis Alfonso (Coord.), *Enfoques actuales sobre Derecho y Libertad en Venezuela*, Academy of Political and Social Sciences, Caracas, 2013, pp. 275-280.

[3]   *Cf.* Bazó Pisani, Andrés E., "Incentivos fiscales y otras políticas tributarias ofrecidas por países en desarrollo. ¿Atraen inversión extranjera o desestabilizan la economía?", in Dupouy M., Elvira and De Valera, Irene (Coord.), *Temas de actualidad tributaria. Homenaje a Jaime Parra Pérez*, Academy of Political and Social Sciences – Venezuelan Association of Tax Law, Caracas, 2009, p. 155.

[4]   *Cf. Ibid.*, p. 153.

sions on whether they are in the nature of incentives or non-incentives to attract foreign investment into a developing country such as Venezuela.

1. *Worldwide and/or Territorial Income*

In direct taxation and, as part of it, specifically in regard to income tax, it is acknowledged that there are two taxation systems: (i) the territorial income-based system, or principle of territorial source, which follows objective relationship criteria, and (ii) the worldwide income-based, or principle of domicile or residence and principle of nationality, which follows subjective criteria.[5]

These systems are being applied jointly in many States. On one part, the territorial income system is applied, by which the domestic-source income of residents or non-residents in the country is taxed (objective criterion), with many of those States concurrently applying the worldwide or global income system to tax foreign-source income produced by their residents (subjective criterion).[6]

This last situation is precisely the case of Venezuela. From its first Income Tax Law, which dates back to year 1942[7], Venezuela adopted the territorial income system –with some exceptions[8]- until in year 1999 when, following an integral reform of income tax legislation[9], the Venezuelan regime additionally adopted, together with the territorial system, the worldwide income system in order to tax foreign-source revenues produced and obtained by residents or domiciled persons in Venezuela.

---

[5]   *Cf.* Evans Márquez, Ronald, *Régimen jurídico de la doble tributación internacional*, McGraw-Hill, Caracas, 1999, p. 6.

[6]   *Cf. Ibid.*, p. 8.

[7]   *Official Gazette of the Republic of Venezuela* N° 20.851, July 17, 1942.

[8]   On these exceptions, vid. Carmona Borjas, Juan Cristóbal, "Principios de la renta mundial y de la renta territorial", in De Valera, Irene (Organizer), *Comentarios a la Ley de Impuesto sobre la Renta, Academy of Political and Social Sciences-Venezuelan Association of Tax Law*, Caracas, 2000, pp. 23-29, and Carmona Borjas, Juan Cristóbal, "Factores de conexión en la legislación venezolana en materia de impuesto sobre la renta", in Sol Gil, Jesús (Coord.), *60 años de imposición a la renta en Venezuela. Evolución histórica y estudios de la legislación actual*, Venezuelan Association of Tax Law, Caracas, 2003, pp. 163-167.

[9]   *Official Gazette of the* Republic *of Venezuela* N° 5.390, Extraordinary Issue, October 22, 1999.

The regulation mentioned above is at present set forth in Article 1 of the 2007[10] Income Tax Law (ITL) along the following lines:

"Article 1: Any annual, net and disposable income obtained in cash or in kind, shall be taxed pursuant to the provisions of this Law. Unless otherwise provided in this Law, every individual or corporation, whether a resident of or domiciled in the Bolivarian Republic of Venezuela, shall pay taxes on income from any origin, whether the cause or source of income is located inside or outside the country. (…)".[11]

In view of the foregoing, it has been properly concluded that the Venezuelan income tax regime comprises three fundamental areas: (i) the taxpayer net operating income from *territorial activities*, which is determined by deducting from territorial gross income the costs and expenses incurred in the country during the fiscal year, (ii) the *inflation adjustments* on taxpayer (non-monetary) assets and liabilities (holding gains), which will increase or reduce the net operating income mentioned in (i) above, and (iii) the taxpayer net operating income from *extra-territorial* activities, which is determined by subtracting from the extra-territorial gross income the costs and expenses incurred outside the country in obtaining that income during the relevant fiscal year. From the tax resulting after applying the assessment procedure indicated above, any applicable *tax credits* will be deducted as well as any *income tax paid abroad* by the taxpayer, provided it does not exceed the highest Venezuelan tax rate, which is thirty four percent (34%).[12]

2. *Domestic and Foreign Dividends*

The dividend tax regime is regulated by Title IV, Chapter II, under "capital gains", and expounded in Articles 66 through 78 of the ITL. It sets forth, among other regulations, the meaning of dividend, how it is taxed and withheld, and certain rules applicable to foreign dividends.

---

[10] *Official Gazette of the Republic of Venezuela* N° 38.628, February 16, 2007.

[11] For a detailed study of territorial and worldwide income effective in Venezuela, vid. Paredes, Carlos Enrique, *El principio de territorialidad y el sistema de renta mundial en la Ley de Impuesto sobre la Renta venezolana*, Andersen Legal, Caracas, 2002, 283 p.

[12] *Cf.* Roche, Emilio J., "Transparencia fiscal internacional", in Sol Gil, Jesús (Coord.), *60 años de imposición a la renta en Venezuela. Evolución histórica y estudios de la legislación actual*, Venezuelan Association of Tax Law, Caracas, 2003, p. 670.

According to the sole paragraph of Article 67 of the ITL, a *dividend* is the portion that corresponds to each share of stock in the profits of stock companies and other assimilated taxpayers[13], such as, for instance, those resulting from participation quotas in limited liability companies.

A *dividend tax* is, pursuant to Article 66 *eiusdem*, a proportional tax that has its origin in such net income of the paying company that is greater than or exceeds the taxed net fiscal income. For these purposes, it is necessary to understand the meaning of: (i) net income, and (ii) taxed net fiscal income. *Net income* is the result (profits) approved by the Shareholders Meeting on the basis of the financial results.[14] Meanwhile, *taxed net fiscal income* means the one that is taxed in accordance with corporate rates.[15]

Under the previously stated rules, the calculation of the shareholder dividend tax can be summarized as follows:

$$\textbf{DNI} = \textbf{NI} - \textbf{(TNFI+EI+DRT)}^{16}$$

---

[13]   According to the First Paragraph of Article 7 of the ITL, entities *assimilated* to stock companies means: limited liability companies, (ii) limited stock partnerships (*comandita simple por acciones*) (iii) civil associations, and (iv) irregular or de facto associations incorporated as stock companies, as limited liability companies, or as limited partnerships.

[14]   For an analysis of the criteria regarding the accounting system that applies for declaring and paying dividends in Venezuela (historical accounting or updated accounting, i.e., inflation-adjusted), *vid.* Roche, Emilio J., "De la entrada en vigencia de la reforma de la Ley de Impuesto sobre la Renta de 2001 y del régimen sobre dividendos", *Impuesto sobre la Renta e ilícitos fiscales. VI Jornadas venezolanas de Derecho tributario*, Venezuelan Association of Tax Law, Caracas, 2002, pp. 159-179; and Romero-Muci, Humberto, "Naturaleza jurídica de los principios de contabilidad de aceptación general en Venezuela y su incidencia en la determinación de la renta financiera para el cálculo del impuesto sobre la renta de dividendos (análisis de los artículos 67 y 91 de la Ley de Impuesto sobre la Renta)", *Impuesto sobre la Renta e ilícitos fiscales. VI Jornadas venezolanas de Derecho tributario,* Venezuelan Association of Tax Law, Caracas, 2002, pp. 181-251.

[15]   *Cf.* Roche, Emilio J., "Parte general del Impuesto sobre la Renta. Relatoría Tema I", in Korody Tagliaferro, Juan Esteban (Coord.), *70 años del Impuesto sobre la Renta. Memorias de las XII Jornadas Venezolanas de Derecho Tributario*, volume II, Venezuelan Association of Tax Law, Caracas, 2013, p. 151.

[16]   DNI: Dividend net income; NI: net income; TNI: taxed net fiscal income; EI: exempt or exone-rated income; DRT: dividends received from third parties. In a similar sense, *Cf.*, *Idem.*

According to Article 73 of the Law, dividend taxation is subject to a thirty four percent (34%) rate and to total withholding upon being paid or credited on account.

Yet, Article 71 of the ITL introduces a very important distinction depending on whether a *domestic dividend* or *foreign dividend* regime is involved. In this respect, the first paragraph of Article 68 states that if dividends are received either (i) from enterprises incorporated and domiciled abroad or (ii) from enterprises incorporated abroad and domiciled in Venezuela, i.e., *foreign dividends*, such dividends will be treated as excluded from the net income for purposes of domestic calculations. As in the case of domestic dividends, foreign dividends are subject to a proportional tax rate of thirty four percent (34%). To this result, the dividend tax paid abroad is applicable.

Lastly, under its Article 72, the ITL provides for a *presumptive regime* on foreign dividends in the case of (i) enterprises incorporated abroad and domiciled in Venezuela or (ii) enterprises incorporated and domiciled abroad and having a permanent establishment in Venezuela, pursuant to which they must pay thirty-four percent (34%) on their net, neither exempt nor exonerated, income in excess of the taxed net income of the fiscal year, unless the branch shall prove to have reinvested and maintained in the country —for a least five years— the difference between the taxed net fiscal income and the net income.[17]

II. TAX HAVENS AND HARMFUL TAXATION

1. Concept of Tax Havens in Venezuela

It could be said that there are as many concepts or definitions of tax havens are there are tax havens, given that the semantics or terminology will depend on the criteria utilized to benefit or not benefit the user[18]. Nevertheless, apart from the difficulty of defining a tax haven, or low-tax jurisdiction, or preferential tax system, or offshore jurisdiction[19], because their

---

[17]   In this respect, *vid.* Vecchio D., Carlos A., *El impuesto al dividendo presunto de las sucursales. Especial referencia a los tratados para evitar la doble tributación*, Venezuelan Financial Law Association, Caracas, 2004, 151 p.

[18]   *Cf.* Roche, Emilio J., "Transparencia fiscal...", *cit.*, p. 666.

[19]   *Cf.* Díaz Ibarra, Valmy J., "Las reglas de transparencia fiscal internacional en Venezuela. Consecuencias de la vinculación de contribuyentes venezolanos con socie-

condition as such is subject to, among other things, political and legislative changes in the location jurisdiction, in truth it is known that it is possible to identify common characteristics in jurisdictions that are tax haven sites, such as (i) rates or aliquots that are either special, reduced or non-existent, (ii) commercial and bank secrecy, (iii) political and financial stability, (iv) absence of foreign exchange controls, (v) developed infrastructures, and (iv) self-promotion.[20]

The ITL does not define in Chapter II, Title VII on International Fiscal Transparency Regime what should be understood as *tax havens* or, as called in the ITL, *low-tax jurisdictions*. Notwithstanding the foregoing, Ruling (*Providencia*) N° SNAT/2004/232[21] has established a method –a mixed and alternative one– for qualifying tax havens based on three criteria: (i) *preferential tax system* (maximum taxation of 20% on income or capital), (ii) *black list* express inclusion (*blacklisted countries*), and (iii) *absence of double taxation agreement with an information exchange clause*. In the presence of any of these criteria, a jurisdiction will qualify as a low-tax jurisdiction or tax haven for Venezuelan purposes.[22]

The topic of tax havens and of jurisdictions with elements of *harmful tax competition*, the slight distinctions of which renders them often alike[23], is especially relevant for the international fiscal transparency regime, as it is located its core, and as from them, its application activates. Therefore, it is important to review the most relevant aspects of this particular regime.

2. International Fiscal Transparency Regime

Also known as *controlled foreign corporation rules*, or CFC rules, this regime consists in viewing entities located in tax havens or low-tax jurisdictions as non-existent or transparent. For this reason, an investor domi-

---

dades en "paraísos fiscales", in Dupouy M., Elvira and De Valera, Irene (Coord.), *Temas de actualidad tributaria. Homenaje a Jaime Parra Pérez*, Academy of Political and Social Sciences–Venezuelan Association of Tax Law, Caracas, 2009, p. 341.

[20]   *Cf.* Roche, Emilio J., "Transparencia fiscal...", *cit.*, pp. 667-669.

[21]   *Official Gazette of the Republic of Venezuela* N° 37.924, April 26, 2004.

[22]   *Cf.* Díaz Ibarra, Valmy J., *op.cit.*, p. 358.

[23]   While in tax havens the collection of income tax is not part of public finances and those places are promoted as an escape for residents of jurisdictions with high levels of taxation, jurisdictions with harmful tax competition elements are often characterized by collecting important sums of income tax and offering tax benefits for specific activities. *Cf. Ibid.*, pp. 341-342.

ciled in Venezuela or non-domiciled in Venezuela but having a permanent establishment therein, must report the income, costs and expenses attributable to such an entity (whether or not the company and its members have, as they in fact do, different legal capacities[24]), even if dividends have neither been declared nor distributed.[25]

As such, it is clear that the objectives of this regime are (i) to improve the application of the worldwide income system, given that tax is applied on such income obtained by the foreign entity that has not paid tax offshore or that has paid it at rates lower than the thirty-four percent (34%) rate of Venezuelan law, and (ii) to avoid deferral of payment of income tax in Venezuela, thus discouraging deferral of declaration and payment of dividends by the foreign entity to the Venezuelan taxpayer. Under this assumption, even if the investor does not receive any dividend payment, due to the fact that the entity is deemed transparent (as if it did not exist), the Venezuelan taxpayer must report the income, costs and expenses, and Venezuelan tax will be applied to the extra-territorial income.[26]

A. *Application Criteria*

Article 100 of the ITL sets forth that taxpayers having investments made directly, indirectly, or through intermediaries, in branches, corporations, real or personal property, shares of stock, bank or investment accounts, and any manner of interest in entities with or without legal capacity, trusts, business associations, investments funds, as well as in any other similar legal body created or organized under foreign Law and located in low-tax jurisdictions, will be subject to the application of this regime.

To these ends, it is a necessary condition that the taxpayer can decide the time for distributing profits or dividends derived from low-tax jurisdiction, or when the taxpayer has control over their administration, either directly or indirectly or through an intermediary.

On its part, Article 102 of the Law provides for those events in which an investment is deemed situated in a tax haven or low-tax jurisdiction, as follows: (i) when the accounts or investments of any type are in institutions located in that jurisdiction, (ii) when having a domicile or post office box in that jurisdiction, (ii) when the person has its actual or principal

---

[24]   *Cf.* Falcón y Tella, Ramón and Pulido Guerra, Elvira, *Derecho fiscal internacional*, Marcial Pons, Madrid, 2010, p. 243.

[25]   *Cf.* Roche, Emilio J., "Transparencia fiscal...", *cit.*, p. 673.

[26]   *Cf. Idem.*

management or administration headquarters, or has a permanent establishment in that jurisdiction, (iv) when incorporated in that jurisdiction, (v) when having physical presence in that jurisdiction, or (vi) when making, regulating, or consummating any type of legal transaction under the laws and regulations of that jurisdiction.

Fiscal transparency rules do not apply if fifty percent (50%) of the income-producing assets of the entity located in a low-tax jurisdiction are fixed assets that produce, and also, if less than twenty percent (20%) of the income obtained by the entity comes from passive receipts (*e.g.* royalties, dividends, leases, etc.). In sum, whenever the entity conducts a business or industrial activity in the foreign jurisdiction, the international fiscal transparency rules will not activate.[27]

B. *Blacklisted Countries*

Under Article 2 of Ruling (*Providencia*) N° SNAT/2004/232, the following are low-tax jurisdictions as they are expressly included in the black list: Anguilla, Antigua & Barbuda, Svalbard Archipelago, Aruba, Ascension, Belize, Bermuda, Brunei, Campione D'Italia, Commonwealth of Dominica, Commonwealth of the Bahamas, United Arab Emirates, State of Bahrain, State of Qatar, Independent State of Western Samoa, Commonwealth of Puerto Rico, Gibraltar, Grand Duchy of Luxembourg, Grenada, Greenland, Guam, Hong Kong, Cayman Islands, Christmas Island, Norfolk Island, Saint Pierre and Miquelon Island, Isle of Man, Qeshm Island, Cook Island, Cocos or Keeling Island, Channel Islands (Guernsey, Jersey, Aldemey, Great Sart, Herm, Little Sark, Brechou, Jethou and Lihou Islands), Falkland Islands, Pacific Islands, Solomon Islands, Turks & Caicos Islands, British Virgin Islands, United States Virgin Islands, Kiribati, Labuan, Macau, Malta, Montserrat, Niue, Palau, Pitcairn, French Polynesia, Principality of Andorra, Principality of Liechtenstein, Principality of Monaco, Kingdom of Swaziland, Hashemite Kingdom of Jordan, Dominican Republic, Gabonese Republic, Lebanese Republic, Republic of Albania, Republic of Angola, Republic of Cape Verde, Republic of Cyprus, Republic of Djibouti, Republic of Guyana, Republic of Honduras, Republic of Marshall Islands, Republic of Liberia, Republic of Mauritius, Republic of Nauru, Republic of Panama, Republic of Seychelles, Republic of Tunisia, Republic of Vanuatu, Republic of Yemen, Eastern Republic of Uruguay, Democratic Socialist Republic of

---

[27]   *Ibid.*, pp. 674-675.

Sri Lanka, American Samoa, Saint Vincent and the Grenadines, Saint Helena, Most Serene Republic of San Marino, Sultanate of Oman, Tokelau, Tristan da Cunha, Tuvalu, Canary Special Zone, and Ostrava Free Zone.

III. THE VENEZUELAN REGIME AND THE ADOPTION OF INTERNATIONAL TAXATION CRITERIA

In 1999, Venezuelan income tax legislation suffered an important change. By an integral reform of this fiscal sub-regime, it moved from an –exclusively– territorial system to a worldwide income system. This significant change was accompanied by the insertion of rules of international fiscal transparency and transfer pricing in the ITL, completing in 2007 the adjustment of the Venezuelan regime to the most modern international taxation trends, with the inclusion of undercapitalization or thin capitalization rules.[28] We will briefly proceed to review below each one of these changes and the adoption of international taxation criteria.

1. *Worldwide Income*

Beyond any doubt, the adoption of the worldwide income system in 1999 by the Venezuelan ITL reflects an important change in the very idea of the country, typically regarded on the list of capital importers. Even though Venezuela is still characterized as an importing country, and even more at present given the multiple internal problems and official measures that discourage domestic production as will be noticed further on, the truth is that in an attempt to conform to worldwide economy globalization and commercial integration of countries, the Venezuelan tax regime has included this modification that actually revisits and takes into account the *principle of taxpaying capacity* set forth in Article 316 of the Constitution[29], as it captures the entire taxpayer income regardless of the location of its source.[30]

---

[28] *Cf.* Díaz Ibarra, Valmy J., *op.cit.*, pp. 352-353.

[29] *Official Gazette of the Republic of Venezuela* N° 36.860, December 30, 1999, later reprinted with some corrections in the *Official Gazette of the Republic of Venezuela* N° 5.453, Extraordinary Issue, March 24, 2000. Its first amendment as well as the whole text of the Constitution was published in the *Official Gazette of the Republic of Venezuela* N° 5.908 Extraordinary Issue, February 19, 2009.

[30] Evans Márquez, Ronald, *Régimen jurídico... cit.*, p. 12.

Said ITL reform and adoption of the worldwide system meant that since 1999 all foreign source income produced and obtained by residents or domiciled persons in Venezuela became taxed in accordance with the new regime.

2. *International Fiscal Transparency*

As previously stated, the purpose of international fiscal transparency, or controlled foreign companies, is to improve the worldwide income system and consists in taxing passive income (*e.g.*, dividends, royalties, etc.) generated from foreign investments located in tax havens or low-tax jurisdictions, to the Venezuelan taxpayer controlling such investment, whether or not the income is distributed to the Venezuelan shareholder.[31] In other words, for Venezuelan purposes, the foreign entity is deemed *transparent* –hence, the name of the regime– and for this reason the Venezuelan taxpayer controlling such entity shall report and pay tax on income, as if it were his own, obtained in the tax haven. These rules constitute a presumptive lifting of the corporate veil (disregard of the legal entity).

3. *Transfer Pricing*

The system of transfer prices was first introduced in Venezuelan income tax regulation with the 1999 reform, following the guidelines of the Brazilian legislation on the matter. With the legislative amendment of 2001, it was changed entirely by adopting the criteria and directives of the Organization for Economic Cooperation and Development (OECD), such as applying to interest the comparable free price or comparable uncontrolled price (CUP) method. With the most recent reform of the ITL, occurred later in 2007, the rules on the matter remain unchanged.

Transfer pricing rules are contained in Chapter III, Title VII, Article 111 through 170 of the Venezuelan ITL. Their purpose is none other than achieving that the financial results –departing from fixed prices and general contracting terms– of transactions (supply of goods, provision of services) between *related parties* be similar for tax purposes to the results that would be obtained between *non-related or independent parties*. All of it involves application of the *arm's length principle*[32], i.e. that no prices

---

[31]   *Cf.* Díaz Ibarra, Valmy J., *op.cit.*, pp. 353-354.

[32]   *Cf.* Andrade, Betty, "La subcapitalización y los precios de transferencia en el régimen venezolano", *Jornadas Internacionales. Cuestiones actuales de Derecho tributario*, Foundation of Administrative Law Studies, Caracas, 2007, p. 218.

–lower or higher than market value– be fixed that may *transfer* and locate a greater benefit in the country with the lowest taxation or a greater expense in the country with higher taxation.[33]

A *related party*, according to Article 116 of the ITL means an enterprise that participates directly or indirectly in the management, control or capital of another enterprise, or when the same persons participate directly or indirectly in the direction, control or capital of both enterprises, following in this sense the guidelines delimited in that respect by the OECD.[34]

These rules, as well as the ones we will comment below, act as mechanisms against tax avoidance and prevent the abuse of forms, with the ultimate purpose of reducing international tax evasion.[35]

4. *Thin Capitalization*

Undercapitalization or thin capitalization rules were introduced for the first time in the ITL with the 2007 reform. These rules or *antiavoidance clauses* are intended to *avoid* (i) the transfer of the income tax base (*profit shifting*) from one jurisdiction to another, (ii) the concealing of dividend payments and consequently the non-payment of dividend tax in the country of origin, and (iii) the creation of a fictitious expense to reduce the tax base of the enterprise that repays a loan.[36] Pursuant to Venezuelan law, a *thinly capitalized enterprise* is that whose debts to a related party from a received loan exceed its stockholders' equity; that is, its debt/equity *ratio* evidences excessive indebtedness of the borrowing enterprise under a financing (loan) transaction with a related party (lending enterprise).[37]

In effect, Article 118 of the ITL limits the deductibility of interest paid directly or indirectly to related parties. In order to determine if the amount of debts exceeds the net equity of the taxpayer, the yearly average balance of the taxpayer debts to independent parties is subtracted from the yearly average balance of its net equity.[38]

---

[33]   *Cf.* Falcón y Tella, Ramón and Pulido Guerra, Elvira, *op.cit.*, p. 231.

[34]   *Cf. Idem.*

[35]   *Cf. Ibid.*, p. 223.

[36]   *Cf.* Fraga Pittaluga, Luis, "Subcapitalización y reclasificación de los intereses no deducibles", in Korody Tagliaferro, Juan Esteban (Coord.), *70 años del Impuesto sobre la Renta. Memorias de las XII Jornadas Venezolanas de Derecho Tributario*, volume II, Venezuelan Tax Law Association, Caracas, 2013, pp. 374-375.

[37]   *Cf. Ibid.*, pp. 375-376.

[38]   *Cf. Ibid.*, pp. 406-407.

Lastly, the Venezuelan rule provides that such portion of the amount of debts incurred by the taxpayer directly or indirectly with related parties, and that exceeds the average balance of net equity, will be treated as net equity in any event. In this manner, it has been considered that, contrary to what happens in other legislations, the Venezuelan rule does not permit to reclassify non-deductible interest as dividends, but it rather incorporates such interest to the net equity of the taxpayer.[39]

IV. DTAs AND INFORMATION EXCHANGE AGREEMENTS

The OECD Model on income and capital provides in Article 26.1 for the *exchange of information* of tax relevance between contracting States, not only for the application of the agreement but also when pertinent for managing any domestic tax –at any political territorial level– even if said tax is not expressly included in the agreement, as long as no imposition contrary to the agreement is involved.[40] It is –precisely– the main source of exchange of information in Venezuela.[41]

1. *Permitted Sources and Types of Information Exchange*

In fact, the actual Double Taxation Agreements (DTAs) ratified by Venezuela[42] constitute one of its sources for conducting *information ex-*

---

[39]   Cf. *Ibid.*, pp. 420-421. In the same sense, *vid.* Castillo Carvajal, Juan Carlos, "Relatoría general. Tema II. Temas especiales de la Ley de Impuesto sobre la Renta", in Korody Tagliaferro, Juan Esteban (Coord.), *70 años del Impuesto sobre la Renta. Memorias de las XII Jornadas Venezolanas de Derecho Tributario*, volume II, Venezuelan Association of Tax Law, Caracas, 2013, p. 57. Against, *vid.* Andrade, Betty, *op.cit.*, pp. 257-260.

[40]   Cf. Falcón y Tella, Ramón and Pulido Guerra, Elvira, *op.cit.*, pp. 197-198.

[41]   For a detailed study of Tax Administration cooperation, with special reference to the Venezuelan case, *vid.* Carmona Borjas, Juan Cristóbal, "Colaboración y asistencia mutua entre Administraciones tributarias", *Revista de Derecho Tributario*, N° 100, Venezuelan Association of Tax Law, Caracas, 2003, pp. 161-219.

[42]   Article 122 of the Venezuelan Organic Tax Code (*Official Gazette of the Republic of Venezuela* N° 37.301, October 17, 2001), sets forth that: "The Tax Administration will have the faculties, powers and duties prescribed in the Tax Administration Act and other laws and regulations and it may especially: (…) 11. Enter into inter-institutional information exchange agreements with local and international agencies provided that the classified nature of such information is protected as set forth in Article 126 of this Code and ensuring that the information supplied will be used by tax competent authorities only". According to Article 126 *eiusdem*: "Any information and documentation obtained by any

change with other States. As the DTAs that Venezuela has entered into follow –basically- the OECD Model, their exchange provisions, in line with Article 26.1 of the model, consist in enabling competent authorities to exchange the information required in order to *apply* the various agreements made, but they are not restricted to the *scope of application* of the DTA and enable information requests on transactions in tax havens and in jurisdictions that have elements of harmful tax competition.

The information received by Venezuela and the States with which it has entered into such agreements must be kept secret, as must the information obtained on the basis of the local Law of Venezuela and the other State, and will be communicated to authorities (including Courts and administrative agencies) competent for the management or collection of the agreement-regulated taxes, the related declaration or execution processes, and the decision of the appeals filed against any submitted claims.

2. *Information Exchange Restrictions contained in the DTAs*

The first limit established by DTAs entered into by Venezuela is that the reports obtained from the information exchange can be used by the authorities only for *these purposes*. As such, by argument to the contrary, any use for *purposes other than those* related to the application of the agreement would entail a violation of the latter.

On the other hand, Venezuelan DTAs establish the typical three limits of the OECD Model directed to not imposing on the contracting States an obligation to (i) take any administrative actions contrary to their administrative practice or legislation or contrary to those of the other contracting State, (ii) provide information that cannot be obtained on the basis of their own legislation or in the exercise of their regular administrative practice or that of the other Contracting State, and (iii) provide information that discloses trade, industrial or professional secrets, trade procedures or information the transmission of which is contrary to public order.

Lastly, beyond the established DTAs limits on information exchange between foreign and Venezuelan Tax Administrations, it is true that no agreement can affect the guaranties set out in the Constitution of Venezuela. For this reason, the *inviolability of home and correspondence*

---

means by the Tax Administration will be classified and will be communicated only to the judicial or any other authority in the cases set forth by the laws. Any inappropriate use of classified information will bring about the application of the respective penalties".

cannot be ignored by the agreements, for being individual and constitutional rights of the taxpayers.[43]

V. SPECIAL TERRITORIAL TAX REGIMES

In general, customs territories are constituted by geographic spaces having a special legislation that creates and delimits their special tax regime with extra-fiscal (tax benefit) purposes, for establishing a certain activity, customs controls and customs duties. For tax purposes, it is possible to distinguish in Venezuela three types of customs territories: (i) *free zones,* (ii) *free ports,* and (iii) *free areas (zonas libres).*

1. *Free Zone Tax Regime*

Free zones are defined in Article 2 of the Venezuelan Free Zone Act[44] as "[T]he area of land physically delimited and subject to a special tax regime (...) where legal entities that for the purposes of this Act are authorized to engage in producing and marketing goods for export as well as in providing services related to international trade". In this manner, the objective of the State is the *development of a specific activity* (industry, trade or service) in an economically depressed area that is artificially delimited in the Act that creates that zone.

The principles contained in the Free Zone Act are expounded in its Regulations[45], which set forth the conditions and parameters for the creation, extension, reduction and termination of free zones.

There are three free zones in Venezuela, to wit: (i) *Zona Franca Industrial, Comercial y de Servicios ATUJA (ZOFRAT)*[46], located in the San Francisco Municipality, city of Maracaibo, State of Zulia, under the authority and control of the Principal Customs of Maracaibo, (ii) *Zona*

---

[43]   *Cf.* León Rojas, Andrés Eloy, "La doble tributación internacional. Diferencia entre países desarrollados y en desarrollo", *IV Jornadas Venezolanas de Derecho Tributario,* Venezuelan Association of Tax Law, Caracas, 1998, p. 324.

[44]   *Official Gazette of the Republic of Venezuela* N° 34.772, August 8, 1991.

[45]   Decree N° 2.492 of 4 July 2003, *Official Gazette of the Republic of Venezuela* N° 37.734, July 17, 2003.

[46]   *Official Gazette of the Republic of Venezuela* N° 36.096, November 29, 1996.

Franca Industrial, Comercial y de Servicios de Paraguaná[47], located in the Paraguaná Peninsula, State of Falcón, under the authority and control of the Principal Customs of Las Piedras de Paraguaná, and (iii) *Zona Franca Industrial, Comercial y de Servicios de Cumaná*[48], located in the Autonomous Sucre Municipality, City of Cumaná, State of Sucre, under the authority and control of the Principal Customs of Puerto Sucre.

2. *Free Port Tax Regime*

On their part, *free ports* consist of a customs exemption regime boosting, via tax benefits and/or economic activity establishment benefits, the *economic development of a portion of territory* that in principle is economically depressed. As opposed to free zones, these areas are territorially delimited by the area of a specific political territorial entity and are created by special law.

Free ports in Venezuela are located in Santa Elena de Uairén[49] and in the State of Nueva Esparta[50]. The first one consists of a preferential tax regime to encourage and promote the social and economic development of the region. This exempting regime covers the activities performed within the duly delimited territory of the free port. The goods entering under this free port regime do not pay import duties, although they are subject to the fee for customs services (1% *ad valorem*), nor are they subject to payment of domestic taxes, provided the goods are shipped for consumption at the free port.[51]

The second one consists of a preferential (exempting) tax regime to encourage and favor the social and economic development of the State of Nueva Esparta. Goods entering under the free port regime are exempt from payment of import duties, Value Added Tax (VAT), taxes on ciga-

---

[47]   *Official Gazette of the Republic of Venezuela* N° 5.145, Extraordinary Issue, April 30, 1997.

[48]   *Official Gazette of the Republic of Venezuela* N° 36.249, July 16, 1997.

[49]   Created by Decree N° 3.112, of 16 December 1998, dictating the Regulations on the Free Port of Santa Elena de Uairén System, *Official Gazette of the Republic of Venezuela* N° 5.288, Extraordinary Issue, January 13, 1999.

[50]   Created by the Free Port Act of the State of Nueva Esparta, of 3 August 2000, *Official Gazette of the Republic of Venezuela* N° 37.006, August 3, 2000.

[51]   Consulted in: http://www.seniat.gob.ve/portal/page/portal/MANEJADOR CONTENIDOSENIAT/04ADUANAS/4.4REGIMENESTERRITOR/4.4.1PUERTOSLIB RES/4.4.1.1 SANTA_ELENA, February 15, 2014.

rettes and manufactured tobacco, alcohol and alcoholic species, matches, and the like –unless domestic law determines otherwise– but are subject to payment of the fee for customs services (1% *ad valorem*).[52]

3. *Free Areas (Zonas Libres) Tax Regime*

Lastly, *free areas* or *zonas libres* are a mixture of the two previously commented regimes, as they are intended for the *development of a portion of the territory by means of a specific activity*, usually in an economically depressed area that is also delimited by the space of a specific political territorial entity.

They comprise the Culture, Science and Technology Free Zone of the State of Mérida (*Zona Libre Cultural, Científica y Tecnológica* (ZOLCCYT))[53] and the Free Zone for Tourist Investment Development of Paraguaná Peninsula (*Zona Libre para el Fomento de la Inversión Turística de la Península de Paraguaná*)[54]. The first of them is located in the State of Mérida in the territory of Libertador, Campo Elías, Sucre and Santos Marquina Municipalities, under the control of the Principal Ecologic Customs of Mérida. Its special preferential tax regime was established to promote the production, dissemination and distribution of the region's cultural, scientific and technological activities. Cultural, scientific and technological goods and services produced in the country, as well as goods and their parts coming from abroad and entering Venezuela with destination to the ZOLCCYT, are subject to the following preferential regime: (i) no customs duties, (ii) exempt from VAT and any other domestic tax directly or indirectly imposed on their import or sale, (iii) no customs service fees, and (iv) no tariff and para-tariff rates, except for those of a health-related nature.

---

[52] Consulted in: http://www.seniat.gob.ve/portal/page/portal/MANEJADOR CONTENIDO_SENIAT/04ADUANAS/4.4REGIMENES_TERRITOR/4.4.1PUERTOS LIBRES4.4.1.2.NUEVA_ESPARTA, February 15, 2014.
[53] Created by the Act on the Cultural, Scientific and Technology Free Zone of the State of Merida, of July 14, 1995, *Official Gazette of the Republic of Venezuela* N° 4.937, Extraordinary Issue, July 14, 1995; expounded by the Regulations on Cultural, Scientific and Technology Free Zone of the State of Merida, of September 9,1998, *Official Gazette of the Republic of Venezuela* N° 36.611, December 19, 1998.
[54] Created by the Act on Creation and Regime of the Free Zone for Tourist Investment Development of Paraguaná Peninsula, State of Falcón, of August 6, 1998, *Official Gazette of the Republic of Venezuela* N° 36.517, August 14, 1998.

The second one (Free Zone for Tourist Investment Development of Paraguaná Peninsula) is located in Paraguaná Peninsula, in the area comprised by the territory of Carirubana, Falcón, and Los Taques Municipalities of the State of Falcón, under the control of Las Piedras-Paraguaná Principal Customs. Its regime consists in that the income obtained by tourist service providers on new infrastructure investments made by persons authorized to operate within the free zone, are exempt for a period of ten years, prior verification that the investment has been made.

VI. TAX MEASURES AND INCENTIVES TO ATTRACT INVESTMENT AND ECONOMIC ACTIVITY INTO DEVELOPING COUNTRIES AND INTO COUNTRIES WITH HIGH LEVELS OF POVERTY

Tax incentives have always represented an important tool of fiscal policy[55], especially in developing countries, where they are used to compensate for other negative factors that may discourage foreign investment.[56] Already since the beginning of year 2000, consideration was being given to the necessity for the country to carefully revise incentive policies to render them in line with postulates of economic reactivation and also to attain levels of competitiveness with other countries of the region.[57]

But reality tells otherwise: Venezuelan is now –and ever more– far from competing with its neighboring countries, precisely due to the fiscal, regulatory, political and economic measures it has been establishing, unfavorable to opening to and welcoming foreign investment.

Presently, a number of fiscal measures are in force in Venezuela *formally* directed to attract economic activities, investments and capitals[58], being both *domestic* (in national laws) as well as *international* (via treaties and

---

[55]   *Cf.* Evans Márquez, Ronald, "Los convenios para evitar la doble tributación internacional y otros aspectos internacionales de la política tributaria venezolana", in De Valera, Irene (Organizer), *Comentarios a la Ley de Impuesto sobre la Renta*, Academy of Political and Social Sciences-Venezuelan Association of Tax Law, Caracas, 2000, p. 58.

[56]   *Cf.* Bazó Pisani, Andrés E., *op.cit.*, p. 172.

[57]   *Cf.* Evans Márquez, Ronald, "*Los convenios para evitar…*" *cit.*, p. 59.

[58]   On the matter, *vid.* Palacios Márquez, Leonardo, "Medidas fiscales para el desarrollo económico", *Revista de Derecho Tributario*, N° 97, Venezuelan Association of Tax Law, Caracas, 2002, pp. 179-224, and Sol Gil, Jesús, "Medidas fiscales adoptadas en Venezuela para el desarrollo económico", *Revista de Derecho Tributario*, N° 97, Venezuelan Association of Tax Law, Caracas, 2002, pp. 225-248.

agreements), such those established with the Southern Common Market (MERCOSUR)[59], the Latin American Integration Association (ALADI)[60] and the Bolivarian Alternative of Latin America and the Caribbean (ALBA), among others, of which Venezuelan forms part and which represent cases of Latin American integration and harmonization.

In effect, one of the main objectives of MERCOSUR, according to Article 1 of the Asunción Treaty is to achieve "[f]ree circulation of goods, services and production factors between the countries through, among other things, the elimination of customs duties and non-tariff restrictions to the circulation of merchandise, and any other equivalent measure", "[e]stablishment of a common external tariff (...)", and "[c]o-ordination of macroeconomic and sectorial policies between States Parties on: foreign trade, agriculture, industry, tax, monies, exchange and capitals, services, customs, transportation and communications, and any others that may be agreed (...)", which evidences the relevance –for tax purposes– of said Treaty.

In this respect, in order to achieve the general objectives and postulates of MERCOSUR, it has been considered that the Venezuelan tax regime should be modified in, among other aspects, the following: (i) progressive harmonization and elimination of para-fiscal contributions, (ii) flexibilization of foreign currency control for countries of the block, (iii) revision of exporter VAT credit recovery system, (iv) implementation of income tax incentives, and (v) entering into DTAs with member countries of the block.[61]

However, apart from the existence and effectiveness of a series of tax measures and incentives prescribed in quite a number of treaties –which will be mentioned further on under *VIII. Investment Protection, Taxation, Bilateral and Multilateral Exchange Treaties*–, and also apart from local laws –as will be analyzed under *VII. Income Tax Credits (Reductions)*–,

---

[59] For a study on the tax aspects of MERCOSUR and, in general, of Latin American integration, *vid.* Valdés Costa, Ramón, "Aspectos fiscales de la integración con especial referencia a América Latina", *Revista de Derecho Tributario*, N° 58, Venezuelan Association of Tax Law, Caracas, 1993, pp. 7-18.

[60] On ALADI and tax harmonization in Latin America, *vid.* Montero Traibel, José Pedro, "La armonización tributaria en los procesos de integración", *IV Jornadas Venezolanas de Derecho Tributario*, Venezuelan Association of Tax Law, Caracas, 1998, pp. 279-311.

[61] *Cf.* Atencio Valladares, Gilberto, "Cuestiones tributarias del Mercosur: aproximaciones desde el Derecho tributario venezolano", *Revista de Derecho Tributario*, N° 141, Venezuelan Association of Tax Law, Caracas, 2014, pp. 8-14.

the Venezuelan Government has systematically adopted a series of guidelines that contribute little to the development and economic stability of the country, or to attract foreign investment or maintain domestic investment, and that without their mention –even succinct– this national report would be incomplete.

On the one hand, there are the tax matters *per se*. In fact, the National Integrated Service of Customs and Tax Administration (*Servicio Nacional Integrado de Administración Aduanera y Tributaria*-SENIAT) (which is the federal tax administration agency and highest competent authority in the area) has designed and implemented a number of measures within the framework of the highly-publicized –and questioned– "Zero Evasion Plan", which consists in imposing fines and penalties including temporary closing on enterprises for their purported failure to comply, in both cases, with formal obligations in indirect taxes.[62] Also to be borne in mind is the number of para-fiscal contributions that have been recently dictated, counting more than thirty to date, which has generated an important increase of taxes that do not integrate in a consistent and organized manner with tax laws and regulations, and that in turn increase the accumulated tax pressure on taxpayers.[63] This would not seem to make much sense when, in addition, one must take into account that Venezuela is a country that depends on its *oil revenues* –rather than its tax revenues-, such oil revenues having represented since 1950 and in the average more than ninety percent (90%) of the *total revenues* of the country.[64]

On the other hand, combined with the fiscal measures, it has become internationally known[65] that since 2001 the Venezuelan government has followed a negative trend in connection with the property right protected un-

---

[62]   *Cf*. Abache Carvajal, Serviliano, "La responsabilidad patrimonial del Estado "Administrador, Juez y Legislador" tributario venezolano especial referencia al paradigmático caso del procedimiento de verificación" (National Report-Venezuela), *Memorias de las XXV Jornadas Latinoamericanas de Derecho Tributario*, volume II, Abeledo Perrot-Latin *American Institute of Tax Law-Colombian Institute of Tax Law*, Buenos Aires, 2010, pp. 349-350.

[63]   *Cf*. Abache Carvajal, Serviliano and Burgos-Irazábal, Ramón, "*Parafiscalidad…*" *cit*., p. 256.

[64]   *Cf*. Ross, Maxim, *¿Capitalismo salvaje o Estado depredador?*, Editorial Alfa, Caracas, 2008, pp. 21-22.

[65]   *Cf*. Rondón García, Andrea, Herrera Orellana, Luis Alfonso and Arias Castillo, Tomás A., "Case Study: Private Property Abolition in Venezuela", International Property Rights Index. 2010 Report, American for Tax Reform Foundation/Property Rights Alliance, Washington, 2010, pp. 55-57.

der Article 115 of the 1999 Constitution. According to the *International Property Rights Index 2012*, Venezuela occupied the last place in the world (130/130) in physical protection of property rights, and was in next to last place (129/130) in respect of intellectual property rights. While in the *International Property Rights Index 2013*[66] Venezuela "improved" in both cases (123/130 in physical protection of property rights and 119/130 in respect of intellectual property rights), it is last (130/130) insofar as legal and political environment, which in turn comprises, among other things, the judicial independence (130/130) and Rule of Law (129/130) indexes. Measures such as occupations, seizures, expropriations, price controls, etc., account for the above.

According to the Venezuelan Property Rights Watch Group, from 2007 to 2011 there have been 3,355 private property violations in Venezuela, distributed as follows: (i) 1,911 violations arising from "rescuing" lands fit for agriculture; (ii) 915 violations against the property of industries and businesses, and (iii) 529 encroachments or attempts of encroachment.

These actions, as can be noticed, instead of attracting economic activity, investment and capitals to the country, have had a negative effect internationally known, in view of the departure of important corporations and economic groups unwilling to continue to tolerate –or, simply, unable to keep in existence with– these guidelines and policies of the State.

VII. INCOME TAX CREDITS (REDUCTIONS)

In the past, various forms of credits (reductions) in the matter of income tax have been established as internal fiscal measures directed to attract economic activity, investments and capitals. At present, two forms of credits are regulated, i.e.: (i) for *new investments* in (1) industrial, agro-industrial, construction, electricity, telecommunications, science and technology activities, (2) tourist services, (3) agricultural, livestock, fishing or fish farming activities, and (4) preservation, defense and improvement of the environment; and (ii) for *excess payments*.

1. *Reductions for New Investments*

By disposition of Article 56 of the ITL a ten percent (10%) tax reduction is granted on the amount of new investments made in the five years

---

[66] Consulted in: http://www.internationalpropertyrightsindex.org/profile? location=Vene zuela, February 16, 2014.

following the effective date of that Law[67], to owners of income arising out of *industrial and agro-industrial, construction, electricity, telecommunications, science and technology activities* and, in general, all industrial activities representing an investment in advanced or cutting-edge technology, in new fixed assets other than lands and used to effectively increase production capacity, or to new enterprises, provided not previously used in other enterprises.

At the same time, pursuant to the aforesaid Law the owners of income obtained from the provision of *tourist services* –enrolled in the National Touristic Register–, are entitled to a seventy five percent (75%) credit on the amount of new investments used in building hotels, lodgings and inns, expanding, improving or refurnishing existing buildings or services, providing any tourist service or training their employees.

In the case of *agricultural, livestock, fishing or fish farming*, the credit will be of eighty percent (80%) on the value of new investments made in the area of influence of the production unit and intended for mutual benefit, both for the unit itself as well as for the community where it is inserted. A similar reduction will be granted to the *tourist activity, for community investments*, when such investments are made by small and medium-sized industries of the sector.

A ten percent (10%) credit, additional to the above, is also established on the amount of investment in assets, programs and activities for the *preservation, defense and improvement of the environment.*

Lastly, it must be taken into account that reductions for new investment in *fixed assets* must be made with figures adjusted by the *inflation adjustment system* rather than at historical cost[68], on one part and, on the other, that all the credits previously mentioned above can be carried over to the next three (3) fiscal years.

2. Credits for Overpayment (tax credit)

The ITL also provides, in its Article 58, that if in case of advanced payments or payments on account arising out of withholding tax the taxpayer has paid more than the tax accrued in the respective fiscal year,

---

[67]   On the various possible interpretations of the five year term for using the credit, *vid.* Roche, Emilio J., "Parte general...", *cit.*, pp. 141-148.

[68]   *Vid.* Ruling of the Supreme Court of Justice, Political-Administrative Chamber, case: *Goodyear de Venezuela C.A.*, March 4, 2008.

there is a right to "subtract" such excess in future tax returns and subsequent fiscal years (tax credit), until concurrence with the amount of such excess or credit, without detriment to the right of refund.

VIII. INVESTMENT PROTECTION, TAXATION, BILATERAL AND MULTILATERAL EXCHANGE TREATIES

Jointly with the DTAs, the Bilateral Treaties for the Protection of Investments (BITs) appear internationally as the minimum legal framework necessary to promote investments in countries and, consequently, must be part of the external economic agenda of Venezuela as basic instruments to develop a State policy aimed at improving the legal conditions necessary for foreign investment[69], in harmony with point VI above (Tax Measures and Incentives...).

As it is well known, one of the factors that can adversely affect investment flow between countries is –precisely- the phenomenon of double or multiple taxation of the same income or capital. This has generated an open and ever growing interest in countries to combat such pathology, as currently evidenced by the more than 2,000 agreements made and in force throughout the world.[70]

1. Countries with which Venezuela has signed BITs

According to the Venezuelan National Council for Investment Promotion (CONAPRI): "[t]he main objective being sought by Venezuela with the signing of these Treaties is to encourage investment and increase the amount of flows of foreign capital towards its territory. In addition, favoring investment entails the promotion of the creation of jobs and technology development or transfer. This objective relies in the undisputable fact that a Bilateral Treaty with clear rules of mandatory execution, aimed at protecting the foreign investor, reduces the risks that may be encountered by the latter".[71]

Currently in Venezuela there are 26 BITs effective with: Germany[72], Argentina[73], Barbados[74], Belarus[75], Belgium-Luxembourg[76], Brazil[77], Can-

---

[69]   *Cf.* Evans Márquez, Ronald, "Los convenios para evitar..." *cit.*, p. 61.

[70]   *Cf. Idem.*

[71]   Consulted in: http://www.conapri.org, February 15, 2014.

[72]   *Official Gazette of the Republic of Venezuela* N° 36.383, January 28, 1998.

ada[78], Costa Rica[79], Cuba[80], Chile[81], Denmark[82], Ecuador[83], Spain[84], France[85], Great Britain and Northern Ireland[86], Iran[87], Lithuania[88], Paraguay[89], Portugal[90], Peru[91], Czech Republic[92], Russia[93], Sweden[94], Switzerland[95], Uruguay[96], and Vietnam[97].

---

[73] *Official Gazette of the Republic of Venezuela* N° 35.578, November 1st, 1994.

[74] *Official Gazette of the Republic of Venezuela* N° 4.853, Extraordinary Issue, February 8, 1995.

[75] *Official Gazette of the Republic of Venezuela* N° 38.894, March 24, 2008.

[76] *Official Gazette of the Republic of Venezuela* N° 37.357, January 4, 2002.

[77] *Official Gazette of the Republic of Venezuela* N° 36.268, August 13, 1997.

[78] *Official Gazette of the Republic of Venezuela* N° 5.207, Extraordinary Issue, January 20, 1998.

[79] *Official Gazette of the Republic of Venezuela* N° 36.383, January 28, 1998.

[80] *Official Gazette of the Republic of Venezuela* N° 37.913, April 5, 2004.

[81] *Official Gazette of the Republic of Venezuela* N° 4.830, Extraordinary Issue, December 29, 1994.

[82] *Official Gazette of the Republic of Venezuela* N° 5.080, Extraordinary Issue, July 23, 1996.

[83] *Official Gazette of the Republic of Venezuela* N° 4.802, Extraordinary Issue, November 2, 1994.

[84] *Official Gazette of the Republic of Venezuela* N° 36.281, September 1st, 1997.

[85] *Official Gazette of the Republic of Venezuela* N° 37.896, March 11, 2004.

[86] *Official Gazette of the Republic of Venezuela* N° 36.010, July 30, 1996.

[87] *Official Gazette of the Republic of Venezuela* N° 38.389, March 2, 2006.

[88] *Official Gazette of the Republic of Venezuela* N° 5.089, Extraordinary Issue, July 23, 1996.

[89] *Official Gazette of the Republic of Venezuela* N° 36.301, September 29, 1997.

[90] *Official Gazette of the Republic of Venezuela* N° 4.846, Extraordinary Issue, January 26, 1995.

[91] *Official Gazette of the Republic of Venezuela* N° 36.266, August 11, 1997.

[92] *Official Gazette of the Republic of Venezuela* N° 36.002, July 17, 1996.

[93] *Official Gazette of the Republic of Venezuela* N° 39.191, June 2, 2009.

[94] *Official Gazette of the Republic of Venezuela* N° 5.192, Extraordinary Issue, December 18, 1997.

[95] *Official Gazette of the Republic of Venezuela* N° 4.801, Extraordinary Issue, November 1st, 1994.

[96] *Official Gazette of the Republic of Venezuela* N° 36.519, August 18, 1998.

Similarly, Chapter VIII of the Group of Three Trade Liberalization Agreement, concerning investments, provides for an Investment Promotion and Protection Agreement between Mexico, Colombia and Venezuela[98] [99].

2. *Countries with which Venezuela has signed DTAs*

Beginning in 1990, Venezuela was open to enter into DTAs with the principal countries of the world[100]. To this date, Venezuela has signed 31 Agreements[101] with the following countries[102]: Germany[103], Austria[104], Bar-

---

[97] *Official Gazette of the Republic of Venezuela* N° 39.170, May 4, 2009.

[98] *Official Gazette of the Republic of Venezuela* N° 4.833, Extraordinary Issue, December 29, 1994.

[99] On January 25, 2012, Venezuela denounced the Convention on the Settlement of Investment Disputes between States and Nationals of Other States, to which it had been a party since 1993. Such denunciation had full legal effects 6 months after its notice pursuant to Article 71 of the Agreement and as result it is not longer possible for a foreign investor to bring to the International Center for Settlement of Investment Disputes (ICSID) the legal disputes arising in connection with its investment in Venezuela, unless the foreign investor has timely accepted an arbitration offer from Venezuela under some Treaty or convention made between the State of origin of that investor and Venezuela.

[100] *Cf.* Evans Márquez, Ronald, "Los convenios para evitar..." *cit.*, p. 61.

[101] It is important to mention that the position of the Venezuelan government in DTA negotiations has been of wide openness to eliminate tax barriers with the contracting States, and that it is even considered that this position should have been more moderate given that the rates granted by Venezuela to those countries have been significantly below the average granted by other developing countries. This has a twofold reading: (i) Venezuela has lost in its collection of those items, which in turn reduces the tax revenues of the State, or (ii) Venezuela offers greater advantages than other countries of the region to foreign investors. *Cf. Ibid.*, pp. 65-66. Another important topic is that the OECD Model was not designed based on the reality of Latin American Countries. For this reason, its implementation by countries like Venezuela has generated no little inconvenience in practice. This explains why, among other reasons, the Latin American Institute of Tax Law (*Instituto Latinoamericano de Derecho Tributario*-ILADT) (www.iladt.org) has taken the excellent initiative and difficult task, by the team including professors Addy Mazz, Antonio Hugo Figueroa, Heleno Taveira Torres, Jacques Malherbe, Natalia Quiñones Cruz, and Pasquale Pistone, of preparing the *ILADT Model of Multila-teral Convention on Double Taxation for Latin America*, which responds to the distinctive features, realities and needs of countries of the region. The Model can be viewed at http://www.iuet.org.uy/docs/Modelo_Multilateral_ILADT_FINAL.pdf, February 19, 2014. On the other hand, for an analysis of DTAs in Latin America based on the Andean Pact, *vid.* Uckmar, Víctor, "Los tratados internacionales en materia tributaria", en Uckmar, Víctor (Coord.), *Curso de Derecho tributario internacional*, volume I, Temis, Bogotá, 2003, pp. 104-110.

[102] Consulted in: http://www.seniat.gob.ve/portal/page/portal/PORTALSENIAT, February 15, 2014.

bados[105], Belarus[106], Belgium[107], Brazil[108], Canada[109], China[110], Korea[111], Cuba[112], Denmark[113], United Arab Emirates[114], Spain[115], United States[116], France[117], Indonesia[118], Iran[119], Italy[120], Kuwait[121], Malaysia[122], Norway[123], The Netherlands[124] (denounced), Portugal[125], Qatar[126], United Kingdom[127],

---

[103]   *Official Gazette of the Republic of Venezuela* N° 36.266, August 11, 1997.

[104]   *Official Gazette of the Republic of Venezuela* N° 38.598, January 5, 2007.

[105]   *Official Gazette of the Republic of Venezuela* N° 5.507, Extraordinary Issue, December 13, 2000.

[106]   *Official Gazette of the Republic of Venezuela* N° 39.095, January 9, 2009.

[107]   *Official Gazette of the Republic of Venezuela* N° 5.269, Extraordinary Issue, October 22, 1998.

[108]   *Official Gazette of the Republic of Venezuela* N° 38.344, December 27, 2005.

[109]   *Official Gazette of the Republic of Venezuela* N° 37.927, April 29, 2004.

[110]   *Official Gazette of the Republic of Venezuela* N° 38.089, December 17, 2004.

[111]   *Official Gazette of the Republic of Venezuela* N° 38.598, January 5, 2007.

[112]   *Official Gazette of the Republic of Venezuela* N° 38.086, December 14, 2004.

[113]   *Official Gazette of the Republic of Venezuela* N° 37.219, June 14, 2001.

[114]   *Official Gazette of the Republic of Venezuela* N° 39.685, May 31st, 2011.

[115]   *Official Gazette of the Republic of Venezuela* N° 37.913, April 5, 2004.

[116]   *Official Gazette of the* Republic *of Venezuela* N° 5.427, Extraordinary Issue, January 5, 2000.

[117]   *Official Gazette of the Republic of Venezuela* N° 4.635, Extraordinary Issue, September 28, 1993.

[118]   *Official Gazette of the Republic of Venezuela* N° 37.659, March 27, 2003.

[119]   *Official Gazette of the Republic of Venezuela* N° 38.344, December 27, 2005.

[120]   *Official Gazette of the Republic of Venezuela* N° 4.580, Extraordinary Issue, May 21, 1993.

[121]   *Official Gazette of the Republic of Venezuela* N° 38.347, December 30, 2005.

[122]   *Official Gazette of the Republic of Venezuela* N° 38.842, January 3, 2008.

[123]   *Official Gazette of the Republic of Venezuela* N° 5.265, Extraordinary Issue, October 1st, 1998.

[124]   *Official Gazette of the Republic of Venezuela* N° 5.180, Extraordinary Issue, November 4, 1997.

[125]   *Official Gazette of the Republic of Venezuela* N° 5.180, Extraordinary Issue, November 4, 1997.

Czech Republic[128], Russia[129], Sweden[130], Switzerland[131], Trinidad & Tobago[132], and Vietnam[133].

It is observed in the above lists that the countries with which Venezuela has signed both DTAs as well as BITs are: Germany, Barbados, Belarus, Belgium, Brazil, Canada, Denmark, Spain, The Netherlands, United Kingdom, Czech Republic, Sweden and Switzerland, thus propitiating – theoretically, at least– investment from those countries in Venezuela.

3. Countries with which Venezuela has signed Bilateral or Multilateral Exchange Treaties

There are several hundreds of treaties signed by Venezuela with countries of Latin America and the Caribbean, Asia, Oceania, the Middle East, Europe and Africa on subjects related –directly or indirectly– to bilateral or multilateral exchange. Therefore, instead of extensively listing such treaties, which cover fields such as petrochemistry, mining, energy, electricity, trade, economics, among others, we prefer to refer the reader to the official source (http://www.asambleanacional. gov.ve/tabs/aproba torias) that lists all signed and effective treaties, and expressly mentions the Approving Law promulgated by the National Assembly which in turns permits direct consultation and furthermore allows to appreciate the current trend of the government on those subjects.

---

[126]   *Official Gazette of the Republic of Venezuela* N° 38.796, October 25, 2007.

[127]   *Official Gazette of the Republic of Venezuela* N° 5.218, Extraordinary Issue, March 6, 1998.

[128]   *Official Gazette of the Republic of Venezuela* N° 5.180, Extraordinary Issue, November 4, 1997.

[129]   *Official Gazette of the Republic of Venezuela* N° 5.822, Extraordinary Issue, September 25, 2006.

[130]   *Official Gazette of the Republic of Venezuela* N° 5.274, Extraordinary Issue, November 12, 1998.

[131]   *Official Gazette of the Republic of Venezuela* N° 5.192, Extraordinary Issue, December 18, 1997.

[132]   *Official Gazette of the Republic of Venezuela* N° 5.180, Extraordinary Issue, November 4, 1997.

[133]   *Official Gazette of the Republic of Venezuela* N° 39.183, May 21, 2009.

IX. TAX RATE STRUCTURES FOR INDIVIDUALS AND CORPORATIONS (*COMPAÑÍAS ANÓNIMAS*) (DOMESTIC AND FOREIGN)

Finally, the Venezuelan ITL establishes two large groups of taxpayers: (i) *individuals* and (ii) *corporations,* and their assimilated entities. From this classification the various rate or aliquot structures according to which those persons pay tax there are determined –in principle–, also adding a special rate list according to the income-producing activity.

1. *Individuals*

Individuals and similar taxpayers will pay tax according to Article 8 of the ITL, based on the rate and other tax types contemplated in Article 50 of the Law, except when derived from the activities mentioned in Article 12 (operation of mines and assignment of such royalties and participations).

In this respect, Article 50 of the Law contemplates rate N° 1 for individuals, expressed in *tax units* (T.U.)[134], in the following terms:

RATE N° 1

1. For the fraction up to 1,000.00: 6.00%.

2. For the fraction that exceeds 1,000.00 up to 1,500.00: 9.00%.

3. For the fraction that exceeds 1,500.00 up to 2,000.00: 12.00%.

4. For the fraction that exceeds 2,000.00 up to 2,500.00: 16.00%.

5. For the fraction that exceeds 2,500.00 up to 3,000.00: 20.00%.

6. For the fraction that exceeds 3,000.00 up to 4,000.00: 24.00%.

7. For the fraction that exceeds 4,000.00 up to 6,000.00: 29.00%.

8. For the fraction that exceeds 6,000.00: 34.00%.

---

[134]   The tax unit (T.U.) is designed as an inflationary correction technique that utilizes a monetary module to restate automatically the nominal fixed values utilized by tax regulations (tax obligations, penalties, etc.). This unit is readjustable by the Tax Bureau, based on the previous year variation of the consumer price index (CPI) in the Metropolitan Area of Caracas, which must be published by the Central Bank of Venezuela at the beginning of each year. *Cf.* Romero-Muci, Humberto, "Uso y abuso de la unidad tributaria", en Sol Gil, Jesús (Coord.), *60 años de imposición a la renta en Venezuela. Evolución histórica y estudios de la legislación actual,* Venezuelan Association of Tax Law, Caracas, 2003, pp. 469-472.

Non-resident individuals, i.e., individuals whose stay in the country does not take longer than one hundred and eighty three (183) days in a calendar year and who do not qualify as domiciled in Venezuela, will pay tax according to the thirty-four percent (34%) aliquot.

2. Companies Engaged in General Business

Pursuant to Article 9 of the ITL companies (*compañía anónimas*) and similar tax-payers (whether domestic or foreign) who perform *general economic activities* (i.e., other than the exploitation of hydrocarbons and related activities), will pay tax under the rate set forth in Article 52 *eiusdem*, also expressed in tax units (T.U.), according to which:

RATE N° 2

For the fraction up to 2,000.00: 15%.

For the fraction that exceeds 2,000.00 up to 3,000.00: 22%.

For the fraction that exceeds 3,000.00: 34%.

3. Companies and Individuals Engaged in Special Hydrocarbon and Mine Exploitation Business

Lastly, those companies (*compañías anónimas*) and similar entities engaged in the exploitation of hydrocarbons and related activities, on the one part, and, on the other, those *individuals* who obtain income from the exploitation of mines and assignment of such royalties and participations, will pay tax according to rate N° 3 set forth in Article 53 of the ITL:

RATE N° 3

a. Proportional rate of sixty percent (60%) for the income specified in Article 12 (individuals).

b. Proportional rate of fifty percent (50%) for income specified in Article 11 (corporations).

Caracas, February 2014

X. BIBLIOGRAPHY

ABACHE CARVAJAL, Serviliano, "La responsabilidad patrimonial del Estado "Administrador, Juez y Legislador" tributario venezolano. Especial referencia al paradigmático caso del procedimiento de verificación" (National Report–Venezuela), *Memorias de las XXV Jornadas Latinoamericanas de Derecho Tributario*, volume II, Abeledo Perrot-Latin American Institute of Tax Law-Colombian Institute of Tax Law, Buenos Aires, 2010.

ABACHE CARVAJAL, Serviliano and BURGOS-IRAZÁBAL, Ramón, "Parafiscalidad, sistema tributario y Libertad", in HERRERA ORELLANA, Luis Alfonso (Coord.), *Enfoques actuales sobre Derecho y Libertad en Venezuela*, Academy of Political and Social Sciences, Caracas, 2013.

ANDRADE, Betty, "La subcapitalización y los precios de transferencia en el régimen venezolano", *Jornadas Internacionales. Cuestiones actuales de Derecho tributario*, Foundation of Administrative Law Studies, Caracas, 2007.

ATENCIO VALLADARES, Gilberto, "Cuestiones tributarias del Mercosur: aproximaciones desde el Derecho tributario venezolano", *Revista de Derecho Tributario*, N° 141, Venezuelan Association of Tax Law, Caracas, 2014.

BAZÓ PISANI, Andrés E., "Incentivos fiscales y otras políticas tributarias ofrecidas por países en desarrollo. ¿Atraen inversión extranjera o desestabilizan la economía?", in DUPOUY M., Elvira y DE VALERA, Irene (Coord.), *Temas de actualidad tributaria. Homenaje a Jaime PARRA PÉREZ*, Academy of Political and Social Sciences-Venezuelan Association of Tax Law, Caracas, 2009.

CARMONA BORJAS, Juan Cristóbal, "Colaboración y asistencia mutua entre Administraciones tributarias", *Revista de Derecho Tributario*, N° 100, Venezuelan Association of Tax Law, Caracas, 2003.

——————————, "Principios de la renta mundial y de la renta territorial", in DE VALERA, Irene (Organizer), *Comentarios a la Ley de Impuesto sobre la Renta*, Academy of Political and Social Sciences-Venezuelan Association of Tax Law, Caracas, 2000.

CARMONA BORJAS, Juan Cristóbal, "Factores de conexión en la legislación venezolana en materia de impuesto sobre la renta", in SOL GIL, Jesús (Coord.), *60 años de imposición a la renta en Venezuela. Evolución histórica y estudios de la legislación actual*, Venezuelan Association of Tax Law, Caracas, 2003.

CASTILLO CARVAJAL, Juan Carlos, "Relatoría general. Tema II. Temas especiales de la Ley de Impuesto sobre la Renta", in KORODY TAGLIAFERRO, Juan Esteban (Coord.), *70 años del Impuesto sobre la Renta. Memorias de las XII Jornadas Venezolanas de Derecho Tributario*, volume II, Venezuelan Association of Tax Law, Caracas, 2013.

DÍAZ IBARRA, Valmy J., "Las reglas de transparencia fiscal internacional en Venezuela. Consecuencias de la vinculación de contribuyentes venezolanos con sociedades en 'paraísos fiscales'", in DUPOUY M., Elvira and DE VALERA, Irene (Coord.), *Temas de actualidad tributaria. Homenaje a Jaime PARRA PÉREZ*, Academy of Political and Social Sciences-Venezuelan Association of Tax Law, Caracas, 2009.

EVANS MÁRQUEZ, Ronald, "Los convenios para evitar la doble tributación internacional y otros aspectos internacionales de la política tributaria venezolana", in DE VALERA, Irene (Organizer), *Comentarios a la Ley de Impuesto sobre la Renta*, Academy of Political and Social Sciences-Venezuelan Association of Tax Law, Caracas, 2000.

EVANS Márquez, Ronald, *Régimen jurídico de la doble tributación internacional*, McGraw-Hill, Caracas, 1999.

FALCÓN y TELLA, Ramón and PULIDO GUERRA, Elvira, *Derecho fiscal internacional*, Marcial Pons, Madrid, 2010.

FRAGA PITTALUGA, Luis, "Subcapitalización y reclasificación de los intereses no deducibles", in KORODY TAGLIAFERRO, Juan Esteban (Coord.), *70 años del Impuesto sobre la Renta. Memorias de las XII Jornadas Venezolanas de Derecho Tributario*, volume II, Venezuelan Association of Tax Law, Caracas, 2013.

LEÓN ROJAS, Andrés Eloy, "La doble tributación internacional. Diferencia entre países desarrollados y en desarrollo", *IV Jornadas Venezolanas de Derecho Tributario*, Venezuelan Association of Tax Law, Caracas, 1998.

MONTERO TRAIBEL, José Pedro, "La armonización tributaria en los procesos de integración", *IV Jornadas Venezolanas de Derecho Tributario*, Venezuelan Association of Tax Law, Caracas, 1998.

PALACIOS MÁRQUEZ, Leonardo, "Medidas fiscales para el desarrollo económico", *Revista de Derecho Tributario*, N° 97, Venezuelan Association of Tax Law, Caracas, 2002.

PAREDES, Carlos Enrique, *El principio de territorialidad y el sistema de renta mundial en la Ley de Impuesto sobre la Renta venezolana*, Andersen Legal, Caracas, 2002.

ROCHE, Emilio J., "Parte general del Impuesto sobre la Renta. Relatoría Tema I", in KORODY TAGLIAFERRO, Juan Esteban (Coord.), *70 años del Impuesto sobre la Renta. Memorias de las XII Jornadas Venezolanas de Derecho Tributario*, volume II, Venezuelan Association of Tax Law, Caracas, 2013.

ROCHE, Emilio J., "Transparencia fiscal internacional", in SOL GIL, Jesús (Coord.), *60 años de imposición a la renta en Venezuela. Evolución histórica y estudios de la legislación actual*, Venezuelan Association of Tax Law, Caracas, 2003.

ROCHE, Emilio J., "De la entrada en vigencia de la reforma de la Ley de Impuesto sobre la Renta de 2001 y del régimen sobre dividendos", *Impuesto sobre la Renta e ilícitos fiscales. VI Jornadas venezolanas de Derecho tributario*, Venezuelan Association of Tax Law, Caracas, 2002.

ROMERO-MUCI, Humberto, "Uso y abuso de la unidad tributaria", in SOL GIL, Jesús (Coord.), *60 años de imposición a la renta en Venezuela. Evolución histórica y estudios de la legislación actual*, Venezuelan Association of Tax Law, Caracas, 2003.

ROMERO-MUCI, Humberto, "Naturaleza jurídica de los principios de contabilidad de aceptación general en Venezuela y su incidencia en la determinación de la renta financiera para el cálculo del impuesto sobre la renta de dividendos (análisis de los artículos 67 y 91 de la Ley de Impuesto sobre la Renta)", *Impuesto sobre la Renta e ilícitos fiscales. VI Jornadas venezolanas de Derecho tributario*, Venezuelan Association of Tax Law, Caracas, 2002.

RONDÓN GARCÍA, Andrea, HERRERA ORELLANA, Luis Alfonso and ARIAS CASTILLO, Tomás A., "Case Study: Private Property Abolition in Venezuela", *International Property Rights Index. 2010 Report, American for Tax Reform Foundation/Property Rights* Alliance, Washington, 2010.

ROSS, Maxim, *¿Capitalismo salvaje o Estado depredador?*, Editorial Alfa, Caracas, 2008.

SOL GIL, Jesús, "Medidas fiscales adoptadas en Venezuela para el desarrollo económico", *Revista de Derecho Tributario*, N° 97, Venezuelan Association of Tax Law, Caracas, 2002.

UCKMAR, Víctor, "Los tratados internacionales en materia tributaria", in Uckmar, Víctor (Coord.), *Curso de Derecho tributario internacional*, volume I, Temis, Bogotá, 2003.

VALDÉS COSTA, Ramón, "Aspectos fiscales de la integración con especial referencia a América Latina", *Revista de Derecho Tributario*, N° 58, Venezuelan Association of Tax Law, Caracas, 1993.

VECCHIO D., Carlos A., *El impuesto al dividendo presunto de las sucursales. Especial referencia a los tratados para evitar la doble tributación*, Venezuelan Association of Financial Law, Caracas, 2004.

CONSULTED WEBSITES

- www.asambleanacional.gov.ve
- www.iladt.org
- www.iuet.org.uy
- www.conapri.org
- www.internationalpropertyrightsindex.org/
- www.seniat.gob.ve

CONTENT

THE GOVERNMENT OF JUDGES AND DEMOCRACY.
THE TRAGIC SITUATION OF THE VENEZUELAN JUDICIARY
Allan R. Brewer-Carías

- L'EFFET PROSPECTIF DES DÉCISIONS DE JUS-TICE / JUDICIAL RULINGS WITH PROSPECTIVE EFFECTS

"JUDICIAL RULINGS WITH PROSPECTIVE EFFECT"
Hildegard Rondón de Sansó

I.C. DROIT COMPARÉ ET UNIFICATION DU DROIT / COMPARATIVE LAW AND UNIFICATION OF LAWS

- LE CONTRÔLE ET LA RECONNAISSANCE DES SENTENCES ARBITRALES ÉTRANGÈRES – L'APPLICATION DE LA CONVENTION DE NEW YORK PAR LES JURIDICTIONS NATIONALES / RECOGNITION AND ENFORCEMENT OF FOREIGN ARBITRAL AWARDS: THE APPLICATION OF THE NEW YORK CONVENTION BY NATIONAL COURTS

RECOGNITION AND ENFORCEMENT OF FOREIGN ARBITRAL AWARDS: THE APPLICATION OF THE NEW YORK CONVENTION BY NATIONAL COURTS
Eugenio Hernández-Bretón

II.B. *DROIT INTERNATIONAL PRIVE / PRIVATE INTERNATIONAL LAW*

- *INFORMATION ET PREUVE DU CONTENU DU DROIT ÉTRANGER / PROOF OF AND INFORMATION ABOUT FOREIGN LAW*

PROOF OF AND INFORMATION ABOUT FOREIGN LAW

Eugenio Hernández-Bretón and Claudia Madrid Martínez

- *LA CORRUPTION DANS LES CONTRATS COMMER-CIAUX INTERNATIONAUX ET SES EFFETS EN DROIT PRIVE / THE CIVIL LAW EFFECTS OF CORRUPTION IN INTERNATIONAL COMMERCIAL CONTRACTS*

THE CIVIL LAW EFFECTS OF CORRUPTION IN INTERNATIONAL COMMERCIAL CONTRACTS
Eugenio Hernández-Bretón and Claudia Madrid Martínez

241

III.A. DROIT COMMERCIAL / COMMERCIAL LAW

CURRENT CHALLENGES FACED BY COMPANIES (SOCIEDADES ANÓNIMAS) IN VENEZUELA
-SPECIAL REFERENCE TO THEIR REGULATION UNDER BUSINESS LAW-
Andrea I. Rondón García

IV.B. DROIT CONSTITUTIONNEL / CONSTITUTIONAL LAW

- LE RECOURS AUX PRÉCÉDENTS ÉTRANGERS PAR LE JUGE CONSTITUTIONNEL / FOREIGN PRECE-DENTS IN CONSTITUTIONAL LITIGATION

LE RECOURS AUX PRÉCÉDENTS ÉTRANGERS PAR LE JUGE CONSTITUTIONNEL
Claudia Nikken

www.ingramcontent.com/pod-product-compliance
Lightning Source LLC
Chambersburg PA
CBHW021554210326
41599CB00010B/444